Mission in Mar

Introducing the Mission in Marginal Places series

Christian mission is facing critical challenges. Diverse, complex and rapidly changing contexts raise fundamental questions about the theology and practice of mission. The vision behind this series is to engage afresh with these questions in a way that will help equip Christian communities of all kinds to develop mission in their own particular situation.

The series incorporates a number of distinctive elements that are critical for contemporary mission. Firstly, Christian mission must give priority to those on the margins of society and questions of 'difference' must therefore be a guiding consideration in all aspects. Secondly, mission must be predicated on a practical or 'lived' theology which grapples with the actual experiences of life in a broad range of contexts. And thirdly, to be both rigorous and credible, mission studies must be in dialogue with the social sciences where much can be learned about the context for mission in relation to, for example, globalization, shifting experiences of 'place' and 'space', self-other relationships, urban studies and changing patterns of marginalization.

At heart, our intention is to help readers ground such theology and understandings into their own personal journey; to reflect on the character and spiritualities needed to sustain such an embodied and highly contextual approach to mission; and to help develop rhythms and practices that will enable such engagement.

The books:

Paul Cloke and Mike Pears (eds), *Mission in Marginal Places: The Theory* (2016)

Paul Cloke and Mike Pears (eds), *Mission in Marginal Places: The Praxis* (2016)

Paul Cloke and Mike Pears (eds), *Mission in Marginal Places: The Stories* (2017)

Paul Cloke and Mike Pears, *Exploring Spiritual Landscapes: Mission in Marginal Places* (2017)

Mike Pears, *The Peaceful Way: Mission in Marginal Places* (2018)

Mike Pears, *Placing the Powers: Mission in Marginal Places* (2018)

Mission in Marginal Places

The Praxis

Paul Cloke and Mike Pears (eds)

Paternoster:
thinking faith

Contents

Introduction (Mike Pears and Paul Cloke)   1

Part I

  1 Understanding the Economic Realm (Paul Cloke)   28
  2 Case Study: A Journey (Chris Sunderland)   56
  3 Case Study: YMCA Exeter Job Club Project
    (Samuel Thomas)   62
  4 The Economic Realm: Editorial Comment
    (Andrew Williams)   69

Part II

  5 Understanding the Political Realm
    (Martin Gainsborough)   78
  6 Case Study: Being Left with Some Difficult Questions
    (Martin Gainsborough)   98
  7 Case Study: Welcoming the Stranger
    (Martin Gainsborough)   100
  8 The Political Realm: Editorial Comment
    (Mike Pears and Paul Cloke)   103

Part III

  9 Understanding the Social Realm (Gordon Cotterill)   110
 10 Case Study: Ilford, London (Naomi Clifton)   134
 11 Case Study: The Coffee House, Sutton
    (Gordon Cotterill and Adam Bonner)   138

12 The Social Realm: Editorial Comment
    (Mike Pears and Paul Cloke)   140

Part IV
   13 Understanding the Environmental Realm
       (Paul Ede and Sam Ewell)   148
   14 Case Study: Clay Community Church, Possilpark,
       Glasgow (Paul Ede)   169
   15 Case Study: Casa da Videira, Curitiba, Brazil
       (Sam Ewell)   175
   16 The Environmental Realm: Editorial Comment
       (Mike Pears and Paul Cloke)   182

Part V
   17 Understanding the Creative Realm (John Hayes)   190
   18 Case Study: Called to Witness (John Hayes)   218
   19 Case Study: Life in a Paper Cup (John Hayes)   223
   20 The Creative Realm: Editorial Comment
       (Mike Pears and Paul Cloke)   225

Author Biographies   232

Introduction

Mike Pears and Paul Cloke

The Approach of This Book

This book aims to identify a series of different arenas, or spheres, through which new forms of practical mission can be considered in socially and geographically marginalized places. However, drawing on the themes introduced in the first book in this series – *Mission in Marginal Places: The Theory* – we want to suggest that any such practical mission needs to be approached with very considerable prayer, care and forethought. Too often, mission has involved attempts to implement preconceived innovations in marginalized territories; innovations conceived *outside* of the communities concerned and imposed on the people therein without any sustained attention to and understanding of local contexts, needs and cultures. This 'dropping in' of plans from the outside has led both to potentially inappropriate mission activities and to the expression of a particular form of power relations between those 'outside' and 'inside' the community. Often inadvertently, Christians perform dominant mission roles that assume both that they know what is best for marginalized people and that ideas and schemes brought in from the outside will have a universal capacity to meet needs whatever the local circumstances.

In contrast, the approach championed in this book involves mission that is earthed in the conditions, events and experiences of the marginalized people concerned. It involves a self-critical realization of how those seeking to undertake mission are themselves wrapped up in the power relations that give rise to marginalization. It requires a posture of engagement that is willing to take time to notice and understand the everyday goings-on in particular mission contexts. It suggests a capacity to set aside our pre-existing orthodoxies of understanding and explaining in order to make space for other kinds of intellectual and emotional world-views. It necessitates a conviction that when we look at the world through our particular 'window', what we see is only one representation of the realities involved. We need also to be able and willing to see the world through other people's 'windows' such that we move beyond imposing our perception and move towards a co-created perception of local cultural context. And, of course, it requires a spiritual attentiveness to insights, discernments and revelations of that which is beyond our understanding, as provided by the Holy Spirit.

What is required therefore is an ability to recognize how wider structures and processes of marginalization are being mapped out and configured in the particular mechanisms, events and cultural specificities of the marginal places concerned. This involves both a reflexive engagement with neighbourhoods and faithful theological performances and narratives built on this engagement. Accordingly, this book attempts to bring together insights that are both social-scientific and theological. From social science we can grasp key understandings of how our 'selves' relate to 'others', how these self–other relations can lead to marginalizing and exclusionary tendencies that often result in geographical differentiation and cultures of belonging/not belonging and in-placeness/out-of-placeness. We can also learn from ethnographic research methodologies that have been developed to enable us to get under the skin of other places and communities. From theology we can learn from the mistakes made in early versions of practical theology, in which theological process moved too quickly beyond a rigorous examination of local context and experience, with the result that theological engagement was based on a superficial grasp of social and cultural experience. As with social-science methodologies, rigorous examination of local complexity is an essential forerunner for both the understanding of marginalization and the theological narratives of participation in and among marginalized people. So, before working our way through different potential arenas of missional activity, we first want to underline the importance of these foundational approaches to understanding marginal places and discerning the appropriateness of theological narratives therein.

Selves and Others: The Power Relations of Marginalization and Exclusion

Suggesting a focus on the self seems at first glance to be indulgent. Surely our focus and passion is for others, and that should be our only legitimate starting point. Starting with others, however, risks unwarranted assumptions about ourselves. Not so very many years ago, social scientists such as human geographers were taught to be 'objective' in their studies, so that anyone else tackling the same subject would come up with the same results. This approach assumes that a person's background, identity, personality, experience and world-view needed to be subjugated to the need for a scientific kind of method. It is clear, however, that the self *does* matter in the ways we seek to understand other people and other places.[1] Who we are impacts on our geographical imaginations, the ways we see the world and assume how it works. Not acknowledging and reflecting on ourselves means not only that we can unknowingly buy into other people's orthodoxies, but also that we can carry the expectation for others to buy into our orthodoxies; we can assume that everybody sees the world as we do and therefore impose our 'sameness' onto others.

In practice, it can be extraordinarily difficult *not* automatically to see things from our own perspective, however hard we try to escape from a focus on the self. However, the risk of imposing our sameness onto others involves a somewhat natural tendency to stereotype people's differences, thereby equating difference with abnormality or deviance.[2] So as well as needing to reflect on our 'selves', we need to understand how we respond to *others*, and in particular how well (or not) we attune ourselves to the difference that they represent. This is true in major areas of social discrimination such as gender, ethnicity, sexuality and age, but it is also pertinent across less obvious social boundaries, as for example, in the distinctions made around the supposedly 'deserving' or 'undeserving' nature of those experiencing poverty and other social hardship.[3]

So how might we start to develop an understanding of otherness? The French anthropologist Marc Auge[4] suggests a two-pronged approach. First, he argues, we need to develop a *sense for the other*, in the same way that we have a sense of direction, or humour, or family, or rhythm. This sense for otherness is thought to be diminishing as broad societal tolerance of difference becomes increasingly challenged by intolerant processes of regionalism, nationalism and narrow-minded political treatment of migrants and asylum seekers. Second, Auge pinpoints the need to develop *a sense of the other*, or a sense of what has meaning, significance and value for others. This requires attempts to understand some of the social meanings that are developed among and lived out within social and identity groups other than our own. This combination of an understanding *of* the other, and an emotional, connected and committed sense of appreciation *for* the other is fundamental to any attempt to achieve solidarity with marginalized people through participation and involvement in their worlds. Rather than attempting to convert 'them' into 'our' world, such solidarity involves a conversion of our 'selves' for the other.[5]

The risk of not converting ourselves in the processes and practices of mission is that we simply attempt to convert others into our world. This might rock considerably the notion of the orthodox evangelist whose role has over the years been understood as just such a sense of the conversion of others. Entire understandings of the process of journeying into Christian faith have been pinned on this word 'conversion'. The key distinction we want to make here is that being 'born again' in Christ (as in the description of the faith-journey of Nicodemus[6]) is a startlingly different idea from being converted into the world-views, assumptions, prejudices and experiences of any particular group of Christians engaging in mission. Yet so often, both in history and in current times, the practice of mission implies just such a conversion into a particular Christian culture, regardless of how that culture narrates Christian faith and whether it is in a way that is meaningful and significant to the 'converts'. The choice presented is often one of 'come over to us or remain an outsider'; thus creating a rather suspect emphasis on particular cultures of 'being converted' rather than on the acceptance of the Jesus message and of participation in the kingdom as indicated by relationship with God rather than relationship with a particular Christian culture.

The wider social and cultural processes of 'converting others into our world' will often result in a marginalization of those who cannot conform to these expectations of conversion. Geographers in particular have sought to understand the mechanisms that underpin social exclusion, that is the situation in which individuals and groups in society become apparently 'unconvertable'; in other words separated from the normal orthodoxies of living and working in that society.[7] A key figure in these studies is David Sibley[8] who describes how exclusion is *simultaneously* material and symbolic; symbolic social disapproval often results in stigma that acts to reinforce, and is reinforced by, material circumstances such as impoverishment. He demonstrated how stigmatized groups were commonly found to dwell in the geographical margins of society, and how those considered socially 'marginal' are either pushed towards geographically marginal spaces, or seek them out in an attempt to avoid confrontation or abuse. Space is therefore 'both an expression of and a means by which exclusionary practices gain purchase and meaning'.[9]

The clear danger here is that unreflexive mission in these marginalized places risks reinforcing, rather than counteracting, the material and especially symbolic forces of exclusion. With the best of intentions, shipping in preconceived 'answers' to marginalized places can potentially signify and practise just those stigmatic assumptions about otherness that give meaning to wider exclusionary practices. Human geographer Tim Cresswell[10] suggests that the human mind makes sense of the world by dividing it up into categories – especially into place categories. Many such categories are not thought or spoken about – they appear somehow 'natural' and are reinforced by orthodox behaviours that comply with the categorization. However, as Cresswell points out, this seeming 'unthinkability' of place categories means that they can become potent ideological weapons, laden with meanings that can create and reinforce relations of domination and subordination. In this way, places are often acted out – performed – through a series of uncritical acts that conform to the expectations of those around us.

Marginal places are no exception. They exist because mainstream places tend to exclude certain kinds of people and their associated behaviours. When we (for the purposes of mission, or for other reasons) move from mainstream places into marginal places, we can – if we are not very careful – unthinkingly carry with us a series of ideas about what is 'orthodox' in the so-called mainstream, which then defines our expectations about what is different in the margins. With the best will in the world, these expectations can serve to reinforce stereotyping and stigma, in assessments of people and places, in analysing what is 'in-place' and what is 'out-of-place', and especially in the diagnosis of what is needed to return people and places to the 'mainstream'.

However, it is important to note that these seeming certainties of order that are constructed by and through place are not inevitable and can be transgressed. Transgression often occurs when marginalized people choose to inhabit (where possible) 'mainstream' places, but it can also occur when marginalized people are treated seriously and legitimately in marginalized places. And this is precisely the potential of these kinds of *redemptive* missional practices – ways of engaging reflexively with marginal places such that Jesus-narratives can be interconnected appropriately with intimate knowledge and understandings of the place experiences of marginal people – which we are seeking to emphasize in mission contexts.

The Role of Ethnography

Over recent decades, social science has turned significantly towards qualitative methodologies that emphasize 'thick description' of particular contexts rather than enumerated analysis purporting to be representative of a wider whole. While particular research techniques, such as interviews, focus groups, even open-ended questions in questionnaires, have been used to develop these qualitative ambitions, the most intensive search for thick description has occurred in the form of ethnography. The term literally means 'people-writing'[11] and is drawn from early forms of anthropological fieldwork in which western researchers typically spent a year or more in some far-off and exotic location, learning local languages, observing local culture and participating in everyday activities. Ideally, this type of research results in an intensive understanding of the way of life and cultural orthodoxies associated with that place; the researcher gains the kind of knowledge that an inquisitive insider might naturally accrue by living there.[12] It will be evident that although ethnography in this form has a sound methodological core, it too is vulnerable to the kinds of self–other relations we have discussed above. If ethnography is to be embraced as a modus operandi in mission contexts, it is crucial both to appreciate its core values, and to apply it in a reflexive and redemptive manner so that it can become a tool of sympathetic engagement rather than an alternative route to converting the other.

A detailed account of ethnography in human geography is provided in the book *Practising Human Geography*.[13] Here, the common characteristics of an ethnographic approach are evaluated in terms of five principal qualities:

1. Ethnography takes local people seriously, regarding them as knowledgeable and situated agents from whom researchers can learn a significant amount about how the world is viewed, inhabited and worked out through real everyday places and communities.
2. Ethnography must involve extended and detailed study that occurs while the researcher is immersed in the place and community concerned. It is therefore a grounded approach by which understandings about local ways of life emerge over time; it cannot be conducted via short-term, flip-in-flip-out, engagements.
3. The precise research methods deployed in ethnography will be opportunist and eclectic, involving sustained observation and

participation, but allowing locally important cultures and events to dictate what is followed up in specific detail.

4. Ethnography involves both what people say they do and why, and what they are *seen* to do and how they explain their actions and opinions to others.

5. Ethnography depends significantly on the researcher, who is required to adapt how she or he acts in familiar circumstances by learning how to act in what are (initially at least) strange circumstances. Understandings of place and community are co-constructed with local people – a process in which different taken-for-granted self-identities, world-views, ways of life, relationships, political and ethical orthodoxies and so on are rubbed up against each other. Resultant narratives depend as much on the researcher themselves as on the characteristics of those being observed.

Clearly, then, ethnographic findings cannot be regarded as the result of any kind of simple process of 'digging up the truth' in a particular context. These findings are what geographers term 'intersubjective truths' – that is they are negotiated iteratively between the researcher and researched, and are dependent upon both parties for their relevance.[14] And those of us who engage in ethnographic practice need to accept the responsibility that accompanies this:

> Novice ethnographers must recognize, develop, complement and sometimes unlearn existing attitudes, habits, sentiments, emotions, senses, skills and preferences. A good ethnographer is someone willing and able to become a more reflexive and sociable version of him or herself in order to learn something meaningful about other people's lives, and to communicate his or her specific findings, including their wider relevance.[15]

Bearing these warnings in mind, then, to what extent can we develop these core characteristics and potentials of ethnography for use in sensitizing mission in marginal places to the importance of local context? We want to suggest that ethnography does indeed offer a set of valuable practical tools with which to develop reflexive engagement in local marginal places. However, drawing on the lessons learned in social sciences such as human geography, ethnographic practices require additional fine-tuning in order to mitigate the continuing influence of self–other relations in our encounters.

Two principal issues require further scrutiny in this context. First, we need to avoid using ethnography to describe local context in terms of *a* people, *a* culture, *a* community and so on. Doing so tends to bolster the kinds of understandings of the world that place people in distinct and discrete places and cultures, and has the potential to carry stereotype over into reflexive engagement. Although local contexts *are* of fundamental significance, they need to be framed from the inside and not from the outside. The processes and expressions of categorization are frequently dangerous in political terms. Communities and places rarely exist as neatly bounded entities with unified characteristics. To assume so is to neglect less-than-visible minorities within places and to ignore the contested nature and needs of marginality. The reality is that most abstract people-grouping terms are relatively meaningless, *and yet* the ways in which such terms are variously defined, deployed and contested in real-world situations can have profound impacts and significance.[16] Culture, for example should not be studied as something that people possess, but rather as a 'powerfully determined idea'[17] bound into specific grounded circumstances and specific contested power relations. It may be necessary to directly challenge stereotypical, popular, culturalist explanations of the living conditions of particular categorized groups in order to better understand the power of categorization in specific circumstances. Equally, people's propensity to self-categorize will be important in this respect.

Second, we need to revisit the thorny issue of how self–other relations influence the practice of being reflexive. Profound questions have been raised in geography about this issue:

What is the relationship between our own background, current position and values, and our own research agenda? How do we know what we know? Through what sort of lenses is our knowledge filtered? Who is included and who is excluded by the social practices and academic subject matter of academic geography? For whom are we writing? And what should be the relationship between our theories and our politics, between our thinking and our action?[18]

For academic geography, read mission in marginal places; and add practical theology and the lingering effects of particular models of church-personship. These questions are awkward, but in human geography they have sparked a particular series of senses of and for the other (to use Auge's terms). Many researchers have focused on recovering and prioritizing marginalized voices so as to unsettle the status quo, and redefine what is relevant and legitimate. This process has resulted in a rethinking of 'what and who counts'. Rather than presenting neat and tidy narratives of self-explanatory categories, ethnography in human geography has legitimized processes that are tricky, annoying, hilarious, confusing, disturbing, mechanical, surprising, messy, iterative, contradictory and most important of all, open-ended. Again, for human geography read mission. These are the very kinds of characteristics that defy categorization, and resist adequate description by numbers. Mission narratives that focus on 'this initiative', 'that project' and 'these numbers of people' will not be served by these foci. But narratives of the everyday lives of marginalized people will be replete with just these tricky, messy, disturbing (and so on) facets of everyday life. And the narratives that result from ethnographic engagement will depend on how we answer the thorny questions about reflexivity. To use ethnography for reflexive engagement in mission contexts will require the unlearning both of many uncritical self–other relations and assumptions, and of the desire to seek out and present tidy narratives of people and place. Instead, periods of open-minded confusion will be a necessary precursor for getting under the skin of local communities.

Spiritual Discernment?

Naturally, the preconditions for undertaking mission in marginal places will necessarily include elements of faith-based understanding that transcend the research power of ethnography to get under the skin of local community. The last part of this introductory chapter uses ideas about practical theology to weave in the spiritual and the theological among these geographies of marginality, stigma and belonging. As a prelude to the discussion of practical theology, however, we want briefly to consider how ethnography can be enhanced by elements of spiritual discernment. Here, we argue that part of the technology needed by reflexively engaged mission will be a focus not simply on that which is tangible and known about the local context, but also on other elements of the context that are distinctly non-rational and other-worldly. Discussion on this point[19] insists that local places consist of far more than just material landscapes of society, economy, politics and culture; in addition we need to take the unseen spiritual world seriously. The term 'spiritual landscapes' has been coined[20] to make this idea more accessible. By the term *spiritual*, we can point to that part of the non-material virtual world in which faith forms a significant part of the move beyond rationality and towards the other-worldly. By the term *landscape*, we can point to embodied practices of being in the world, including ways of seeing, but extending beyond sight to a sense of being that includes all senses (including discernment), and to an openness to be affected by what surrounds us. Therefore, by the term *spiritual landscapes*, we can point to a disposition to be moved and affected by things other than the material, present world around us; something other-worldly and noticeable in a performative 'presencing' of some sense of spirit.

As an example, the American theologian Walter Wink[21] has written about the power of evil in terms of an outer visible structure (an 'exteriority') and an inner spiritual reality (an 'interiority'). He argues that the interior and exterior aspects of evil operate simultaneously, but that the invisible spiritual dimension of the powers of evil is often neglected.[22] While material structures of domination are often very visible in local contexts, the interior spiritual realities of such domination are discernible only as a kind of haunting enslavement that operates in the spiritual landscape to incarcerate humanity. Spiritual landscapes, then, are a tension between presences and absences, and between the performance,

perception and creation of the present in any particular context. The
material is present and the spiritual is seemingly absent, but the ghostly
presence of the unseen spiritual is influential in how we understand
our local contexts, and how we continue to develop them through our
actions. Geographers are currently fascinated by this idea that being
'human' in particular places involves both the visible/tangible and the
virtual/intangible, and accounts of affective powers that are literally ineffable since they cannot be named. The church, of course, has names
for these seemingly ghostly presences and absences and it seems vital
that these kinds of spiritual landscapes should form an integral focus in
the fulfilment of its prophetic and missional responsibilities.

But how do we access these spiritual landscapes as part of the wider
ethnographic foundation of reflexive engagement in mission? We address this issue specifically and in much greater detail in *Placing the
Powers* (Book 6 of this series) but one way forward – again drawing
on experience in the social sciences – is to engage with the idea of *psychogeographies* as a way of opening out practices of discernment. Originally described by the philosopher Guy Debord[23] in terms of the
conscious or subconscious effects of the geographical environment on
individual emotions and behaviour, psychogeography has developed
into a kind of divining of the unconscious cartographies of different
places, both through imaginary and literary responses to a place, and
through embodied practices of walking through that place.[24] A familiar example would be Iain Sinclair's[25] poetic accounts of the hidden
underside of London, based on walks and treks around the wilds of
the East End and the adjoining Essex deltas. Perhaps less well known,
but an excellent example of how these psychogeographies can be sen-
sitized to spiritual landscapes, is John Davies'[26] narrative of walking
coast-to-coast across the north of England, following the route of the
M62 motorway. As part of his journeying, Davies notes, for example, ghostly presences and absences presenting themselves in different guises: '[B]e they the ghosts of communities no longer physically
present in particular places but still active, "dead roads" which had
been cut off by the building of the M62 across them, [or] the "spirits
of place" which I tried at times to describe in my diary entries.'[27]

It is clear here that there is a deliberate spiritual element to his journey, with the author leaning heavily on his faith in 'a God who came to earth, who *incarnated* himself in the ordinary life of the common people'.[28] Psychogeography for Davies then, is a reading of everyday place and displacement in terms of a sacramental understanding of engaging with God in and through everyday experiences, conversations and events, both in terms of loss and suffering, and in terms of the presence of a powerful spirit of grace. As he puts it: 'My fantasy is that once you have learned to "read the everyday" then you are well equipped to start seeing the signs of "heaven in the ordinary" in the previously unpromising places where people interact . . . and in the events which engage them there.'[29]

In Davies' account we can begin to see how psychogeographical surveying can address the spiritual interiorities of places and landscapes, noting the contours of presence and absence, but also being alerted to the tiny hints of incarnational grace that blossom in among other geographies of power, exclusion and marginalization. We can suggest, therefore, that these combined practices of walking, surveying, prayerfulness and openness to the discernment gifts of the Holy Spirit begin to offer a methodology of practice that adds another layer to ethnography. Such methods require careful scrutiny and attention to the specificities of local context, but they will certainly involve both ethical and aesthetic spaces of connection in order to bear witness to, and testify about the inhumanity of misused power, and to the redemptive possibilities of incarnational grace. It is these kinds of grace-filled and Spirit-led ethnographies that we suggest are an absolutely crucial foundation to the reflexive engagements required for mission in marginal places.

Practical Theology and Marginality

Throughout this series of books we will be seeking to develop a series of critical reflections on the role of practical theology as a guiding force behind mission in marginal places.[30] In the context of the above discussion, it is both obvious and very significant that the developing field of practical theology exhibits important connections, crossovers and synergies with the issues of self–other relations and ethnographic practices in the social sciences. That is, many of the key issues around processes and practices of exclusion and marginality are receiving parallel attention from social scientists and theologians, and there is much to be learned from a cross-fertilization of the understandings that arise from these studies. In the lead-up to more detailed accounts of the different spheres of mission practice that might figure in the search for incarnational grace in particular local contexts, we want to emphasize two particular aspects of how practical theology synergizes with these social-scientific insights.

First, we want to point out an important correlation between practical theology and ethnography that relates to the concept of experience. The process of practical theology is commonly understood to begin with experience, which is to say that it is 'earthed', that it works from the ground up. Mary McClintock Fulkerson expresses this well in saying that 'theologies that matter arise out of dilemmas – out of situations that matter. The generative process of theological understanding is a process provoked, not confined to preconceived fixed categories'.[31] Terry Veling proposes that practical theology 'necessarily attends to the *conditions* of human life. It is concerned with the unique, the particular, the concrete – this people, this community, this place, this moment, this neighbour, this question, this need, this concern.'[32] Thus the critical challenge for practical theology is in its ability to effectively and rigorously investigate a given context and the experience of those within it. We have noted a tendency in the practice of practical theology to move too quickly from the investigation of a particular experience, by assuming that the understanding of experience is straightforward or self-evident, so that the theological process starts with a superficial understanding of experience. It is precisely this point of challenge that ethnography addresses in offering a practical and rigorous method for investigating the complexity of everyday experiences with an emphasis on attentiveness to experience, both the experience of those in the context itself and of the research community. This rigorous approach to understanding human experience is especially valuable to the Christian community whose conviction it is that faith is not simply something to be believed but something to be lived; it is a set of convictions to be lived out through the life of the community, it is an embodied and faithful performance.[33]

Second, for Christian communities that are intentionally located in marginal contexts, we see the importance of a practical theological engagement with issues of difference. Many of these communities are placed in such a way that they are on the interface between social and spatial constructions of difference, that is, the actual physical and relational spaces which they occupy are on the boundaries between people of difference. Such an intentional placing of a community often involves a critical element of disruption or transgression in the normal everyday arrangement of things, both in their own lives and in their adopted community.[34] By not conforming to the normal social landscape, they are considered as 'out-of-place'. The dissonance that results and the accompanying feelings of discomfort both within the Christian community and wider community should not be ignored or brushed aside. The sense of discomfort or of being out-of-place is not simply about adjusting to new cultural surroundings – something to learn to be accustomed to – rather the experience of disruption and discomfort becomes the very place that opens up the potential to see differently. Fulkerson talks about this kind of experience of disjuncture as a 'wound', but recognizes that it is precisely the site of a wound that has the potential to generate 'creative thinking'.[35] A simple example of this kind of approach can be found in the small Christian community on an estate in Bristol that one of us (Mike) is a part of, where time is taken to regularly explore the question, 'What has disturbed, or troubled, you this week?'

It should be clear, then, that the task of theology for the marginally located Christian community is not an additional activity to be undertaken as time allows. Neither is it discrete or detached in relation to the practical aspects of the lives of those who are part of it. Rather the theology of these communities is integral to every aspect of their situations both through thoughtful theological reflection upon their own experiences, not least via a reflexive involvement in their neighbourhood, and through faithful 'theological performance' in their following of Jesus.[36] Practical theology assumes the performative nature of faith and it follows, for those who understand that God has a 'bias to the poor', that this performance will be worked out in a complex and deep collaborative engagement with those in marginal locations. In a number of cases this may entail relocating to a different physical place. Indeed, it is clear that for most, if not all, of those who have relocated to marginal places, the very act of relocation and the subsequent journey of discovery is itself an expression of practical theology. Our assumption is, therefore, that practical theology will embody an inbuilt disposition towards marginal situations and that there will be a natural attentiveness therein to experiences of difference and belonging, being in-place or out-of-place and the related areas such as identity and power.

In other words, we are arguing for a theology that is thoroughly conversant with context, and that can be characterized by:

- an ethnographic attentiveness to people of difference;
- an embodiment of the reflexive Christian community in a marginal place; and
- an open-minded engagement with social-scientific as well as theological notions of difference/belonging, in-place/out-of-place.

This practical theological posture will shape the engagement of the Christian community with its context in a number of distinctive ways which are, we suggest, foundational for the transformation patterned on God's shalom, the emergence of a prophetic community, and the development of non-coercive, ethical involvement in society (performance). These various aspects will be developed in more depth in Books 4 and 5 of this series – *Exploring Spiritual Landscapes* and *The Peaceful Way* – but in the context of this introduction, we want to underline five key principles.

1. Seek to understand the patterns which shape everyday life

Communities seeking to engage with the best of practical theology will need to make serious attempts to 'get under the skin' of their local context to find out what is really going on. They will need to adopt a questioning stance that asks: 'Is what appears to be going on with that situation, actually what is going on?'[37] Insights of this nature are, by definition not easily gained. They involve developing new perspectives on familiar and apparently obvious aspects of life. But by doing so, an attentive community will begin to see how unequal arrangements of power are embedded in the everyday places around them in such a way as to exclude certain 'kinds' of people from places of privilege; they will discern how institutional policies and practices which are lauded as 'fair' or 'just' actually tip the scales against those most in need. In other words, practical theology facilitates the recognition of 'sites of privilege' where 'certain people or groups benefit from structural inequalities'.[38] In these ways it becomes apparent how the normal socio-spatial structure of everyday life in fact sustains landscapes of injustice and inequality which often go largely unnoticed, or at least undiscussed, in the course of everyday life. The ability to notice or see these patterns and to bring them into public conversation is an important part of being a prophetic community.

2. Learn to develop a reflexive posture

This journey of engagement will involve a community in the troubling realization of their own short-sightedness, their own inability to 'see'. There are strong resonances here with a host of gospel accounts in which would-be disciples need first to have their own eyes opened before they can participate with Jesus' mission of transformation.[39] The shock of 'seeing' is the realization that we too have been both participants in and beneficiaries of the very structures that exploit and marginalize the poor. Fulkerson talks about this 'not seeing' as a kind of 'obliviousness that comes with dominance': 'Obliviousness is a kind of not-seeing that is not primarily intentional but reflexive. As such, it occurs on an experiential continuum ranging from benign to a subconscious or repressed protection of power.'[40] The thoughtful use of ethnographic methods combined with theological reflection opens up an effective and practical way for a community to embark on the transformational journey of seeing. It makes available theories and practical tools for gaining a deeper sense of how the 'self' is related to the context. This 'reflexive' posture embodies the conviction that others cannot be known or understood through objective observation or rational analysis but only through relational proximity. The reflexive sense is conveyed by Miroslav Volf's notion of 'the will to embrace [which] precedes any "truth" about others and any construction of their "justice"'.[41] The sense conveyed through this is that a person cannot know the other until they have come into social and spatial proximity with them but, equally, neither can that person wholly know themselves until they have come into proximity (or embrace) with the other. Reflexive practice deals precisely with this encounter and is predicated on an understanding of Matthew 7 that self-judgement, or seeing-of-the-self, is a prerequisite for a clear-sighted assessment of others.

3. Allow co-creativity to be a guiding principle in encounters with others

It follows that the knowledge of the context is 'co-created' as people of difference come together in the same relational space. In Fulkerson's eloquent terms, 'a shared space of appearance' comes into being through the self–other encounter 'transform[ing] obliviousness and its social harms'.[42] Although this view might be contentious to some, it must be understood that knowledge, even prophetic knowledge of the situation, is not the preserve of the Christian community especially when that community comes from a position of dominance. Rather, knowledge is formed through the encounter, that is (to think of it spatially) in the space between the self and the other. As Fulkerson puts it: 'What is needed to counter the diminishment and harm associated with obliviousness is a place to appear, a place to be seen, to be recognized and to recognize the other. Being seen and heard by others, being acknowledged by others . . . [is] essential to a community of faith as an honouring of the shared image of God.'[43]

The co-convening of knowledge in this way demonstrates well the sense in which practical theology makes no distinction between the theoretical and the practical. Neither is there a tidy linear separation between learning theology, studying the context and doing mission and witnessing transformation. Rather, all these activities happen concurrently as a reflexive Christian community is embodied in socially and spatially marginal contexts.

4. Be attentive to the work of the Spirit in the space between the self and the other

The practice of practical theology has to embrace a faithful participation in the work of the Holy Spirit; that is to say, the co-creating space of appearance that emerges through the self–other encounter is precisely the space in which the Spirit is found to be at work. This sense that the Spirit resides in the 'space between' resonates with Veling's insistence (expanding on Martin Buber's idea that 'all real living is meeting') that the Spirit resides between the self and the other: 'The Spirit is not in the I, but between the I and the Thou. Whether we speak of love, or understanding, or forgiveness, or peace – these cannot happen except that they happen between us, except that they become a matter of concern for both of us.'[44]

While this idea of the 'space between' is difficult to define, being itself comprised by 'millions of moments of encounter',[45] it is nonetheless the space in which the Spirit resides. Practical theology therefore involves not only an attentiveness to the other, and also a reflexive attentiveness to the self, but perhaps most importantly it requires a faithful attentiveness to the person and work of the Spirit in the 'between' space.

In his classic book, *The Go-Between God*, John Taylor discusses how the commonplace experiences of everyday encounters with other people, ideas or landscapes can bring about a 'flash of recognition' that has the potential to change our lives in such a way that they become true turning points:

> In every such encounter there has been an anonymous third party who makes the introduction, acts as a go-between, makes two beings aware of each other, sets up a current of communication between them. What is more, this invisible go-between does not simply stand between us but is activating each of us from the inside. Moses approaching the burning bush is no scientific observer; the same fiery essence burns in his own heart also. He and the thorn-bush are caught and held, as it were, in the same magnetic field.[46]

We recognize this third party who is the 'ground of our meeting' as the Holy Spirit, the one who is: '[T]he elemental energy of communion itself, within which all separate existences may be made present and personal to each other. The first activity of the Spirit is annunciation. It is always he who gives one to the other and makes each really see the other.'[47] Thus the Spirit not only opens my eyes to Christ, but also to the presence of Christ in the other; to be open towards God means also being open towards the other – 'one cannot choose to be open in one direction and closed in the other'.[48] This openness or vulnerability in two directions – towards God and other – is, in a practical theological sense, at the heart of what 'doing theology' is all about.

5. Nurture a living dialogue between lived experience and understanding Scripture

The practical theological commitment to a patient ethnographic engagement with place described here will also entail willingness to re-read Scripture. It is perhaps for many of us a shock to find the extent to which our familiar readings of Scripture carry the same deeply embedded cultural assumptions that serve to maintain unequal power relations between self and other. Rather than inspiring a prophetic imagination which contests established patterns of marginalization and exclusion, readings of Scripture from centres of power will, more often than not, present modes of discipleship which fail to seriously challenge the status quo.[49]

To draw once again on Fulkerson's terms, the 'obliviousness that comes with power' affects not only the ability to see our own contemporary contexts but also closes our eyes to the way in which the biblical text itself radically addresses the exclusionary and unjust structures of those same contexts and our own collaboration with them. Conversely the 'shared space of appearance' which comes into being through the self–other encounter calls us to see Scripture through fresh eyes. Critically, this new sense of seeing may not be understood as the discovery of new 'truths' or certainties, but rather the bringing onto the horizon of new questions. Such questions may arise from our specific contexts and be addressed to Scripture, or conversely we may see afresh the questions posed in Scripture which may be addressed to our particular places and experiences.[50]

The practical-theological emphasis of the question is seen well in Mark 8:14–30. After rebuking the disciples for their inability to 'see' (vv. 17–18) and healing a blind man (vv. 22–6), Jesus presents the disciples with a question, and its position at the central point of Mark's story suggests it as one of the fundamental questions of faith: 'Who do you say that I am?' (v. 29). It is clear from the way that the narrative unfolds that Peter's seeing of Jesus as 'the Christ' was at odds with Jesus' own way of suffering and death (v. 31). Indeed, as the story unfolds further it becomes clear that the disciples' understanding of Jesus as Messiah relates strongly to their own position in the religious and social hierarchy and their ambitions for greatness (8:33–8; 9:34–5; 10:35). Thus their own journey of faith, recounted in the stories and teaching that unfolded as they travelled the road to Jerusalem, entailed a radical rereading of their own Scripture which included a far-reaching reappraisal of their long-held beliefs about the Messiah.

In a similar way, encounters with those in marginal contexts press us to ask primary questions about our own understanding of Jesus.

Black liberation theologian Anthony Reddie echoes the question of Mark 8:29 by asking, 'Who is Jesus for you?' In doing so he seeks to bring to sight the extent to which prevailing perceptions of Jesus are still predominantly in terms of 'cultural whiteness'. He argues that many 'work with an image of Jesus that looks like them . . . that reinforces their own culture' so that even in our post-colonial context the idea of a 'white Jesus' still functions – albeit unwittingly – to sustain a western cultural hegemony. Reddie provokes us to reflect on our own image of Jesus and challenges us to consider again how a richer appreciation of Jesus might lead us to a deeper participation in the kingdom of God in complex urban areas.[51]

Mission Praxis

We use the term 'praxis' to convey the idea of an approach to mission which is grounded in the ordinary places and everyday experiences of socially and geographically marginalized communities. By drawing on contemporary developments from social sciences and practical theology we are presenting praxis as theoretically and methodologically rigorous, cultivating particular attentiveness to the power relations that define marginality. However praxis also conveys ideas about how the Christian community (or researcher) are themselves embodied in such places and how a practical spirituality characterized by vulnerability and open-heartedness might open up new ways of 'seeing' and 'being with' others.

These ideas are an essential precursor to the following chapters in which we have invited authors to explore five realms of mission: the economic, political, social, environmental and creative. In each case authors engage with the subject through their own embedded experience. The chapters are not therefore intended to present an overarching or comprehensive view of the subject but we hope that, as authors struggle with their own situated experiences of marginalization and exclusion, fresh insight will be found about approaches to mission in marginal places.

Notes

1 P. Cloke, 'Self-other', in *Introducing Human Geographies* (ed. P. Cloke, P. Crang and M.Goodwin; London: Routledge, 2014), pp. 63–80.
2 See, for example, E. Goffman, *Stigma* (Penguin: Harmondsworth, 1990).
3 See O. Jones, *Chavs: The Demonization of the Working Class* (Cambridge: Verso, 2012); M. O'Hara, *Austerity Bites* (Bristol: Policy Press, 2014).
4 M. Auge, *A Sense for the Other: The Timeliness and Relevance of Anthroplogy* (trans. Amy Jacobs; Palo Alto: University of Stanford Press, 1998).
5 P. Cloke, 'Exploring Boundaries of Professional/Personal Practice and Action: Being and Becoming in Khayelitsha Township, Cape Town', in *Radical Theory/Critical Practice: Making a Difference beyond the Academy* (ed. D. Fuller and R. Kitchin; Praxis E-press, 2004), pp. 92–102.
6 John 3:5.
7 C. Philo, 'Social Exclusion', in *The Dictionary of Human Geography* (ed. R. Johnston, D. Gregory, G. Pratt and M. Watts; Oxford: Blackwell, 2000), pp. 751–2.
8 D. Sibley, *Geographies of Exclusion: Society and Difference in the West* (London: Routledge, 1995).
9 J. May, 'Exclusion', in *Introducing Human Geographies* (ed. P. Cloke, P. Crang and M. Goodwin; London: Routledge, 2014), p. 656.
10 See T. Cresswell, *In Place/Out of Place* (Minneapolis MN: University of Minnesota Press, 1996); T. Cresswell, *Place: A Short Introduction* (Oxford: Blackwell, 2004).
11 K. Hoggart, L. Lees and A. Davies, *Researching Human Geography* (London: Arnold, 2002).
12 S. Herbert, 'For Ethnography', *Progress in Human Geography* 24 (2000): pp. 550–68.
13 P. Cloke, I. Cook, P. Crang, M. Goodwin, J. Painter and C. Philo, *Practising Human Geography* (London: Sage, 2004). See also, I. Cook and M. Crang, *Doing Ethnographies* (London: Sage, 2007).
14 It needs to be noted that the terminology of researcher/researched can also be laden with power relations, often with researchers holding the power over their 'subjects' in terms of the questions that are asked and the narratives that are produced.
15 Cloke et al., *Practising Human Geography*, p. 170.
16 See D. Mitchell, 'There's No Such Thing as Culture: Towards a Reconceptualization of the Idea of Culture in Geography', *Transactions IBG* 20 (1995): pp. 102–16; P. Shurmer-Smith, 'Introduction', in *Doing Cultural Geography* (ed. P. Shurmer-Smith; London: Sage, 2002), pp. 1–7.

[17] Mitchell, 'There's No Such Thing', p. 108.

[18] L. McDowell, 'Multiple Voices: Speaking from Inside and Outside "The Project"', *Antipode* 24 (2002): p. 56.

[19] J-D. Dewsbury and P. Cloke, 'Spiritual Landscapes: Existence, Performance, Immanence', *Social and Cultural Geographies* 10 (2009): pp. 695–711.

[20] Dewsbury and Cloke, 'Spiritual Landscapes', pp. 695–711.

[21] W. Wink, *Naming the Powers* (Minneapolis, MN: Fortress Press, 1984).

[22] P. Cloke, 'Emerging Geographies of Evil? Theo-ethics and Postsecular Possibilities', *Cultural Geographies* 18 (2011): pp. 475–93.

[23] G. Debord, 'Introduction to a Critique of Urban Geography' (1955) http://www.library.nothingness.org/articles/4/en/display/2

[24] M. Coverley, *Psychogeography* (Harpenden: Pocket Essentials, 2006).

[25] See, for example, I. Sinclair, *Lights Out for the Territory* (London: Granta, 1996).

[26] J. Davies, *Walking the M62* (2007) http://www.johndavies.org

[27] Davies, *Walking*, p. 13.

[28] Davies, *Walking*, p. 9.

[29] Davies, *Walking*, p. 10.

[30] On practical theology see: Mary McClintock Fulkerson, *Places of Redemption: Theology for a Worldly Church* (Oxford: Oxford University Press, 2007); Christian Scharen and Anna Marie Vigen, *Ethnography as Christian Theology and Ethics* (London and New York: Continuum, 2011); John Swinton and Harriet Mowat, *Practical Theology and Qualitative Research* (London: SCM, 2006); Terry A Veling, *Practical Theology: On Earth as It Is in Heaven* (New York: Orbis, 2005); Pete Ward, *Participation and Mediation: A Practical Theology for the Liquid Church* (London: SCM, 2008).

[31] Fulkerson, *Places*, p. 13.

[32] Veling, *Practical Theology*, p. 18.

[33] Swinton and Mowat, *Practical Theology*, pp. 5–6.

[34] For the concept of 'transgression' see Cresswell, *In Place*, pp. 11–28.

[35] Fulkerson, *Places*, p. 13.

[36] For 'faithful performance' see Swinton and Mowat, *Practical Theology*, p. 4.

[37] Swinton and Mowat, *Practical Theology*, p. v; Veling, *Practical Theology*, p. 60.

[38] Scharen and Vigen, *Ethnography*, p. xx.

[39] See, for example: Matt. 7:1–6; Mark 8:17–30; Luke 10:21–37; 18:35–43; 24:31.

[40] Fulkerson, *Places*, pp. 15, 19.
[41] Miroslav Volf, *Exclusion and Embrace* (Nashville, TN: Abingdon, 1996), p. 29.
[42] Fulkerson, *Places*, p. 21.
[43] Fulkerson, *Places*, p. 21.
[44] Veling, *Practical Theology*, p. 55.
[45] Veling, *Practical Theology*, p. 55.
[46] John Taylor, *The Go-Between God: The Holy Spirit and Christian Mission* (London: SCM, 1972), pp. 16–17.
[47] Taylor, *Go-Between*, p. 18.
[48] Taylor, *Go-Between*, p. 19.
[49] Rasiah S. Sugirtharajah, *Voices from the Margin: Interpreting the Bible in the Third World* (New York: Orbis, 2006), pp. 494–8.
[50] For the 'priority of the question' in practical theology see Veling, *Practical Theology*, pp. 60–63.
[51] Anthony Reddie, 'Telling the Truth and Shaming the Devil: A Postcolonial Take on Urban Mission in the 21st Century'. Seminar delivered in Bristol on 23 June 2015 and available through http://urbanlife.org/project/webinars

Part I

1

Understanding the Economic Realm

Paul Cloke

Contemplating Mission in the Economic Sphere

Kathy Galloway[1] describes Christian spirituality as an emotionally profound amalgam of instincts, intuitions, longings and desires that animate and inspire us; it is the force that moves us, but it also encompasses a sense of those deep concerns and motivations that attract our attention. She goes on to argue, however, that spirituality is more than these 'interior' characteristics. It is also wrapped up in 'exterior' everyday choices and actions where intentions are reflected in actions; where we practise what we preach.[2] Spirituality, then, is as much about how we spend our money, time and abilities as it is about our prayers and formal worship. Indeed, the latter cannot with any conviction be divorced from the former. However, the economic sphere often seems to be a tricky arena for the living-out of Christian spirituality; an area of life in which it frequently seems difficult if not impossible to translate the interiority of the Christian message into the exteriority of ordinary life and mission. Globalized capitalism is now so all-pervasive, and its inherent self-sustaining messages about there being no alternative are so powerful, that the idea of working towards more spiritual alternatives opens up a vast chasm between hope and reality.

For some, the contemporary economic system can be accepted as entirely compatible with Christian faith. For example, we frequently encounter the notion that:

> The Bible as a whole supports an economic system that respects private property and work ethic . . . Both the Old Testament and New Testament teach about private property and good stewardship of property . . . In reviewing the notion of Christian economics, the Bible teaches that workers deserve their pay, and that those who work hard are rewarded, while those who are lazy remain poor . . . Competition through comparative advantage also reinforces our worth and dignity in the sense that our work and diligence contribute to the welfare of society as a whole. Comparative advantage allows us the opportunity to become the best producer of a service or product. Thus, competition that leads to cooperation and the recognition of the individual worth harmonizes with the Christian worldview, which sees human beings as the image-bearers of God.[3]

And just in case we would like to pigeonhole such views as belonging to a particular brand of conservative prosperity theology, it is worth pausing to reflect that much of the exterior spirituality of the institutional church reflects these values rather more closely than might be expected, especially given that public statements about interior spirituality are often keen to emphasize issues of justice and fairness. So, even for those of us who believe that the biblical tradition is both clearly very sceptical about accumulated wealth and self-serving economic priorities, and prioritizes relationships with the poor, needy, trapped and lost, it is often hard to translate those intuitions and instincts into the kind of longings and passions that inspire us to forge new kinds of everyday economic decisions and practices. In many ways, we ourselves are trapped – in a systemic mindset that limply accepts the inevitability that markets are paramount, that individuals need to be responsible for their own economic plight, and that aside from righteous charitable responses there is little that can be done by applying mission objectives to the economic sphere. Our task, then, is a very substantial and significant one; to release the Scriptures – and

ourselves – from bondage to the current context of religious individualism and political conservatism.

   This chapter offers no easy remedies; merely gentle encouragements
to understand the current context of globalization and economic austerity not as inevitable outcomes of social and political waywardness
but as the result of deep-seated practices of market-worship, and to
revisit the revolutionary power and potential of Christian justice and
grace in economic matters. Only then will the economy become a
fundamental part of mission practice.

Understanding Globalization

Although aspects of what can be thought of as a world economy have
existed throughout human history, the degree to which economic activity is interconnected across the globe in the twenty-first century
is far more significant than ever before.[4] Examination of the clothes
we wear, the food we eat, the cars we drive, the holidays we take,
the internet we use and so on reveals that our lives are connected
to and dependent on globalized networks of production, consumption, communication and migration. Transnational links have rapidly been developed into a larger *interdependent* system that links the
fates of people all around the world.[5] Mission in the marginal places
of urban Britain will inevitably encounter many of the localized impacts of globalization, not least because economic interdependency
has been accompanied by shared *political* concerns that have shaped
policy-making, and are therefore responsible for shaping how lives are
actually lived in different global locations.

   Despite the economic crash in 2008, in which unregulated global
trading nearly destroyed the banking system across the globe, globalization remains a political imperative. It is presented as an inevitable
and self-evident truth about the contemporary world that continues
to demand political priority because no other options are available.[6]
Governments around the world have therefore been aligning their national policies to a global logic that economic growth and prosperity

depends on integration with global markets and liberating business from national regulation that hampers its globalized activities. Economic globalization, then, is significant because political leaders have used the idea to help them pursue *political* goals. National policies relating to trade, labour, finance and welfare have been radically reformed so as to support the globalizing market economy; as a result there has been an urgent prioritizing of free trade, privatization and deregulation, and a shrinking of the welfare state, all of which have been deemed necessary if nation-states are to prosper among conditions of global competition.[7]

The term used by social scientists to describe this package of government policies is 'neoliberalism': *liberalism* to convey a return to old ideas about liberating economic markets; *neo* suggesting a rejection that such economic freedom should depend on the safety net of a fully functional welfare state.[8] Neoliberal government, then, describes tendencies towards minimalist and market-friendly policies that to some extent are willing to abandon control over national economies in order to conform to the metrics of a globalizing economy. The broad result will often be the advancement of the interests of social and business elites, pervasive social inequality, the translation of social institutions and relations into marketplace transactions,[9] and the subordination of policy goals relating to welfare and environmental protection. However, it would be a mistake to think that globalization takes the form of a simple top-down force that renders politics the same everywhere in the world. One size does not fit all and, in practice, neoliberal policies are significantly shaped by national and local conditions, and the outcomes of these policies are achieved through much more mundane and everyday technologies and practices.[10] It will be local contexts that best reveal how people are being made variously into entrepreneurial, personally responsible, voluntaristic and resilient neoliberal subjects, and how other people are marginalized and excluded by these expectations.[11]

A common claim from its supporters[12] is that globalization will result in a levelling of the global playing field, as competition within international trade will eventually reduce disparities in wages and living conditions at a global scale. This prospect of economic nirvana is, however, most frequently dangled in front of us by business elites themselves, whose interests are best served by a vision of the world without unevenness and asymmetry. The truth is that we live in a starkly unequal world in which the two hundred richest people have wealth equivalent to the combined annual income of about 40 per cent of the world's population. By any reasonable calculation, neoliberal policies of trade freedom, privatization and welfare austerity will all impact most on the poorest groups in any setting. However, the power of discourses about globalization for policy-making and business elites is that if we can be convinced that neoliberal policies are necessary in order to achieve a level playing-field, then it follows that the problems, crises and suffering of the marginalized and excluded can be blamed on the poor themselves – victims can be characterized as 'undeserving' people who lack the individual qualities needed to join in with the new globalizing environment. In this way, globalization might alternatively be understood as *exacerbating* inequality.

Will Hutton[13] describes neoliberalized countries like the UK as suffering a crisis of purpose. We have been told for decades that the route to universal wellbeing is to abandon the expense of justice and equity in order to allow the market to go unobstructed, yet the loss of public and collective action has had the inevitable consequence of producing an amoral deficit of integrity, a carelessness about others and an increased propensity simply to look after ourselves. The neoliberal politics of globalization, then, have promoted *social inequalities* that have led to an evaporation of trust, a lack of common purpose, a distortion of what is acceptable in money markets and banking, significant levels of indebtedness and a political vulnerability to extreme populism (from right and left). He argues that inequality represents both a stark warning about the growing dysfunctionality of the austere market economy, and (if left unaddressed) the principle obstacle to changing the unworkable nature of our society; in other words inequality has now reached levels that present huge ethical and moral challenges to us as human beings. Far from creating a level playing-field, the austerity of market-centred economics and politics has turned out to be a socially divisive contributor to processes of marginalization and exclusion.

If globalization has been responsible for exacerbating *social inequalities*, it is important to recognize that it has also changed the nature of *geographical space*. Matthew Sparke[14] identifies three main ways in which globalization has created new kinds of geographies that result in new ways to territorialize peoples' lives. First, growth-oriented capitalist markets result in *uneven development* due to a continual moving beyond fixed geographic constraints in order to find cheaper inputs, new markets and ways to speed up the turnover between producing goods and selling them.[15] At all scales, different levels of development result from these processes, meaning that certain continents, countries, regions, cities and suburbs will benefit less from globalization than others at any one time. Underdevelopment not only exacerbates income inequality, unemployment and poverty, but also in some settings expands the populations of the displaced and imprisoned, representing a type of expulsion[16] – from professional livelihood, from living space, even from the very biosphere that makes life possible.

Second, globalization has been associated with the phenomenal growth of *global cities*,[17] fuelled by urban development that is directly organized by the financial speculation of investors, and by expectations among wider communities of governments, planners and transnational property-buyers about the future investment value of real estate. Global cities bear the hallmarks of neoliberal influence on urban government, benefiting from public–private partnerships, entrepreneurial city management and investment-oriented policy. Although one side of global cities is represented by wealth and neoliberal management, the other side can be characterized in a third geographical outcome of globalization, namely *spatial splintering*. New forms of possession by investors inevitably lead to the dispossession of other people, most graphically understood in the fractured-off landscapes of the dispossessed–informal squatter settlements and slums, impoverished estates and neighbourhoods, the sites of the marginalized. The enclaves of privilege that have benefited from neoliberal reforms stand in contrast to their inverse urbanism–spatial concentrations of poverty, poor housing, unemployment and social dislocation.[18] Although political accounts of spatial splintering tend to focus on the role of deviant gang cultures and criminality, what should perhaps be emphasized more is how neoliberal development of cities *causes* social dislocation and exclusion. Splintered spaces should first and foremost be recognized as places of extreme poverty, poor employment opportunities and exploitation, where inhabitants face insecurity, poor health and wellbeing and a lack of citizenship rights. That is, the neoliberal politics of globalization has inscribed inequality into the global city. As Chris Hamnett has argued, 'While some people may be living in a postmodern urban lifestyle playground, others have to live in a post-industrial wasteland.'[19]

The obsession with globalized economic markets has therefore been inextricably linked with deployment of neoliberal political strategies and practices that have permitted market economics to subjugate issues of human wellbeing and welfare. Far from creating a level playing-field, these trends have exacerbated both social inequality and geographical unevenness, splintering off the poor and the marginalized even further from the mainstream. For those involved in urban mission, this picture of globalization presents both an essential context for action, and the basis for serious questioning about how a Christian narrative can offer radical alternatives to the bankruptcy of neoliberalized orthodoxies.

Critiquing Market Worship

Clearly globalization has been made up of more than economics. However, it follows from the above account that the story of globalization has at its root an extravagant respect for and devotion to the almost supernatural power of capitalist markets. Such excessive esteem and reverence is shaped by a very familiar set of rituals and creeds, declaring the market to be the one true arbiter of opportunity, reward and value, and constantly anxious about how the market will react to any particular set of circumstances. Given these terms of allegiance, it is easy to see that the market has in effect been the subject of worship – its power and authority revered as reigning supreme across the earth. However, notwithstanding claims of harmonious compatibility with a Christian world-view, market worship is not only idolatrous, but also a major source of unhelpful human values that require careful critique from Christian perspectives, of which three can be summarized here.[20]

First, market worship skews our appreciation of *what it is to be human*. As Nathan McLellan has emphasized, 'the human person cannot be reduced to a consumer'.[21] That is, consumption must not be permitted to define what it means to be human. Yet one of the defining characteristics of market worship is that people become mere 'personifications of economic relations',[22] being valued in terms of their position in economic hierarchies and their capacity to access commodities. Just as capitalist markets use money to obscure the reality and value of things by turning them into commodities, so the value of people becomes distorted by the apparent importance of what they can, and can't, buy. Commodities, then, are treated as a fetish – as if they have special mystical powers, including those to alienate people from the real value of things, and to alienate humans from their true value by overemphasizing their role in terms of the production and consumption of things. As Michael Watts has stated: 'Commodities surround us and we inhabit them as much as they inhabit us. They are everywhere, and in part define who and what we are. It is as if our entire cosmos, the way we experience and understand our realities and lived existence in the world, is mediated through the base realities of sale and purchase.'[23]

For Christians, being human cannot simply mean a series of unlimited desires that can never fully be satisfied, for we believe that human fulfilment is discovered in relationships with others in and through Jesus. Moreover, it follows that the *places* where these relationships take place are also an important part of being human. Capitalist markets have paid little attention to the role of 'place' in economic life,[24] preferring to think of place as a chessboard in which the pieces can be shuffled around to best suit economic strategy. Market worship therefore has negated the role of *humans-in-place*, paying little attention to the

unique contexts in which traditions, cultural practices and local characteristics affect how people and communities continue to be formed.

Second, and relatedly, market worship skews our appreciation of
what is real and important by converting the world into that which
can be measured by economists. Bob Goudzwaard[25] maintains that in
adopting the language of economics, market worship renders invisible
key qualitative aspects such as, for example, the world of social interactions between people, the importance of therapeutic relations with
the natural and built-up environment, and the value of good health,
active community and cultural wellbeing. In other words, markets
fail to prioritize that which money can't buy,[26] ignoring requirements
either where costs outweigh financial benefits, or those where no
price is set. In the latter case, therefore, market worship will not value
the sustainability of nature, cultural heritage, or even human love
and dignity. No price implies that these things are free to use, and
free to exploit. This casting aside of non-market values has created
both a specific moral deficit in those areas that can only be expressed
qualitatively, and a more general lack of reasoned public debate over
moral and ethical issues. Our political discourse has become mostly
vacuous in that it lacks moral, ethical and spiritual content – each of
which require an ability to look beyond numeric values. Indeed, part
of the appeal of worshipping markets is that typically they neither
differentiate between moral or ethical preferences nor take too much
notice of potentially marginalizing and excluding impacts on social
practices, human relationships and the locations and communities in
which these take place.

Third, market worship skews our capacity for *accountability and
responsibility* for economic outcomes and problems. The science of
the market ascribes a certain type of causality; prioritizing the events
or specific circumstances that have caused problems to happen rather
than who is responsible for, or the cause of, these events. As Goudzwaard explains:

> If we are confronted with an important economic problem, let us say
> inflation, the growth of poverty, the rise of debt-burdens, or the growth

of unemployment, we have learnt ourselves and others not to bother about questions of responsibility for those evils. We 'explain' those phenomena in terms of the level of savings or consumption, the level of interest, the level of government expenditures. The economist's world is a world free of accusations, free from any analysis of accountability for what happened.[27]

This screening out of responsibility, and consequent normalizing of a kind of market forgiveness for irresponsibility, tends also to negate important ethical discussions about alternative kinds of behaviour, especially debates involving the need for redemption of previous guilt.

Market worship, then, has resulted in economic systems that pay little heed to ethical questions of inequality, marginalization and exclusion. Indeed it has resulted in manifestly unfair outcomes, with outrageously excessive rewards for the few, and unemployment, low wages, insecure work conditions, exploitation and impoverishment for the multitude. It is, as Michael Hardt and Antonio Negri[28] have argued, nothing less than the building of a new globalized empire by the world's 1 per cent;[29] an empire that accepts no boundaries and limits and subjugates the multitude to its purposes and control. Any such empire will have periodic moments of meltdown[30] as we have seen in the financial and economic crisis of 2008, and it is at just these moments when we get the clearest glimpse of deep public unease about the moral and ethical consequences of market worship.[31] Indeed, world-leading economists such as Amartya Sen and Joseph Stiglitz[32] are now telling us that free-market capitalism is something of a fantasy, given that most economies depend on transactions and payments for welfare benefits, education, health care and the like occurring *outside of* the free market, relying on rules of citizenship rather than ownership. Sen argues for the recognition of a kind of economic citizenship based on agreed social values that can be defended ethically. Stiglitz talks about 'moral growth', that is an economic system based on tolerance, social justice and solidarity that ensures that benefits are shared equitably. The key question is how these kinds of alternative economic models can be put into practice in a world where the downward pressure of globalization continues to prompt governments towards welfare austerity and economic individualism in which there often seems to be little room for a commitment to ethical values of justice.

Hopelessness into Hope: An Interlude

So to recap: the globalization of the economy and the accompanying hot pursuit of neoliberal forms of government are resulting in grossly unfair economic inequalities and an accompanying reluctance to provide welfare to the victims of marginalization and exclusion. Questions are coming to the surface about the dubious moral basis of economic life, and about the potential for new forms of ethical citizenship that might form the basis of an alternative socio-economic order; but frankly these issues seem so hopelessly huge that it is much easier to ignore them than to find a viable starting place from which to make them an integral element of mission in marginal places. In their book, *Hope in Troubled Times*,[33] Bob Goudzwaard, Mark Vander Vennen and David Van Heemst tackle this need for a hopeful starting place, and offer three practical guidelines for enacting a vision (but certainly not a blueprint) for Christian activism:

1. The periscope guideline

Christian discipleship in among a globalized economy is somewhat akin to being in a submarine submerged below the water, with only a narrow and limited view of the surrounding bigger picture. A periscope allows us to scan the wider horizon, and naturally a return to key biblical principles and values would provide such a perspective. The trouble is that being implicated in market worship has already influenced our norms and warped our values. To some extent the power of biblical ideas of justice, love, truth, freedom, solidarity and economic management has 'become emptied and then refilled for the sole purpose of legitimating certain ends and justifying the means required to implement them'.[34] Only by reclaiming the original meanings of these powerful ideas are we able to regain our periscope on the wider horizon of God's economy.

2. The minesweeper guideline

Sometimes our response to injustice is to engage in mirror-image reactions. For example, there has been a clear tendency in recent years to analyse the cause of economic decline in terms of the inward migration of people from other lands rather than deeper market mechanisms. The argument goes something like this: the reason why 'we' struggle to access accommodation, employment and a decent standard of living is because 'they' have taken over our houses, jobs and school and hospital places. The response to our mistreatment is to mistreat others, resulting in this example in widespread vilification of those who seek refuge among us. If 'mines' are laid in our territory we can fight back – as a form of self-orientated escalation – or we can call in the minesweeper to trace the threat and disarm the mines. However dire the conflict, there are local possibilities for peace, rooted in the conviction that God's economy requires truth-telling, admitting, confessing and forgiving rather than escalation.

3. The rope-ladder guideline

The globalized economy tends to result in forms of injustice, exclusion and deeply entrenched poverty that are both pervasive and mutually reinforcing. The resultant gloom can easily sponsor pessimism, hopelessness and helplessness, even among Christians whose discipleship relies on the hopeful promises of God. The rope-ladder pictures for us the way in which spirals of decline can be tackled one step at a time; small steps of love, peace and justice can have a greater radiating effect than we imagine. Places of despair can become places of blessing if we change our mindsets from all-or-nothing, premeditated, grand schemes, to small steps of grace empowered by God's Spirit rather than self-aggrandized human design.

These three guidelines offer a helpful and hopeful response to the question of how to contemplate bringing Jesus-narratives about humanity, spirituality and responsibility to bear on mission in the economic sphere. Using the periscope guideline it is important to rediscover the radical meaningful power of biblical ideas about economic morality and ethicality. Surveying this wider horizon allows us to 'sweep for mines' not only in the supposed orthodoxies laid down in globalization and neoliberal policy, but also in our own self-centred responses to economic conditions. Only then can we start taking small steps up the rope-ladder by outlining possible economic applications for love, peace and justice as part of mission in marginal places.

Christian Narratives on Economic Justice[35]

It is all too easy to allow theology to become an economic issue, rather than vice versa. Full immersion in an everyday context of markets and commodities sends us sleepwalking into belief that money is a neutral means of exchange, credit innocently allows you to go shopping and debt is a normal way of living life–fantasy assumptions that Ann Pettifor labels 'Alice in Wongaland'.[36] However, economics *is* a theological issue; the parable of the talents (Matt. 25:14–30; Luke 19:11–28) alerts us to the kind of theological awakening required. Read at face value, the parable appears to endorse ruthless business practices, entreating Christians to profit as much as possible through hard work and normalizing the idea that the poor will become poorer because of their individual ineptitude in the economic system. If (as seems commonly to be the case) 'the master' is translated as a figure for God, the narrative suggests a severe, hard-hearted and ruthless deity, akin to an absentee landlord whose only concern is to maximize profit. Read in such a way, the parable warns us to use our talents[37] profitably for God, but it is our immersion in globalized market economics that provides the uncritical basis for assuming that the narrative points to the glories of a system that rewards venture capital. The parable is far more coherent when turned upside down and understood as a cautionary tale about the mercenary selfishness of systems of indebtedness, in which the servant who declined to participate in the money-market games of the greedy master is the one following the Jesus-narrative by paying a high price for speaking truth to power. As Ched Myers and Eric DeBode conclude:

> To read in it a divine endorsement of mercenary economics and the inevitable polarization of wealth is to miss the point completely – and to perpetuate both dysfunctional theology and complicit economics in our churches . . . we meet Christ mysteriously by feeding the hungry, giving drink to the thirsty, welcoming the stranger, clothing the naked, caring for the sick, and visiting the imprisoned. In other words we meet Christ in places of pain and marginality; the 'outer darkness'. The whistle-blower's punishment kicks him out of the rich man's system, but brings him closer to the Lord, who dwells with the poor and oppressed.[38]

As the alternative understanding of this parable suggests, theology can provide Christians with radical perspective that helps them both to avoid unthinking conformity to the world as if its current state is inevitable or sanctioned by God, and to develop a sense of being conformed instead to Jesus-narratives that speak judgement over systems of oppression and exclusion.

While the Bible does not provide us with a set of economic rules, there is a guiding thread running through the scriptural narrative that can help shape mission in the economic sphere. That thread has been brought together within the idea of *Common Wealth*[39] – the earth is created by God and belongs to God, and contemporary conditions of human selfishness and power-hungriness do not and cannot change that reality. Common wealth connects up moments of prophetic biblical truth:

> from the created gift of the world to the laws which challenged debt enslavement and dispossession; from the wisdom tradition which looked

sceptically on wealth and thankless labour, to the prophets who directly
challenged the oppression of the poorest members of society, and the injustice handed out to paid workers; from the early Christian community,
holding all in common, to the vision of a 'New Jerusalem', a world freed
from exploitation.[40]

In this way we can make sense of Old Testament scepticism about the
accumulation of wealth and the exploitation of labour (Lev. 25) and
seek to understand how to respond to its principle that no one should
have too much and no one should have too little. The proclamation
of a year of Jubilee,[41] involving a redistribution of wealth, cancella-
tion of debt and freedom for bonded labourers, has been applied with
some success by the Jubilee 2000 campaign to the issues of global-scale
debt,[42] but its educational value in exposing debt-affected poverty and
espousing biblical notions of debt-forgiveness has yet to be applied
more radically in among the marginal people and places of the UK.
Similarly, the clear perspective of the Old Testament prophets on the
need to be aware that standards of living are not being maintained
through exploitation and oppression,[43] and on the hypocrisy of false
piety in contexts of economic injustice[44] have figured in the words but
rather less so in terms of the missional deeds of the institutional church.

For Christians this narrative thread of common wealth is personified
by the life and teaching of Jesus, who turned upside down common
assumptions about wealth, value and forgiveness, and who confronted
an imperialist and idolatrous economic system through a sacrificial
way of peace and truth. Jesus radically appreciates and appropriates
the thread of common wealth and economic justice found in the Hebrew Bible. His ministry accepts the task of bringing in Jubilee,[45] and
is critical of the rich who accumulate wealth at the expense of the
poor.[46] In Jesus' story of the rich man and Lazarus, he asks out loud
how did the rich man become so rich, and the poor man become so
poor, and in so doing he invites his followers to contemplate what they
already know. The rich man benefited from exploitation, buying land
from impoverished peasants, who were then forced to sell their labour
back to the rich, and were pushed into destitution in hard economic

times. Yet, rather shockingly for us in our money-driven culture, Jesus is clear that it is the poor (and not the rich) who find favour with God. The embodiment of this transforming vision can be glimpsed by attempts in the early church to live out aspects of common wealth in a community setting,[47] and it is the further embodiment of the radically alternative power of God's loving justice and grace that should form the core of contemporary mission in the economic sphere.

Christian Involvement in Alternative Economic Pathways

Inevitably, when it comes to illustrating the sorts of contemporary activities that respond to a transforming vision for the economic sphere, the examples often appear to be unable to match the scale, gravitas and radical nature of the theology concerned. However, the reaction of 'is *that* all we can do?' bears witness more to the overwhelming power of contemporary market worship than to the truth that with God all things are possible. This is where the rope-ladder guideline comes into its own, emphasizing the hopefulness that can be vested in small steps guided by theological principles of justice and grace. What follows is a series of illustrations of the kinds of small steps that might be contemplated. As might be anticipated by the approach to mission advocated in this book, the following examples do not form any kind of blueprint for mission; incarnational presence and discernment in a community will gradually reveal its culture and needs, and local economic responses should certainly be informed by local conditions. However, as a starting point, there are at least five areas of participative activity through which biblical narratives on economic justice can be imagined as part of local mission.

Prophetic protest

Speaking truth to power is one of the most crucial elements of biblical narration of justice; and it is crucial for Christians both to stand in solidarity with oppressed and marginalized people, and to participate fully with forces resisting distorted market-based ideology. Accordingly, there are two very practical reasons for ensuring that prophetic protest becomes part of mission in marginal places. First, the need for justice occurs at various scales, and the interdependence of globalized economies means that local acts can have foreseen and unforeseen circumstances in other parts of the globe. Participation in larger-scale campaigns – for example against sweat-shop production of consumer goods, or against international human trafficking, or in favour of fair trade – bears the mark of radical witness against exploitation and in favour of international responses that favour exploited workers wherever they may live.[48]

Second, a blinkered focus on one particular community, however needy, runs the risk of failing to connect up local response to wider issues of justice. One of the lessons of research into homelessness,[49] for example, is that providing local services for homeless people needs to be twinned with wider campaigning in favour of better national welfare policies for such people. Otherwise the amelioration of local need contributes little to longer-term and more structural policy reform. Therefore, acts of localized kindness to and embrace of marginalized others need to be connected up to more structural discussions of injustice, and prophetic protest helps to make that link.

One further advantage of engaging in larger-scale prophetic protest is that it provides a wider understanding of and opportunity for the role of the church in exercising spiritual critique beyond the local community. Research on the Occupy London Stock Exchange protest in 2011 shows a very considerable Christian presence among the protesters, even though there was eventually a disagreement between Occupy and the authorities of St Paul's Cathedral, where the protest took place.[50] In practice, being part of the Occupy movement enabled Christian protesters to pose three significant challenges to the positioning of the wider church vis-à-vis a radical critique of injustice in the globalized economic system. First, they questioned whether the priority of the church (as represented in this case by St Paul's) should be maintaining its own institutional and financial practices, or highlighting the economic and social damage being inflicted by the financial institutions that surrounded it. Second, they opened up serious doubts about whether the supposed sanctity of formal church buildings was more important than the alternative sanctity of dwelling in everyday places of need, and if necessary critiquing the religious institutions and practices of the time. Third, they contrasted the idea of faith as a set of dogmatic beliefs with more everyday, lived kingdom-practices that defined faith in terms of joining with the multitude of common people in order to resist the forces of empire, to prioritize the needs of the poor and to dance on injustice. Prophetic protest, then, invokes a subversive remembering of the church's identity and calling, and re-equips a radical discipleship for localized mission.

Alternative welfare

Biblical narratives suggesting radical responses to the plight of oppressed and marginalized people may well involve attempts to bridge the gap between shrinking state welfare and the basic needs of local people. The last thirty years have witnessed a remarkable rise in the involvement of faith-motivated organizations and people in responding to the welfare needs of impoverished and exploited people.[51] Indeed Christian groups are now prominent providers of care and welfare for people experiencing homelessness, food poverty, unemployment, trafficking, addiction, refugee or recent migrant issues and many other aspects of social exclusion. In addition, Christians are active in providing services for young and elderly people in their communities. Sometimes such involvement in practice means joining in with already-established national models of service provision, for example, opening a new branch of the Trussell Trust network of food banks, or collaborating with existing providers (such as the Salvation Army or the YMCA) of shelter and housing for homeless people or job clubs for the unemployed.[52]

Such activities are often linked with schemes which provide services of *alternative community navigation*; that is providing advice that puts needy people in touch with people in the public or private sector who can deal with their economic plight. Churches have been particularly active in the navigation of indebtedness, advising those with heavy debts about how to change their consumption habits and reach agreement with those to whom money is owed. On other occasions, alternative welfare activities result in smaller-scale, locally organized schemes that stem directly from identification of the needs of particular families or individuals, and some action will not be in the form of 'schemes' at all, relying on everyday practices of befriending or 'buddying' to introduce postures and patterns of inclusion into marginalized settings.

Participation in alternative welfare often results in crucial contributions to the lives of local people with particular needs, but if these activities are realistically to reflect Christian theologies of economic justice, there are a number of factors that require careful and prayerful evaluation to avoid them becoming schemes-for-schemes'-sake or, worse, expressions of self-satisfying charitable collusion with wider patterns of market worship. For example, there is currently a move in government towards the active encouragement of voluntary organizations to take up the slack left by neoliberal welfare cuts and austerity economics – what is commonly termed the 'Big Society'. These changes afford Christians the opportunity to contribute to Big Society in an expression of 'we are all in this together'. However, the rhetoric of Big Society basically masks oppressive business as usual; it has been recognized as 'divide and rule dressed up as high-minded community spirit'.[53]

A faith response, then, cannot simply be an expression of charity in among unjust economic ideologies. It has to be an earthed and embodied expression of revolutionary excessive grace. This requirement can also raise questions about simply joining in with major national Christian organizations, however worthy. For if the cost of membership is to be obliged to use business models and managerial rules and regulations that restrict the expression of grace, or shape it into something compatible with market worship, then that may be a price that dilutes or even negates biblical narratives of economic injustice.[54] These issues require prayerful discernment; there is often no clear-cut answer. The notion of providing welfare benefits to needy people is crucial in itself, and such provision often both sensitizes volunteers to alternative theologically inspired ethics, and alerts them to some of the more structural politics concerned.[55] Generally, however, welfare work in the meantime needs to be carried out in full recognition of the theological and ideological imperatives at work in local situations.

Alternative consumption

If replacing state welfare risks replication of neoliberal market economics, community activities that promote alternative, and more collaborative, forms of consumption offer the prospect of a more radical alternative to exploitative market economics. To some extent, aside from significant initiatives in support of consuming fair-trade products, alternative forms of consumption are only just creeping onto mission agendas in the UK, yet there seems to be considerable potential here for genuine Christian resistance to market ideologies via more communitarian approaches.

For some, action on consumption will take the form of direct opposition to the role played by advertising in their locality in creating and maintaining market-based consumer culture. Such *adbusting* will often involve different forms of art as protest, including humorous but message-oriented modification of on-line or billboard advertising designed as a form of *culture jamming* to interrupt the normal experience of consumerism by turning around the received meanings from advertisers.[56] For others, incarnational mission can lead to the establishment of local shared economies of consumption. For example, fuel poverty can be addressed through sustainable forms of community energy aimed at reducing the cost and usage of energy resources. Community-led action can often tackle challenging issues around energy, with community groups well placed to understand their local areas and to bring people together with common purpose. Initiatives include: community-owned renewable electricity installations such as solar photovoltaic panels or wind turbines; joint switching to a renewable heat source such as a heat pump or biomass boiler; and collective purchasing of alternative fuel and associated smart technologies.[57]

Another fruitful area of mission via alternative consumption lies in the area of community-based food initiatives. With rising food prices, and the control of agri-businesses and supermarkets over an increasingly centralized and industrialized system of food supply, the UK food economy reflects all the hallmarks of unjust and exploitative market worship. Yet recent developments in community-based food schemes offer interesting alternative models of consumption.[58] These include *food cooperatives* organizing the joint purchase of food for resale within the community, in turn often linked to initiatives to improve the quality of nutrition through, for example, the making available of inexpensive fruit and vegetables, and accessing organic and local produce. Other enterprises make attempts to include communities in the growing of their own food, by promoting an *allotment culture*, or by cultivating *community gardens* as urban growing spaces which are run and maintained by members of the community and produce food that can be distributed on the basis of participation and need rather than purchasing power.

These kinds of activities have endless possibilities for innovation. They open out opportunities for voluntary participation and for making use of urban land that might otherwise be underutilized, and can sometimes evolve into social enterprises in which profits are ploughed back into the community. They can also strengthen community cohesiveness, offer opportunities for embrace of marginalized others, and (most crucially) model something of God's just and grace-filled economy of common wealth.

Alternative business

For some, the chosen path towards an expression of common wealth theologies will be to do business differently. Over recent years there has been a minor explosion of *social enterprise* in countries such as the UK, defined broadly as entrepreneurial activity aimed at generating social value and creating sustainable change rather than focusing on producing monetary profit.[59] To some extent, the boom in social enterprise has become almost a business in itself. For example, the city of Plymouth is reported to have 150 social enterprises, spread across a wide range of sectors including education, health, the arts, the environment, food, finance and housing, employing seven thousand people and producing an income of £500 million.[60] On closer inspection, this social enterprise sector embraces large-scale organizations such as the university and community providers of health care and homes as well as large numbers of smaller businesses, but the guiding principle is a constrained pursuit of gain, and a heightened sense of altruistic moral consideration.

While it is certainly the case that not all religious enterprises are social enterprises, faith-motivation has been recognized as a significant driver for social entrepreneurship.[61] Establishing social enterprise as part of broader mission in marginal places offers a variety of opportunities to live out alternative theologies of common wealth, and to model counter-cultural economic ethics. In this way, social enterprise is being used to create both economic value (through creating employment, or enhancing employability) and social value (through providing relevant services) in local communities. In addition, setting up social enterprise provides a pathway towards relational embeddedness in these communities, offering opportunities to establish a relational presence through conducting business in ways that are different from the orthodoxy of market worship.[62]

The tricky element to this particular model of living out biblical narratives in the economic realm is to find ways of sustaining a modus operandi that resists being immersed into the seemingly all-embracing commercial expressions of market economics. All too often, institutions and individuals unwittingly become increasingly businesslike in their competitiveness and their overriding concern for securing an ongoing role for the enterprise which they have created. Market worship is insidious and cloying, and sometimes the best of intentions are unable to resist its power. However, performed faithfully (and often benefiting from accountability to wider mission communities beyond the economic realm), alternative ways of doing business can be a fruitful element of mission in marginal places.

Alternative finance

Alternative systems of finance are difficult to contemplate given the all-pervasive power of money in the contemporary setting of consumer culture and market worship. Yet as Ann Pettifor[63] argues, what is desperately required in these circumstances is a deliverance from the enslavement of commodification and indebtedness; a prioritization of life and flourishing over the ownership and hoarding of money and things, and a prophetic insight from the theology of economy instead of blind acceptance of the politics and culture of having and hoarding. Small steps towards such a vision are being taken in the area of ethical banking in which socially responsible investment permits lenders and borrowers to establish financial relations with some kinds of agreed ethical values. However, although niche ethical providers such as the Triodos and Charity banks have succeeded in maintaining this ethical stance in among the mainstream marketplace, it is unfortunate (and perhaps inevitable) that larger-scale institutions such as the Co-operative Bank have had to dilute these principles in order maintain a profitable place in the system.

While ethical banking represents a small step forwards in the enactment of justice through financial relations, a more radical pathway to incorporate mission into an economic sphere of excess grace can be found in different segments of what has come to be known as the 'solidarity economy'. Solidarity in economic relations seeks to meet human needs through economic activities – like the production and exchange of goods and services – that reinforce values of justice, ecological sustainability, cooperation, and democracy. In the words of the organization *solidarity nyc*, solidarity economies offer a series of important and distinctive ethical characteristics:

> Instead of enforcing a culture of cut-throat competition, they build cultures and communities of cooperation. Rather than isolating us from one another, they foster relationships of mutual support and solidarity. In place of centralized structures of control, they move us towards shared responsibility and democratic decision-making. Instead of imposing a

single global monoculture, they strengthen the diversity of local cultures and environments. Instead of prioritizing profit over all else, they encourage a commitment to shared humanity best expressed in social, economic, and environmental justice.[64]

These values closely reflect the biblical theology of common wealth, and so those seeking to extend mission into the economic sphere are already benefiting from an awareness of the modus operandi of the solidarity movement. Alternative finance can be made available, for example, via *crowdfunding*, in which individuals donate small amounts (usually without expecting to receive any return) to meet the larger funding requirements of a particular charitable project, or *community shares*, where members of the community can invest in local community projects such as a local shop or energy project that provides a social return.

More familiar in Christian circles are *credit unions*, of which there are now about five hundred in the UK, many with church-based connections. These are not-for-profit community-based savings and loans cooperatives, offering a fairer lifeline in less well-off communities to people grappling with financial problems. As such they provide a more ethical alternative to the payday and doorstep lenders who otherwise profit hugely from the emergency money needs of the poor. Even more radically, some solidarity economy schemes attempt to displace money altogether, usually by establishing local or on-line systems of bartering and swapping that permit the acquisition of necessary goods or services in cashless transactions. In addition, *time banks* have become popular in some communities. Here time is used as a unit of local currency, as participants give or receive help in exchange for time credits. Research has suggested that time banks encourage reciprocal volunteering and active community participation especially among marginalized people in marginalized places.[65]

It needs to be reiterated here that these various forms of Christian involvement in the economic sphere do not present a ready-made programme of potential initiatives in mission. It is all too easy to prefigure what is required in a marginalized community before gaining a listening-and-learning understanding of what is needed and how those needs are shaped by local cultures and spiritual landscapes. Equally, a key potential failing in mission is to become locked into some kind of perceived necessity to innovate continually, and to report quantifiable successes at regular intervals. Mission in the economic sphere requires an emphasis on embedded participation rather than flashy schemes, and consistent sensitivity to theological prompts to common wealth rather than short-term success-for-success'-sake.

Notes

1   K. Galloway, *Sharing the Blessing: Overcoming Poverty and Working for Justice* (London: SPCK/Christian Aid, 2008).

2   For further discussion of interiority and exteriority, see W. Wink, *Naming the Powers* (Minneapolis, MN: Augsburg Fortress, 1984).

3   Quoted from http://www.allaboutworldview.org/christian-economics. htm (accessed 2 Aug 2015).

4   See, for example, A. Jones, 'Economic Globalization', in *Introducing Human Geographies* (ed. P. Cloke, P. Crang and M. Goodwin; London: Routledge, 2014), pp. 413–26.

5   P. Dicken, *Global Shift* (London: Sage, 2010); D. Mackinnon and D. Cumbers, *An Introduction to Economic Geography: Globalization, Uneven Development and Place* (Harlow: Prentice-Hall, 2011).

6   See, for example, T. Friedman, *The Lexus and the Olive Tree* (New York: Picador, 2012).

7   These processes have been transparent, for example in the demands made by EU leaders for austere changes to the Greek economy as the price of financial bail-out in 2015.

8   See D. Harvey, *A Brief History of Neoliberalism* (Oxford: Oxford University Press, 2007).

9   As in, for example, the privatization of health and social care. See, for example, C. Leys, *Market-Driven Politics* (Oxford: Verso, 2013); A. Pollock, *NHS plc* (Oxford: Verso, 2009).

10 W. Larner, 'Neoliberalism', *Environment and Planning D: Society and Space* 21 (2003): pp. 509–12; A. Williams, M. Goodwin and P. Cloke, 'Neoliberalism, Big Society and Progressive Localism', *Environment and Planning A*, 46 (2014): pp. 2798–815.

[11] Although there is also a need to engage in larger-scale (even global) resistance to these outcomes.

[12] T. Friedman, *The World Is Flat* (New York: Farrar Straus Giroux, 2005).

[13] W. Hutton, *How Good We Can Be* (London: Little, Brown, 2015).

[14] M. Sparke, *Introducing Globalization* (Wiley-Blackwell: Chichester, 2013).

[15] See, for example, D. Harvey, *Spaces of Global Capital* (Oxford: Verso, 2006); N. Smith, *Uneven Development: Nature, Capital and the Production of Spaces* (Oxford: Verso, 2010).

[16] S. Sassen, *Expulsions* (Cambridge MA: Harvard University Press, 2014).

[17] D. Massey, *World Cities* (Cambridge: Polity, 2007); S. Sassen, *The Global City* (Princeton NJ: Princeton University Press, 2001).

[18] As Neil Smith has argued, these two sides of the city are often directly linked through 'revanchist' (that is, associated with revenge) geographies in which urban elites organize heavy-handed policing and regulation aimed at reclaiming or gentrifying the spaces previously occupied by poorer sections of the population.

[19] C. Hamnett, 'Urban Form', in *Introducing Human Geographies* (ed. P. Cloke, P. Crang and M. Goodwin; London: Routledge, 2014), p. 704.

[20] But see P. Oslington, ed., *Oxford Handbook of Christianity and Economics* (Oxford: Oxford University Press, 2014).

[21] N. McLennan, 'What is Capitalism?'(n.d.). Quoted from http://marketplace.regent-college.edu/ideas-media/business-economy/what-is-capitalism (accessed 31 July 2015).

[22] G. Ward, *The Politics of Discipleship: Becoming Postmaterial Citizens* (London: SCM, 2009) pp. 93–4.

[23] M. Watts, 'Commodities', in *Introducing Human Geographies* (ed. P. Cloke, P. Crang and M. Goodwin; London: Routledge, 2014), p. 391.

[24] See M. Shuman, *Going Local: Creating Self-Reliant Communities in a Global Age* (London: Routledge, 2008).

[25] B. Goudzwaard, 'Christianity and Economics', Lecture for the Scholarly Conference 'Shaping the Christian Mind', Australia (1996) http://allofliferedeemed.co.uk/Goudzwaard/BG68.pdf (accessed 31 July 2015). See also B. Goudzwaard, *Capitalism and Progress: A Diagnosis of Western Society* (Grand Rapids, MI: Eerdmans, 1996).

[26] M. Sandel, *What Money Can't Buy: The Moral Limits of Markets* (London: Allen Lane, 2012).

[27] Goutzwaard, 'Christianity and Economics', p. 6.

[28] M. Hardt and A. Negri, *Empire* (Cambridge, MA: Harvard University Press, 2001).

[29] See also D. Dorling, *Inequality and the 1%* (Oxford: Verso, 2014).

30 D. Harvey, *The Enigma of Capital* (London: Profile Books, 2011).

31 J. Atherton, C. Baker and J. Reader, *Christianity and the New Social Order* (London: SPCK, 2011).

32 A. Sen, *The Idea of Justice* (London: Penguin, 2009); J. Stieglitz, *The Price of Inequality* (London: Penguin, 2013).

33 B. Goudzwaard, M. Vander Vennen and D. Van Heemst, *Hope in Troubled Times* (Grand Rapids, MI: Baker, 2007).

34 Goudzwaard et al., *Hope*, p. 182.

35 Here, I want to acknowledge my indebtedness to the Ekklesia manifesto, 'Common Wealth: Christians for Economic and Social Justice' http://www.ekklesia.co.uk/CommonWealthStatement (accessed 21 July 2015). The wider notion of 'common wealth' has been explored in M. Hardt and A. Negri, *Common Wealth* (Cambridge, MA: Harvard University Press, 2011).

36 A. Pettifor, 'No, This Is Not the Road to Recovery. It's the Road to Wongaland', *The Guardian* (16 August 2013).

37 A talent was one of the largest values of money in the Greek world – the equivalent to more than fifteen years' wages. A literal interpretation of the parable is therefore nonsensical.

38 C. Myers and E. Debode, 'Towering Trees and Talented Slaves', *The Other Side* (May–June 1999). Quoted in 'The Parable of the Talents: A View from the Other Side' http://godspace-msa.com/2010/05/18/the-parable-of-the-talents-a-view-from-the-other-side/ (accessed 3 July 2015).

39 Ekklesia, 'Common Wealth'.

40 Ekklesia, 'Common Wealth'.

41 See also Deut. 15:1–15.

42 See, for example, J. Gaventa, 'Levels, Spaces and Forms of Power: Analysing Opportunities for Change', in *Power in World Politics* (ed. F. Berenskoetter and M. Williams; London: Routledge, 2007); M. Mayo, *Global Citizens: Social Movements and the Challenge of Globalisation* (London: Zed, 2005).

43 Amos 2:7.

44 Isa. 58:3,6.

45 Luke 4:16–21.

46 Luke 16:19–31.

47 Acts 2:43–7.

48 See, for example, the work of No Sweat (www.nosweat.org.uk); Hope for Justice (hopeforjustice.org); and the Fairtrade Foundation (www.fairtrade.org.uk).

49 See, for example, P. Cloke, J. May and S. Johnsen, *Swept Up Lives?* (Chichester: Wiley-Blackwell, 2010).

50 P. Cloke, C. Sutherland and A. Williams, 'Postsecularity, Political Resistance and Protest in the Occupy Movement', *Antipode* 48 (2015): pp. 497–523.

51 See, for example, P. Cloke, J. Beaumont and A. Williams (eds.), *Working Faith* (Milton Keynes: Paternoster Press, 2013); J. Beaumont and P. Cloke (eds.), *Faith-Based Organisations, Welfare and Exclusion in European Cities* (Bristol: Policy Press, 2012).

52 See, for example, the opportunities available for volunteering at the Trussell Trust (www.trusselltrust.org/volunteer), The Salvation Army (http://www.salvationarmy.org.uk/volunteering) and the YMCA (http://www.ymca.org.uk/volunteer).

53 Ekklesia, 'Common Wealth'.

54 A. Williams, P. Cloke, J. May and M. Goodwin, 'Contested Space: The Contradictory Dynamics of Food Banking' *Environment and Planning A* (Online First), DOI: 10.1177/0308518X16658289; P. Cloke, S. Thomas and A. Williams, 'Faith-Based Action against Poverty', in *Working Faith* (ed. P. Cloke, J.Beaumont and A. Williams; Milton Keynes: Paternoster Press, 2013), pp. 25–46.

55 P. Cloke, J. May and A. Williams, 'The Geographies of Food Banks "in the Meantime"' *Progress in Human Geography* (Online First), DOI: 10.1177/0309132516655881.

56 J. Heath and A. Potter, *The Rebel Sell* (North Mankato, MN: Capstone, 2006).

57 See, for example, http://alternativetechnology.org.uk/CommunityEnergy.htm

58 T. Pinkerton and R. Hopkins, *Local Food: How to Make It Happen in Your Community* (Totnes: Transition Books, 2009).

59 See, for example, C. Leadbeater, *The Rise of Social Enterprise* (London: Demos, 2001).

60 Details of the Plymouth Social Enterprise Network can be accessed at http://plymsocent.org.uk/about/

61 An interesting account of religious social entrepreneurship is provided in R. Spear, 'Religion and Value-Driven Social Entrepreneurship', in *Values and Opportunities in Social Entrepreneurship* (ed. K. Hockerts, J. Mair and J. Robinson; Basingstoke: Palgrave, 2010), pp. 31–51.

62 An example from Bristol is found in Chapter 2.

63 A. Pettifor, *Just Money* (Margate: Commonwealth Publishing, 2014).

64 Accessed at http://solidaritynyc.org/#/resources/

65 G. Seyfang, 'Time Banks: Rewarding Community Self-Help in the Inner City?' *Community Development Journal* 39 (2004): pp. 62–71.

2

Case Study: A Journey

Chris Sunderland

It was 1998 and I was leaving parish ministry. I had served, for the best part of a decade, as vicar to folk in a tower-block estate in Barton Hill in Bristol. They were good people, often surviving in the toughest of life circumstances. And I was tired. Well, actually, not just tired, but full of grief, for the community and its burdens that I had shared over the years. I also felt that I had to try to make faith count in a different way. The traditional Anglican method seemed so hopelessly compromised in our developing post-Christendom society. The set of expectations that a vicar was working with were no longer acceptable to most people. So I set out to find a new path.

The early years of the new century saw the completion of an M. Phil. as a chance to get my head around the deep changes that the Enlightenment had brought to our way of thinking. I then tried to distil this into a book called *In a Glass Darkly*; my first attempt to reposition faith in public life. In terms of my inner life, I was encouraged by contact with the Northumbria Community and their interest in storytelling in relation to faith. I began to mine the Bible in new ways and learnt to 'tell' portions of it as part of discussions about public life. So I would be a slightly raving Jeremiah denouncing his king for failure to be concerned for the poor and needy. Or I would 'tell' the dreadful political struggles of David in the context of contemporary events in the Middle East. Those who knew me in these days would have noted how 'dark' the stories were that I told. I think

I was working through some of my own grief at the time, because I remember the day when I woke up and felt, very consciously, 'I don't need to tell those dark stories any more.'

These early years were deeply formative and not very obviously fruitful. I would gather small groups in pubs, usually consisting of the more radical type of believer and play out some conversation about public life. Looking back on it, the topics we discussed are still of primary interest. They went under titles like 'Weapons of Mass Delusion', 'Death by Performance Indicators', 'A Surveillance Society', 'Immigration, Threat or Opportunity'. I actually published the structure of these conversations so as to encourage others associated with churches to do this type of thing, but there was little take-up. I think it all felt like a bridge too far for most church people.

So it was around 2008, having been through a phase of what you might call spiritual formation that I began to understand that the truly great struggle we were all facing was to be about the human relationship with creation. I remember both the challenge and the joy that this realization brought. I now knew what my life was to be about. As I saw it at the time, this calling to embrace the concerns of creation was the next great mission of the church. Just as the church had made such a profound contribution to Jubilee 2000, Make Poverty History and Drop the Debt campaigns in relation to the developing world, so surely it would rise to the challenges being presented by climate change and the whole litany of environmental issues associated with our relationship with the earth and its creatures? Looking back now in 2015, it is probably the greatest sadness of my life to recognize that the main body of the church is resolutely human-centred and refuses to see creation concern as anything other than an 'add on' to its interests. Yet back then I was full of hope. Ann Pettifor, who had led Jubilee 2000, was appointed lead for Operation Noah, the churches response to climate change. So the wheels were ready to turn.

I began with an attempt to form a Christian community called EarthAbbey and with a Bristol-based city-wide campaign called Chooseday, which was a behavioural change initiative around leaving cars at home on a Tuesday. The campaign achieved some traction. We had a great banner on the Council House and the hospital, we became reasonably well known, and I began to learn some of the skills of leading a movement for change. Meanwhile the church agreed to license a former vicarage garden to EarthAbbey, as a community-growing project and a team of us were also working each other's gardens over to grow food, in an initiative called Grow Zones. It was a great start, and a learning opportunity for me. I began to see that the church was hesitant to whole-heartedly embrace the sort of projects I was proposing, but also that the truly radical people in our city were outside of the church and deeply suspicious of formalized Christianity. Yet these people did have a spiritual heart. They were very much not materialists. They were committed to radical expressions of community life, suspicious of leadership and hard to organize. These experiences had a strong influence on my own faith journey.

I recall a set of meals we had put on as EarthAbbey, specifically designed to introduce different ways of approaching environmental issues and moving on from simple, individual behavioural change to a vision for deeper transformation of society itself. We talked about permaculture, with its vision for growing food and society in harmony with the earth. We discussed community-supported agriculture and its potential to derive a different type of food business. Several of my friends went on to do things along these lines but, I recall, at the end of the last meeting, pointing to the potential for a local currency to give people a taste of a different form of money, that was embedded in the local economy and could produce a new values-led community of exchange. And I told the group I would have a crack at it.

Next stop was to pay a visit to one of the leading figures in the Transition movement in the city. It was clear that a local currency had to be done at scale if it was to be seen as significant and attain public confidence. The pioneering initiatives in Totnes, Lewes, Brixton and Stroud had shown that there was enormous public interest in these projects, but also that it was hard to get to an adequate scale with just a paper currency. So I said, 'We need to do a currency that is city-wide and uses both electronic and printed media'. That was our root commitment that stayed with us through the next three years of preparation for launch.

Gradually a team grew around this core idea. Others had been thinking along similar lines. They were not necessarily people of faith. It was clear to me by this time that projects like this, if they were to achieve real public impact, had to be truly inclusive from the start. In post-Christendom society, it is very hard for any project that is actively identified with a faith organization to become more than a niche concern. So, our team grew from two, to four, to eight, until by the time of launch we had around twenty people working their socks off to make the Bristol Pound, as we had called it, a reality. The interesting thing about this group of people is that almost no one was paid.

There was an energy in the team that remains to this day. I reckon it is based on two things. The first is being very clear about what you are going to do and not being distracted from this core purpose. The second is to recognize and nourish the shared values that you all hold in regard to this project. Our team were all people who held a deep and abiding concern for the earth. They saw that the dominant economic system was truly at the heart of the problems we were facing and that we had to try to model something different. The phrase 'Shared Values Clear Purpose' sums up this approach to team-building.

The Bristol Pound was launched on 19 September 2012 to enormous acclaim. It was on all the TV channels, even Ukrainian TV! The Lord Mayor, dressed in all his regalia, gathered with the media outside the exchange building in Bristol, the historic heart of trading in the city. He held up a paper Bristol Pound and declared, 'What will anyone give me for my Bristol Pound!' Joe Wheatcroft from Source, a food shop, brought out a loaf of bread. An exchange was done and the cameras whirred. Meanwhile people queued up for their Bristol Pounds. The first person said 'I will have 500 Bristol Pounds please.' And we were flabbergasted by the response over the course of the day. At the same time the electronic accounts were switched on. They are managed by Bristol Credit Union, and use a mobile phone exchange system as well as allowing on-line trading much as in BACS.

I have reflected on why the public response at launch was so positive and I put it down to the years of preparation. It was doing the hundred-page feasibility study that covered all the details. It was visiting the Bank of England to talk through the legalities. It was working up the electronic system, which we did in partnership with the Brixton Pound. It was engaging with our local authority so that they had agreed to accept business rates in Bristol Pounds. And perhaps most of all, it was taking the time to build a team of people, variously skilled, but fired up to make this happen. I recall the three weeks before launch. Our office went quiet. There was a profound concentration. This thing was about to happen. The electronic system was being tested. Cafés and pubs, etc. were being recruited as places to exchange sterling for Bristol Pounds. Our trader manager was teeing up businesses ready to join.

So where are we now? As I write this in January 2015, there are over 700 businesses and 1,300 individuals that are part of the scheme. Paper Bristol Pounds are circulating in the city, accepted on the buses and many traders are familiar with them. Tourists also love them. The electronic system is the heart of our exchange. In the four weeks over Christmas our total exchange was something like 30,000 BPs across the city. That may sound a lot, but actually, across a city our size, it is still small beer. We recognize the need to expand our reach considerably over the coming months and years.

As a result, our team are currently working on bringing in an energy supplier, working to achieve major public procurement contracts in Bristol Pounds, developing a new business-to-business credit facility and also – a project that I have personally been working on – focusing on encouraging people to source food from local producers. I see food as a key driver of change for many of us. It has the potential to make us aware of the earth and, historically, has always been the centre of human social development. So we have developed a new cooperative, called Real Economy. Our aims are to bring people in touch with local producers, encourage uptake of fresh food, with minimal waste, through using buying groups that order their food using a bespoke webtool that we have developed.

Our particular interest with Real Economy is to develop our buying groups in areas of high unemployment and little food choice. Bristol Pound has mostly taken off among educated people in the slightly more well-off areas of the city, but this demographic sector has never been our intended focus. So with Real Economy we have the aim to restore the balance, developing community life through buying groups in some of the most challenging areas of the city and bringing a whole range of people together through the cooperative to encourage new enterprise, pop-up markets and any interests our members would want to promote. We see the cooperative as a new expression of a solidarity economy, a 'can-do' approach to life under austerity. I write this in the week that the first five buying groups are making their orders . . . We shall see where it goes.

'So what of faith?' I expect some readers are asking. I see my work as an expression of faith in the public arena. I have never felt more clearly called to anything in my life than the work I am now engaged in. I remain keen to work with faith and faith communities and give one day a week to this work, but I recognize the limitations of faith organization-branded approaches to life in a post-Christendom society. I believe that we are living in an age of deep change, that is a 'prophetic' age, when some are called to go to the margins and attend to, in Brueggemann's words, the 'reimagination of society'.

3

Case Study: YMCA Exeter Job Club Project

Samuel Thomas

YMCA Exeter is one of 114 YMCAs in England and one of the oldest in the world, originally founded in 1848. Today it draws heavily on its Christian ethos and mission and while we work particularly with young people, YMCA Exeter's vision is to 'see communities transformed into places characterized by love, joy, peace and hope where all people can become everything they were created to be'.

The Job Club Project was initially birthed out of YMCA Exeter's Supported Housing Project, conceived as an additional service that would add value to the ongoing personalized support plans drawn up around each young adult living at the YMCA. Out of a desire to see these residents 'make the most of their day', reduce isolation and engage in meaningful activity, the housing staff team put on a weekly drop-in where residents could access computers, chat to a staff member about any ideas or aspirations they had for further training, education or work. The job club was incentivized with a free bacon sandwich and coffee and this, combined with a friendly informal approach from staff, led to overall good levels of participation.

In 2011, YMCA Exeter was approached by Devon Community Foundation to deliver a similar service in four local neighbourhood wards known for having high levels of socio-economic deprivation. Since then the Job Club Project has operated with two main strands: one developed for the specific needs of the young adults living at the YMCA; and a community-embedded model designed for a broader age group and open to all. This expansion into differing communities has led to encounters with a broad range of people who experience some form of exclusion from the labour market for a variety of reasons, and who often have multiple and complex individual needs. In its current form the Job Club Project consists of seven job clubs delivered across four sites every week, complemented with a further two additional services of a skills-based workshop and a pilot into-work mentoring project. The teams facilitating the clubs comprise of one paid member of staff working alongside several volunteers.

The work is challenging! In the years of running the job clubs we have encountered on a small, local scale some of the wider issues surrounding paid labour and employment, and, in relation to this, many of the ongoing tensions and challenges faced by the YMCA Exeter Job Club team seem to reflect two main questions:

- How do you tackle the sanctions-based culture of 'job-seeking' and best support and encourage those who are embedded within and reliant upon such a welfare model?
- How might we assist and encourage those who are not just having difficulty accessing the labour market, but who face the kind of complex and often multiple issues that mean they find themselves a long way from being 'ready for work'; for whom there is often a significant chasm between what they have to offer and what employers are looking for?

In the face of these challenges, we have learned that the ethos of the Job Club Project and the related practices is of key importance. Phrases that might helpfully describe what lies at the heart of the job club approach would include: emphasis on being 'person-centred', working collaboratively and holding to a hopeful perspective.

Each person accessing one of the job clubs is given one-to-one time and there is a careful welcome and induction process. There is no 'one-size-fits-all' model or quick fix, and the foundation of the approach enacted in the job clubs is one of compassion, incredible

patience, and a sincere desire to see those who attend live more enriched lives. This is epitomized in the comments of one of the Job
Club Project team describing the purpose of the project:

> When we work with our clients our goal is not just to see them get
> jobs. We want them to live lives that are full and to build their personal
> resources so that they can be confident and caring of themselves and
> others. We journey with our clients for as long as they need us, accepting
> them, but also challenging those things that limit them. Our work is pur-
> poseful, but also person-centred. We empower our clients by equipping
> them to do things for themselves so that they can become independent of
> us and do what they want to do and be who they want to be.

Some individual personal barriers to securing paid employment (interview techniques, for example) can be easily overcome, while other
barriers (such as significantly low self-esteem or lack of confidence)
require a more holistic approach. In these situations the ability of staff
and volunteers first to generously welcome, and then encourage individuals to lift their sights to acknowledge their own capabilities, raises
spirits and gives the club its sense of togetherness and camaraderie.
With some job club users there is no instant remedy to unemployment but the culture of support and perseverance instils a sense of
hope in those accessing the service.

Being hopeful is key, as is a continual iteration of what it means to
be human. In practice this means holding and enacting an approach
in the job clubs that values what people bring to the club: a 'come as
you are' mantra; an acknowledgement that everyone is more-than-
a-worker. Someone brings their dry sense of humour, another their
ability to recall obscure historical facts. Essential to the make-up of
the job clubs is a wider set of non-market values. Everyone has a
chance. Everyone is equal. Everyone has something to contribute.

The importance of this stance has been particularly notable when
folk come as referrals from the local Job Centre Plus. Many individuals who make regular use of a job club are dependent upon the financial benefits they receive as 'job seekers' from the local Job Centre Plus

(e.g. Job Seeker's Allowance). However in many cases the surveillance and individual scrutiny each individual endures at a Job Centre Plus shapes clients' perceptions of why help is offered and what can be gained from the process of job-searching. Typically those who come via this route can present themselves as nervous, anxious and concerned as they first walk into a YMCA Job Club, articulating that if they 'do not apply for so many jobs they will have their benefits cut'. Immediately the job club team have to assure them that as a local Christian charity we are distinct from Job Centre Plus. This often includes moments of reassurance that we will endeavour to support them the best we can and are not going to 'report back to the job centre'. The fear, anxiety and confusion that clients come with takes a number of weeks to unravel and dispel. Critical to this process are the small encounter moments within the service that embody an approach that speaks of a more hopeful and less 'strings attached' expression of support.

In some cases the actual identity and self-narrative of the person have been rewritten by the process of being a job-seeker claimant. The challenge in these circumstances is how to draw out a different way of being and believing in oneself that is not wrapped up in the continual rather automated and governed process of compliance. How do we best support individuals entrenched within this system so that they themselves feel empowered and envisioned to make the most of paid work rather than continuing to make decisions through compliance and a feeling of being controlled? This is a difficult challenge and one that needs continual re-examination. While the answer is most probably in providing alternative frameworks of power and empowerment, the practicalities of how this theology is worked out need to be carefully considered. It's an ongoing challenge and one that too often gets buried amidst the 'busyness' of trying to deliver a service, deal with the unexpected, chase the next funding grant or deal with the immediacy of peoples' vulnerability and poverty.

A collaborative culture has emerged as another key ingredient in the health and success of the Job Club Project. The job club environment, its results and successes are not the product of one individual, paid or voluntary, rather the creative collaboration of a pooled skill set. This collaborative approach is rolled out both within the team, within the actual job club through encouraging clients to be co-contributors, and beyond it through seeking strategic partnerships with other agencies across the employment support landscape. Central to the ethos of the Job Club Project is an ambition to see 'clients' involved in the delivery of the service (through various volunteer roles) and able to help shape its direction themselves (through a client steering committee). Alongside this is the recognition that volunteers have a great deal to offer and need to be used to their full potential. Students, workers and those who have retired all have something to bring, whether this is in making the most of their gift of hospitality, their ability to patiently listen, or troubleshoot with the computers, or their skill in building and refining CVs. A good team culture has emerged from having a clear sense of vision, a culture of praise, regular training, and setting aside times to get to know each other better through social events.

More widely, allegiances with a variety of statutory, voluntary and private companies and individuals have all helped shape the service. Not all have been successful, but where these alliances are positive such rapprochements bring innovation, creativity and resilience to what is often a difficult task in a very tough labour market environment.

Where the Job Club Project continues to struggle is around the complex issue of sustaining paid employment for those who would be seen as having 'successfully' secured a job through the club. This is a major challenge, particularly pertinent within the context of YMCA Exeter's support of young people, but one that is applicable across the demographic and in all cases appears to be due to the combination of two different factors: first, external labour market conditions (e.g. zero hours contracts, seasonal work, migrant labour); and second, personal circumstances such as a particular social network or lack of it, substance misuse, personal expectations and changes to statutory benefits.

How do you best support people as they navigate their way through the current volatility and ferocity of the labour market?

The current conditions that underpin unskilled and blue-collar work in the UK are far from complementary to the needs and difficulties faced by those on the social and economic margins of British society. When YMCA Exeter clients do secure paid work it is often seasonal, minimum wage and/or based upon a zero hours contract. Therefore moving from a place of long-term unemployment (with all the associated personal costs of physical and mental health concerns, debt issues and personal isolation) to a position of holding down a job in such an environment is an extremely daunting task. Many case examples can be drawn from YMCA Exeter that suggest how difficult this transition can be. While it is all very well providing a caring, understanding and compassionate environment within a job club, the project has little or no control over the work environment into which the individual becomes embedded. In some cases individuals find the task of their newly found job too stressful and as a result feel there is no other option available to them but to quit. Bullying in the workplace and a lack of tolerance for individual differences add to the personal difficulties they are already working hard to overcome.

This case study presents a local response to unemployment by highlighting one of YMCA Exeter's community projects. It outlines the nature and ethos of the Job Club Project and looks at some of the key aspects and challenges that have emerged from this missional engagement as we have tried to be attentive to local economic conditions and to respond in a meaningful and practical way. The example of YMCA Exeter Job Clubs highlights how necessary it is to consider the whole person when combating issues of unemployment and exclusion from the labour market, and the need to build a culture of intentional collaboration both within the actual job clubs and beyond with partner agencies and the wider employment support landscape. This localized response to a far-reaching global issue hopefully brings into being local spaces of care that begin to redraw the nature of what is possible through an emphasis not on the status quo – competition, consumption and 'self-first' – but on compassion, consideration and empathy for and alongside the vulnerable other.

However, as the case study also shows, these hegemonic neoliberal forces are not easily overcome through the development of alternative frameworks of local activism. The following questions are still pertinent to what we do:

- How might we best support and encourage job-seekers who are embedded within and reliant upon a punitive sanctions-based welfare model?
- How do we best support someone on the margins of the current labour market into long-term sustainable employment?

These two challenges must be met with a hopeful and determined response that draws upon the spirit and grit of making the impossible possible but they also remind us to be cautious of a quick-fix, one-size-fits-all model that does more for our own consciences than it does for the actual individual who walks through the door looking for support in finding paid employment.

4

The Economic Realm: Editorial Comment

Andrew Williams

Redeeming Economics

The question of mission and the economic sphere attracts much ambivalence, even suspicion, in western Christianity on a number of grounds. There are some who continue to adhere to the idea that faith is private and personal, and therefore antithetical to social or political involvement. Particular eschatologies uphold a premillennial view of 'the world' not as the fallen order being redeemed by God, but as a material, perishable existence and thus non-spiritual. This has sponsored political *quietism*, in which escapist, negative or conformist postures towards society draw on ideas about the kingdom of God being reserved for the eschatological future. Yet in recent years there has been a sea change in eschatological ideas about the kingdom of God,[1] with the emergence of *transformational* approaches which acknowledge that the outworking of the kingdom of God can transform society in the here and now. Evangelicals, in particular, display a renewed openness to embrace the biblical call to seek justice and reconciliation between people to God, to each other and the environment.[2] This movement can be traced in a host of new socially engaged expressions of faith in areas of welfare, environmentalism and humanitarianisms.[3] However, mapping the politics of church groups and organizations working in these arenas reveals the divergent ways the economic sphere and mission can potentially connect. Most visible in elements of evangelical Christianity in the USA, there is an unapologetic de-fence of free-market fundamentalism, and its ideologies of individual-ization, private property and moral responsibility.[4] Yet elsewhere, and even within US evangelicalism, there are Christian groups embodying more collectivist sensibilities, who identify in the Jesus-story various expressions of socialist, liberal and neo-anarchistic politics.[5]

In Chapter 1, Paul Cloke outlines examples that illustrate the greater willingness among Christians across denominations in the UK to engage the economic sphere both as a site of and a tool for mission. Any attempt to begin explaining this shift will inevitably be culture-specific, so I will focus discussion on the area of Christianity I know best: contemporary evangelicalism in the UK. Here we can identify two factors that have played a significant role in increasing the propensity for individuals and churches to become more engaged in issues of economic justice. The first concerns the changing the-ology of evangelical belief and praxis, especially its broad political leanings. Much can be said about key figures who have helped shift Christian moral and political concern from an apparent fixation on issues of abortion, sexuality and marriage, onto issues of economic and social justice, as well as their role in opening up a debate that for some believers has led to a revision of, even repentance for, previ-ously held moral standpoints. While these trends are important, they need to be understood within the wider move from Christendom to post-Christendom, whereby Christians find themselves as now 'one voice among many' and can no longer expect or benefit from the familiarity of cultural privilege and control over government. While some Christians lament the erosion of legislative powers with a sense of loss or even hawkishness,[6] others celebrate throwing off the binds of established religion and its theologies of cultural and economic privilege that domesticated the good news to fit a particular charita-ble and nationalist expression. In this contemporary moment, there are new opportunities for the church to embody a more radical, trans-national movement of believers.

Second, in a context characterized by heightened diversity and plu-rality of belief, faith and identity, urgent questions have arisen about how Christians might deal with 'difference' in ways that avoid forms of cultural imperialism or separation, and instead enter into reflexive and postsecular-styled encounters with 'others' so as to develop understanding, respect and common purpose. Equally, it is important to examine the different ways in which the 'individualization and commodification' of spirituality has itself shaped forms of evangelical praxis. Here Paul Cloke's discussion of 'market worship' and how the (capitalist) economic market has infiltrated how we see God, see ourselves, and how we relate to others is insightful. If the neoliberal enculturation of our desires, attitudes and passions as possessive consumers is taken as formative of the contemporary spiritual context; if market worship is found equally in the social and economic relationships of the church as in society; then, there is little wonder why younger and older Christians alike express dissatisfaction with 'business as usual' models of church that – perhaps inadvertently – provide merely a spiritual consolation for the individual rather than embodying an alternative community of praxis.

The combination of these factors has led to what Paul Cloke identifies as the emergence of 'theo-ethics'; a shift towards a more socially engaged faith that eschews previously conversion-oriented agendas in favour of an *embodied enactment of the essences of belief, such as agape and caritas*, among marginalized groups in contemporary society.[7] In Chapter 1 and elsewhere, Paul Cloke develops the concept of 'theo-ethics' to draw attention to the move from propositional modes of belief and ecclesial practice, towards more performative theologies that incorporate tradition and immanence in the form of virtue ethics.[8] The spaces in which theo-ethics are enacted can open out important sites of collaboration across religious and non-religious difference, as like-minded individuals and groups themselves identify synergy between their own world-view, religious or not, and the hopeful politics and relationships found in radical expressions of Christian theo-ethics.[9] For this reason expressions of theo-ethics often attract individuals for whom 'church attendance' in whatever guise is no longer, or never was, a meaningful expression of their own religious or spiritual beliefs.

Paul Cloke identifies alternative spaces of welfare as key sites in the city in which faith-motivated people and groups join others to practically serve and care for people who often find themselves marginalized or stigmatized by the very government policies designated to help them (homeless people, unemployed, asylum seekers, sex-workers, victims of indebtedness), and in doing so embody particular theo-ethics of grace, simply defined here as a self-sacrifice and unconditional love. Take the moralization of welfare, for example, whereby government policy, increasingly driven by authoritarian-libertarian ideas of 'just rewards', seeks to redefine the very parameters of what we think of as good, right and just. In his 2010 address to the Conservative Party conference, David Cameron stated: 'Fairness means giving people what they deserve – and what people deserve depends on how they behave.' Notions of deservedness soon became entrenched in welfare policy. Those who were unwilling to help themselves – for whatever reason – were singled out for tougher sanctions and illiberal measures. In this economy the persistent widow would be deemed irresponsible for not being willing to accept her losses to 'get on and get ahead' (see Luke 18:1–8), while Lazarus sitting at the gate of the rich man would be deemed a scrounger and has only himself to blame for the sores on his body (Luke 16:19–31). Theo-ethics of grace, then, embody a word of judgement on a system that restricts the offer of acceptance, hospitality or physical wellbeing itself to some crude behavioural credit-rating that assigns whether or not one is 'deserving' or 'undeserving'. Paul Cloke notes that in a variety of different arenas (protest, welfare, environmentalism) it seems the subversive voice of public theology is being heard again when it is grounded in practice.

Most importantly, Chapter 1 deals not just with the economic sphere as a site of care and protest, but also identifies the practical challenges and opportunities present in embodying new ways of doing economics. Faced with the goliaths of global capitalism and corporate power that saturate the physical and spiritual landscape, the question of experimenting with new economic projects might be seen as entirely futile. However, Paul Cloke suggests that the economic sphere should not be mired by its association to a narrowly defined hegemonic set of capitalist relations, or regarded as an inherent threat to the purity of mission. This fails to recognize the multitude of every-day economies[10] that we inhabit, including: alternative market econ-omies and alternative capitalist economies (forms of enterprise where private accumulation of surplus is not, or not the only, core business); sharing economy; gifts/gifts-in-kind; non-monetary exchange; house-hold flows, charity, gleaning; and theft. Perhaps we need to find new ways of recognizing or even speaking about the diverse economies that make up the economic sphere, and develop ways to experiment with the economic as a site of mission.

The notion of 'redeeming economies' is helpful here in focusing attention on the mission of God in bringing redemption, renewal and restoration to economic spheres. It refers to the kingdom-styled transformative work that particular forms of economic relations can achieve. Redeeming economies encompass prophetic campaigning, civil disobedience and protest that challenge the trade of goods that should not, and will not, play any role in God's economy; for exam-ple, the trade in armaments, human trafficking and harvested human organs. It also speaks of the need to challenge and reform a raft of unjust economic practices, be they the legislation surrounding credit and pay-day loans; intensive animal farming; or even reworking the ethics on which our own church institutions are organized. The eco-nomic sphere, however, should not simply be regarded by Christians as a site of protest but as a tool for reconciliation and redemption.

While caution is needed not to valorize any one economic model as inherently 'sacred', the call here is to experiment locally with eco-nomic practices that can bring about redemptive purposes. Prom-inent examples include economic cooperatives in Israel–Palestine where local cafés seek to encourage spaces of encounter and dialogue by offering half-price meals to Palestinian and Israeli customers who sit and eat together. Or the 'Urban Farms for Ethiopian New Im-migrants' in the cities of Beer Sheva and Kiryat Gat, which provide access to a livelihood and a means for inclusion for one of Israel's most marginalized populations through its community gardens and local exchange trading systems. Within these alternative economic spaces, the encounters and economic relations between participants and members are as important as the production of goods.

Examples of the transformative aspects of redeeming economies are well illustrated in more formal economic cooperatives such as Delicious Peace in Uganda, where Jewish, Muslim, Christian and non-religious farmers self-organize to share resources and profits into a variety of public health and education projects. The cooperative directly sells its coffee to independent artisan coffee houses in the USA. While a cynic might dismiss this as nothing more than the commodification of the interfaith 'brand' to sell coffee, looking a little deeper reveals the multitude of interactions and exchanges within this economic space: profit-sharing; economic self-determination and self-organization; fairtrade; consumption networks opting out from corporate-dominated supply chains; spaces of cooperation, dialogue and conflict resolution; building bridges beyond fundamentalisms; and cultivating reflexive engagement and tolerances across social, religious and ethnic differences.

Such examples of cooperative economies or social enterprises are not a substitute for structural critique of capitalism; but they do offer a strategic way of 'doing something' that reworks, subverts or resists hegemonic spaces of production in ways that offer real opportunities to individuals and groups often affected by systemic injustices in global neoliberal economies.

Too often our involvement in the social and economic spheres is limited by our imagination of what is possible. As a result we reproduce the 'ready to go' projects or national franchises, being drawn to what is easy and 'feasible' without serious reflections on local needs and alternative models. With regard to the ever-expanding role of food banks, for example, one might draw inspiration from how other European countries tackle food insecurity. In Tuscany, a region pioneering alternative food networks, we find a range of initiatives, including Gruppi di Acquisto Solidale (Solidarity Purchasing Groups), Campagna Amica (a network of short food-supply chains), Libera (a network of farms, civil society groups and cooperatives that work land confiscated from the mafia), Caritas Solidarity Shops (which provide emergency food assistance), and Orti Etici (a social cooperative of organic farmers who employ disabled people).[11]

Obviously there will be questions about how easy it is to translate such schemes from a region which boasts rich institutional and food activist histories, yet lessons remain of how we can rework existing models of charitable food banks into something more collectivized, be it through solidarity purchasing groups, communal food hubs, or something else. Building links and sharing knowledge and technical skills would help navigate the difficulties of setting up similar projects elsewhere. By looking elsewhere we might be drawn less to charitable models that address residual needs of the few, and instead experiment with collectivist food networks that address the social as well as the food needs of the many.

Notes

[1] On the changing theological landscape of Christian faith motivation see, Paul Cloke, Sam Thomas, Andrew Williams, 'Radical Faith Praxis?' in *Faith-based Organisations and Exclusion in European Cities* (ed. Justin Beaumont and Paul Cloke; Bristol: Policy Press, 2012), p. 109.

[2] See David Bosch, *Transforming Mission* (Maryknoll, New York: Orbis Books, 1991); Tim Keller, *Generous Justice* (London: Hodder & Stoughton, 2010); Shane Claiborne and Tony Campolo, *Red Letter Christianity* (London: Hodder & Stoughton, 2012); Jim Wallis, *God's Politics* (New York: HarperCollins, 2005); Cynthia Moe-Lobeda, *Resisting Structural Evil: Love as Ecological-Economic Vocation* (Minneapolis: Fortress Press, 2013).

[3] See prominent church-led anti-poverty campaigns such as Jubilee 2000, Micah Challenge and Make Poverty History, the proliferation of Christian involvement in areas of welfare (food banks, Christians Against Poverty) as well as the more longstanding advocacy work of CARE, Church Action on Poverty, Barnado's and Housing Justice.

[4] This is exemplified in Wayne Grudem, *Politics – According to the Bible* (Grand Rapids, MI: Zondervan, 2010); Barry Asmus and Wayne Grudem, *The Poverty of Nations: A Sustainable Solution* (Wheaton, IL: Crossway, 2013). For a critical account of these developments in the USA see Jason Hackworth, *Faith-Based: Religious Neoliberalism and the Politics of Welfare* (Athens, GA: University of Georgia Press, 2012).

5   Jim Wallis, *God's Politics* (New York: HarperCollins, 2005); Alexandre Christoyannopoulos, *Christian Anarchism: A Political Commentary on the Gospel* (Imprint Academic: Exeter, 2011).

6   This is not purely an American phenomenon. In the UK, political movements such as the Christian People's Alliance, the Christian Institute and the Christian Party (the latter fielded candidates in seventy-one constituencies in the 2010 election) have sought to exploit the perceived marginalization of (supposed) Christian values in Britain in order to push policies that seem utterly inconsistent with the teachings of Jesus (see Simon Hill, 'Why I'm Not Voting for the Christian Party', Ekklesia (6 May 2010) http://www.ekklesia.co.uk/node/12072 (last accessed 21 Jan 2011).

7   Paul Cloke, 'Theo-Ethics and Faith Praxis in the Postsecular City', in *Exploring the Postsecular: The Religious, the Political and the Urban* (ed. A. Molendijk, J. Beaumont and C. Jedan; Leiden: Brill, 2010), pp. 223–43.

8   See Cloke et al., 'Radical Faith Praxis'.

9   Andrew Williams, 'Postsecular Geographies: Theo-Ethics, Rapprochement and Neoliberal Governance in a Faith-Based Drug Programme', *Transactions of the Institute of British Geographers* 40(2) (2014): pp. 192–208.

10 J.K. Gibson-Graham, *A Postcapitalist Politics* (Minneapolis, MN: University of Minnesota Press, 2006).

11 For a more detailed account of alternative food networks in Tuscany, and their capacity to address food insecurity by re-socializing food production and consumption practices along more socially and ecologically just lines, see Gianluca Brunori, Adanella Rossi and Francesca Guidi, 'On the New Social Relations around and beyond Food: Analysing Consumers' Role and Action in Gruppi di Acquisto Solidale (Solidarity Purchasing Groups)', *Sociologia Ruralis* 52 (2012): pp. 1–30. Also see Roberta Sonnino, 'The New Geography of Food Security: Exploring the Potential of Urban Food Strategies', *Geographical Journal* (2014), DOI: 10.1111/geoj.12129; Roberta Sonnino and Christopher Griggs-Trevarthen, 'A Resilient Social Economy? Insights from the Community Food Sector in the UK', *Entrepreneurship and Regional Development: An International Journal* 25 (34) (2013): pp. 272–92.

Part II

5

Understanding the Political Realm

Martin Gainsborough

*[H]ow can anyone change the world and society at its
roots without taking away freedom? . . . There must
be a place, visible and tangible, where the salvation of
the world can begin . . . Beginning at that place, the
new thing can spread abroad, but not through persua-
sion, not through indoctrination, not through violence.
Everyone must have the opportunity to come and see.
All must have the chance to behold and test this new
thing . . . What drives them to the new thing cannot be
force, not even moral pressure, but only the fascination
of a world that is changed.*[1]

Introduction

What do we think politics is? There is, of course, the classic definition
that it is about who gets what, when and how.[2] But what is it to act
politically? Here, people tend to rush to a fairly predictable and likely
rather circumscribed list, including voting, writing to one's MP, joining a campaigning group, or going on a march. There is, of course,
nothing much wrong with these things and they are one way to engage in the political realm. However, there is also a sense in which
they do not take us to the heart of what it is to act politically or even

to what politics is. As a professional political scientist, I would say that politics is much more ubiquitous – everything is political – and hence to act politically takes us into a much wider realm of activity.[3]

Imagine, for a moment, that you are a church in a 'run-down' part of town – an inner-city area or an outer estate – where poverty is widespread, where people are often not working, where there is a higher incidence of long-term illness and people die younger than the population at large, where people are often very locally focused, and may not have the skills, confidence or desire to engage with the 'standard' national or international issues. What do you do? How do you love and honour the people? How do you seek to build the kingdom of God in that place and, importantly, what are the particular issues one needs to be sensitive to if one wishes to do mission with integrity there?

These are some of the questions that this chapter grapples with, in the process trying to tease out what is 'political' about mission in marginal places. The chapter is unapologetically focused on the experience of one local church, and on a single project within the parish in which the church is focused. One of the things that will become clear in this chapter – and is a theme of the book as a whole – is the importance of being attentive to place, to context and to local culture, as the very hallmark of good mission. It is important that our research methodologies reflect this too. However, in the chapter, we will seek to extrapolate from the particular to make points which I hope will have more universal relevance, even while remembering that every context is distinctive.

Engaging in some auto-ethnography, the chapter first looks at some of the common pitfalls of institutions and actors who intervene in areas of poverty and deprivation in the name of 'development' or 'tackling poverty'. This is not to suggest that all development is bad but it is to highlight some common and often downplayed problems with it which are all too real. This analysis is based on the author's experience as an academic and practitioner of both 'international' and 'national' development, but the point is that the pitfalls are common wherever in the world one is operating.

Having completed this analysis, the church is then introduced into the mix, considering it, like the organizations reviewed in the previous section, as an actor with power, capable, unless it is careful, of acting pathologically or doing violence to the people it is called to serve. However, the chapter argues that Christian theology, if reflected on carefully and prayerfully, such that it is allowed to shape and govern our actions, offers resources which may help the church avoid some of the worst excesses of contemporary development.

I then tell the story of the project on which this chapter is based, known as Drop In, from its conception to the present day. I map its high points and its low points, and some of the things we have wrestled with and/or come to understand through it.

The final section seeks to tease out the wider significance of this analysis for our understanding of the politics of mission in marginal places, asking how exactly Drop In is 'political' and what its significance is.

Some Pathologies of 'Development'

In 2005–06, I worked for the United Nations Development Programme in Hanoi, Vietnam, as Senior Technical Adviser on a project reviewing twenty years of economic and political reform in that country. It was a fascinating time and I learnt a lot about Vietnam and its people. It was also an excellent opportunity to observe the workings of the international aid community up close, with all its different agencies from the IMF and the World Bank, to the many bilateral or government aid agencies, and the numerous NGOs.

In 2010, back in England, I began work as a priest in an inner-city area of Bristol. I remember experiencing the same sense of excitement and fascination as I had when I first arrived in Vietnam many years earlier and started the business of getting to know a new culture and new place. Whether Vietnam or inner-city Bristol, people spoke a different language. Their reference points and even their values were not necessarily the same as mine although we found plenty in common (and to laugh about!). However, as I began the business of getting to know the parish, something else struck me, namely I experienced a strange sense of déjà vu in that I noticed huge parallels between the many local agencies operating in the parish in the name of tackling poverty, raising school standards or helping the elderly, and the agencies I had encountered – and been a part of – in the international aid community in Vietnam. Inner-city Bristol or Hanoi, Vietnam – when analysing how 'elites' operate, there did not seem a great deal to choose between them.

So, what are parallels that I saw? The first thing to say is whether in Vietnam or Bristol I saw a great deal of goodwill, hard work and commitment: individuals genuinely trying their best to make a difference. However, looked at from the level of systems or structures and institutions, I saw things which were much more worrying.

First, there is the way in which areas of poverty, whether it be Vietnam or inner-city Bristol, attract a multiplicity of *outside* agencies who descend on an area, set up offices, and design projects and programmes to try and 'put things right'. That is, while such agencies are not 'of the place', they purport to be able to speak and act on local people's behalf. We particularly see this at times of humanitarian crisis in the Global South but the phenomenon is just as real in areas of poverty in the Global North.

Second, I noticed how, whether in Bristol or Vietnam, these same agencies compete with each other – 'jockey for position' – as they go after the many revenue streams which follow poverty, and seek to carve out their exclusive 'project' niche. In the same vein, while the language within these circles is very much about 'co-ordination' and 'collaboration' between agencies, and avoiding 'duplication of effort', what often lies behind such talk is a much more Machiavellian attempt to gather intelligence on competitors and to neutralize threats. In the international aid industry, I observed competition between agencies more often than collaboration.[4]

Third, whether in Bristol or Vietnam, these same agencies tend to follow the fads and fashions of the day, switching chameleon-like their 'interests' whenever the received wisdom (and the money) about how to tackle poverty, social cohesion, youth unemployment or whatever changes.

What we have then is a series of *externally derived* blueprints – external that is to the community where the programmes are rolled out – which cast judgement on what the problems are in a given place and how they ought to be tackled. Again, whether in Bristol or Vietnam, they claim to be based on evidence or community consultation but in practice this evidence usually rests on selective storytelling which suits the interests of those doing the intervening. Where community consultation does take place its findings are often prejudged or skin-deep. Consequently, whether it is in Bristol or Vietnam, or anywhere else we care to mention, the same policy prescriptions are routinely rolled out. Witness, for example, how the post-Washington Consensus 'governance' agenda looks pretty much the same wherever in the world it is.[5] Put like this, whatever the talk of being sensitive to culture, context or place, what one finds is that the said interventions are profoundly intolerant of difference. Take, for instance, UK education, there is little or no scope for a community – particularly a marginalized community – to say that it does not fully sign up to Ofsted-laid-down norms about what constitutes a good education, and yet different communities see such things differently.[6]

Lastly, whether in Bristol or Vietnam, what one notices in both cases is that huge amounts of money are spent in the name of tackling this or that problem and yet the said problems never seem to go away.[7] This in turn raises questions about what the whole endeavour is about in the first place and the extent to which, systemically speaking, the agencies ostensibly operating to tackle problems are feeding off them instead. Of course, there are many possible explanations for why problems do not go away but that the developmental community at home or abroad may be parasitic off the very problem itself is worth taking seriously.[8]

With reference to the so-called 'developing' world, scholars have written about how the very words we use to divide the world – north/south, developed/developing, first world/third world – depict one part of the globe as suffering from a 'lack' or as 'passive' or 'inferior', and hence needing of outside 'help', and yet this same help – the developmental actors referred to above – maintains power structures which favour parts of the world which are economically richer.[9] At the same time, academics writing on the UK have noticed the way in which working-class populations in inner-city areas and outer estates are frequently demonized as feckless, lazy or the cause of their own problems, in an analysis which again prepares the ground for outsiders to intervene to put them right.[10]

If this, however, is the analysis of much contemporary developmental practice, how might we do better, and in particular what are the implications for the mission of the church?

The Church as a Political Actor

The first issue to consider is why it might be helpful to conceive of the church as a political actor alongside all the other actors we have just reviewed as opposed to, say, the more customary 'missional actor', which it obviously is too.

The reason to do this is because it helps us to conceive of the church as an actor with power. If the previous section of the chapter was in effect about exploring the ways in which much contemporary development practice inflicts a kind of violence on people by imposing something generated from outside, by failing to listen, and failing to be open to difference and the multiplicity of ways which distinctive communities might realize public goods (theirs not ours), then it is important to be alert to the ways in which the church may also fall victim to such pathologies.[11]

Benedict Anderson famously wrote about the state, the business, corporation, the university *and the church* that they each 'harbour self-preserving and self-aggrandizing impulses', which are '"expressed" through its living members, but cannot be reduced to their passing personal ambitions'.[12] To speak in this way is to say something about the nature of institutions, notably how they tend to behave, especially when they feel threatened. Whatever else we may say about the church – and Rowan Williams helpfully refers to the church as 'a place or dimension in the universe . . . cleared by God through Jesus in which people may become what God made them to be'[13] – it is worth remembering that it is more than capable of acting pathologically even if the church is not reducible to such behaviour.[14]

While we can all too easily lay out what some of those pathologies may be, in that they are the same as they are for any developmental actor, the key question for the purposes of this chapter is: What, if anything, are the dangers for the local church operating in a marginal place? Many of the dangers facing churches are in fact generic ones and therefore are not determined by anything to do with marginality (for example, too small a vision, manipulative or exclusivist theologies, insensitive or inappropriate evangelism, various kinds of competitive behaviour, and so on).

At the same time, for the church operating in a marginal place, there is a special onus on it, and particularly its leadership, to be sensitive to its powerfulness. In an inner-city or outer-estate area, the priest or minister will nearly always be an 'outsider' (that is to say, they are unlikely to have been born and bred in the area). Also, they may well have more in common in social class or educational terms with local elites (head teachers, GP surgery leadership, local council officers) than with the people they are there to serve. It is, therefore, all too easy to lapse into a paternalistic mindset which sees the church as 'helping' the 'helpless other', to not listen, or to ride roughshod over indigenous ways of thinking, instead imposing the church's own off-the-shelf methodologies or blueprints for doing mission (Alpha, Messy Church, etc.).[15] Moreover, when one is coming in contact with people who are vulnerable, hungry or suffering from mental illness – all of which are everyday occurrences in areas of poverty – important and difficult questions arise about what is appropriate in terms of evangelism, and how the church might conduct itself in ways which truly honour the freedom of the person before them.

In this section, we have sought to tease out the ways in which the church is an actor with power, highlighting some of the dilemmas and pitfalls which may arise. We have argued that if it is not careful the church is just as much in danger of being like any other organization, clamouring to make itself heard, jockeying for position, competing with other organizations, and committing violence on people. In the next section, we explore ways in which, notwithstanding such risks, Christian theology offers resources which, if reflected on carefully and prayerfully, might enable the church to engage in mission that is life-giving.

Mission in Marginal Places: Some Resources from Christian Theology

To explore the question of what resources Christian theology offers the church that might help it avoid some of the pitfalls associated with any kind of intervention designed to bring about change is to trespass into a topic which knows few bounds! That said, we are reflecting on the politics of mission in marginal places and while some of what we say will almost certainly have relevance beyond marginal places, this focus can be used to guide our discussion somewhat.

To think about the way in which Christian theology might have something to offer here is to reflect on what our theology tells us about power. It is also to reflect on what our theology tells us about life/full life. It is to reflect on what our theology says about our relationship with our fellow human beings. Let me briefly deal with each in turn.

Power

God, the ultimate power in the universe, the source of all that is, is revealed most clearly to us in Jesus dying a criminal's death on a cross. What a bizarre and wholly counterintuitive notion this is, to put it mildly! It is through the cross, again utterly strangely, that we see the world transformed, death defeated, resurrected life.[16] However, what does the cross say about relationships of power – the very things we have been reflecting on as we have considered interventions in the name of development or in the name of mission? All we can say, at this stage, is that notions of powerfulness and powerlessness are turned on their head. It is a strand which clearly runs through the Beatitudes (Blessed are the poor, meek, the persecuted, etc.). Similar ideas are clearly evident in 1 Corinthians 1: 'Not many of you were wise by human standards; not many were influential; not many were of noble birth. But God chose the foolish things of the world to shame the wise; God chose the weak things of the world to shame the strong' (vv. 26–7), and so on.

But what does this turning on its head of notions of powerfulness and powerlessness achieve? What does it say which may be relevant as we think about mission in marginal places?

What it achieves is to shake up notions of our own powerfulness or powerlessness. At best, it makes us aware of how our own worldly notions of power are not the way it is, and that God's purpose is worked out differently. This is acutely relevant in a context of marginality where the church, or the leader/minister, is very often viewed as a member of the elite – as an 'agency' or an individual with power, to be consulted or briefed alongside other agencies in respect of matters of local concern.[17] Leaders/ministers need to take great care that this kind of thing does not go to their heads, and they develop a too cosy relationship with the establishment, especially in a context where local people may not question them simply by virtue of the fact that they are 'the ministers': 'God chose the weak things of the world to shame the strong.' Our own powerfulness is a great danger.

Life

While the cross is critical to Christianity in terms of stopping us – by God's grace – from degenerating into all the power games, all the deceptions and all the lies we tell ourselves, which dominate so much of human existence, Jesus at the same time as promising the cross (Mark 8:31) will not stop speaking about life – abundant life (John 10:10). However, it is a particular kind of life, which it appears can only be had by a kind of self-forgetfulness or a self-emptying: 'For whoever wants to save his life will lose it, but whoever loses his life for me will find it' (Matt. 16:25; Mark 8:35; Luke 9:24; John 12:25). Again, things are turned on their head. It is the very opposite of what we would expect. It is only by going against our (worldly) instincts – the will to power, status and control – and not looking out for self that we can by God's grace find life. If this way of thinking can be internalized, and allowed to inform our practice, it surely strikes at the heart of many of the pathologies of development/mission we have highlighted above, notwithstanding the fact that bringing such ideas to bear in our practice is clearly a big 'if'.

Neighbour

After notions of powerfulness/powerlessness turned on their head, and of life only to be had by relinquishing self, our third resource found in Christian theology which may aid us in avoiding some of the worst pitfalls of development/mission has to do with ideas about human interdependence, particularly as it relates to the weakest members of society. In 1 Corinthians 12, Paul famously talks about the church as being like a body, with no one part of the body being dispensable. However, Paul goes further than this, arguing that wholeness for the body of Christ or the church, and indeed I would add for the whole of the created order, cannot be had if one member is not living that full life. 'If one part suffers, every part suffers with it; if one part is honoured, every part rejoices with it' (v. 26). This too seems a power-ful image when considering mission in marginal places, which again may aid the church as it seeks to act in the manner of Christ. That is, if one member of the body is hurting, if one member of the body is not reconciled to their neighbour, if one member of the body is not reconciled to God, this is of profound concern as it interferes with the peace of the world and my own ability to be reconciled with God.

Let us now turn to our case study, looking at what is known as 'Drop In' as an example of how one church has sought to respond authentically in its context. Of interest is the extent to which Drop

In has succeeded in internalizing some of the theological motifs high-lighted above and in turn the light which Drop In sheds on the politics of mission in marginal places.

Drop In

Drop In is a project at St Luke's Church, Barton Hill, where the author is vicar. It was established in 2010 in a bid to make contact with a group of people we were aware of but did not have much contact with and who we would not expect to come to our Sunday church service. Drop In works with some of the most marginalized people in our community, especially men, with a high incidence of alcohol, drug abuse and mental health issues. Very few earn. Most are on benefits. Some are homeless, living in hostels or are sofa-surfing.[18] In the early days, it was not easy to make contact with the people we were trying to reach. However, we were helped by a local man who had a gift for talking to anyone – in his own distinctive style! He was very good at breaking down barriers between us and them. Indeed, this local man has been quite a thorn in our side, in a good way, throughout the history of Drop In, critiquing what we are doing and telling us when we have got it wrong.

Drop In takes place in the church crypt which was converted for youth work about a decade ago. It is a fairly un-churchy space with a couple of big rooms, kitchen/dining area, a few break-out rooms, and graffiti art on the walls.

Drop In meets twice a week on a Sunday and a Wednesday, starting at 11 a.m., finishing at 1 p.m. on both days. Sunday was the day for the original Drop In, running in parallel with our Sunday morning service. Wednesday is a more recent development, introduced to try to take our relationship with people a step further in terms of more intentionally showcasing the Christian faith.

On Sunday, there are bacon and egg sandwiches, tea and coffee, and people play pool. Pool is the mainstay of Drop In. There are newspapers (tabloids) and the radio is on (Heart FM or something similar). Everything is paid for by the church and hence is free of charge for those who come. There is a prayer board and usually some lit candles or candles to light. People are invited to write up prayers and we 'offer the prayers to God' at the end of the session when everyone stops and observes a few minutes of quiet.

Wednesday Drop In has a similar format to Sunday but with a slightly different vibe. People play pool and drink tea and coffee as on Sunday. However, instead of prayers we have a simple act of Holy Communion followed by lunch.

Holy Communion starts with a short reading from the Bible. The Bible reading is introduced with a few sentences aimed at connecting it up with people's lives and making it accessible to people who may not have an active faith or be sure what they think about God. At Communion, we use grape juice rather than wine, given that so many people have issues with alcohol.

New people are always told they are welcome to receive Communion if it feels meaningful to do so but equally people can receive a blessing or simply sit out. We try hard to create an atmosphere where all of the above is acceptable ('Please don't feel you have to receive Communion to please the vicar!', I often say). We have considered exploring more innovative ways of doing Communion. However, to date, our approach to Communion is fairly traditional, with the principal focus being on making sure the words we use are accessible. We also enjoy the fact that after the liturgy of Communion we immediately share a meal together.[19]

People who come to Drop In generally reflect positively on the experience, saying it offers a different kind of space from other places they visit. One recent comment, which was reported to me, was: 'I love coming on a Sunday morning. I look forward to it all week and always feel looked after.'

People who come to Drop In often make a comparison with another nearby project which offers a cooked lunch. They say Drop In is less edgy than the other project. We have very little 'trouble' at Drop In, whereas the word is it 'kicks off' more often at the neighbouring project.[20]

Drop In is smaller than the neighbouring project mentioned above – say twenty to thirty people come through our doors each week – and our premises can easily accommodate the people who come. Consequently, people can stay for the full two hours at Drop In as there is no pressure on people to vacate the premises so others can come in, as there is at the neighbouring project.

A lot of the people we meet are used to getting short shrift from people in power (e.g. via the benefits system, the housing people or the GP surgery receptionists). Drop In seeks to cut a different tone. We emphasize unconditional welcome and acceptance. While we have asked ourselves whether we should be doing more to help people come off drugs or tackle their alcohol addiction, we have more or less concluded that part of Drop In's strength is that it simply lets people be. Other agencies engage in more interventionist work. It is not what Drop In is for.

There is, of course, a danger that our interaction is just another paternalistic exchange or that the church is yet another external actor seeking to impose its will. We try to avoid this. We try to break down barriers between the 'helpers' and the 'helped'. Apart from helping cook, a key role of the volunteers is to chat to people over a cup of tea, lunch or a game of pool. Getting to know people takes time but over the years we have become more adept at being friendly while not asking too many questions of people who may initially be suspicious of us (as just another agency with power). Moreover, volunteers who support the project are encouraged not to see it simply in terms of them 'helping' others but to be open to the way in which the exchange is more reciprocal (i.e. we too are enriched or made whole by the encounter with our neighbour).

At the same time, people who attend Drop In are encouraged to help with setting up and/or the washing-up so that they give as well as receive. While there is a bit of a gender divide in Drop In (women cook, men play pool and drink tea!), people on the whole are willing to help when asked.

The question is: How does Drop In speak theologically and what light does it shed on the politics of mission in marginal places?

Analysis: The Theology and Politics of Drop In

In worldly terms, Drop In may not appear to add up to much. In one sense the juggernaut of state power and transnational capitalism, and its local variants, just steamroller on, ignoring Drop In or paying it little attention. Drop In does not 'tackle' the problems of poverty or inequality on its own. In many respects, it scarcely makes a dent.

However, in another sense – and perhaps from a God's-eye perspective – Drop In is valuable. It clearly makes a difference to the lives of those who come. It may not be a big operation. But we value Drop In for its relative smallness as this offers an opportunity to get to know people on an individual basis, and to talk – things which are often hugely lacking for people on the margins.

Drop In is a space where people can just be, where we have consciously made a decision not to try to fix people. Drop In is not locked into welfare state or other criteria about eligibility or who qualifies or who does not qualify for food – and this is intentional. Anyone who comes can have a bacon sandwich or lunch, without question or judgement.

More theologically, Drop In seeks to be a place where notions of powerfulness and powerlessness are turned on their head, where we try to model some notion of self-forgetfulness, or caring for each other, within and perhaps beyond the Drop In community, and where we try to cultivate a sense that when our neighbour suffers we are all somehow less whole before God.

That we celebrate Holy Communion in Drop In is significant in terms of how we understand Drop In. We hope that through the telling and retelling of the Christian story we provide a window onto how the world might be, and help those who come catch a glimpse of God and in turn imagine their world changed (Rev. 21:1–4). In this sense, Drop In has a subtle but distinct activist element to it.

A new heaven and a new earth

Writing about capitalism, Daniel Bell explores how we might 'open up a space of liberation' in relation to capitalism's more destructive effects.[21] While the problems of capitalism are not our principal focus, Bell's ideas are instructive for what we are talking about. According to Bell, part of capitalism's strength lies in the way in which it captures and subverts the way we think 'tempt[ing] us', in Bell's words, 'to a pessimism that severs the nerve of liberative practice'.[22] That is, by subverting the way we think, it stops us believing that the world can be organized differently. However, Bell goes on to say that because part of capitalism's power lies in the realm of its ideas, it is also where it is weak: 'In other words, that capitalism is an ontological and not merely economic discipline does not mean that its victory is in fact total; rather the ontological nature of the struggle broadens opportunities for resistance insofar as it opens up a plethora of fronts on which capitalism may be contested.'[23]

We would argue for something similar taking place in Drop In – small and insignificant in one sense though it is – but also whereby through the practice of Communion we tell a different story, and thereby offer a window onto a world changed. Offering people the opportunity to take part in Communion, including people who are unsure about where they stand in relation to Jesus Christ, is not meant to be a passive activity, or something 'done' to them. Rather, the hope is that as the Christian story is told and retold week by week, and as people enter into Jesus' life, death and resurrection, letting them connect with their own lives and the lives of the people they meet, they may see the world in a different light.

William Cavanaugh has written about Holy Communion as a practice which challenges the false order of the state and offers an alternative.[24] He argues that the state's promise of salvation – the kind of things politicians offer in abundance at election time – is a false copy of the salvation offered by the church, and a promise of salvation that can never be delivered.[25] In particular, Cavanaugh says that the state and the church tell radically different foundational stories about the nature of the world and what it is to be human in it. The state story, Cavanaugh says, emphasizes the individuality of the human race – fallen individuals with no common ends needing government (Leviathan) to save them from each other. The church story, by contrast, recalls a time of primal unity before the Fall, arguing that redemption comes through a restoration of that unity through participation in Christ's body.[26]

The practice of Communion, Cavanaugh says, challenges the state's story and points to an alternative. Specifically, Cavanaugh says

Communion is where notions of 'mine and thine' are 'radically effaced', that at Communion one is united not just to God but to one another – that is, there is no liberal state body in which a 'centre' seeks to maintain the independence of individuals from each other – and that Communion also redefines who your neighbour is.[27]

In addition, Cavanaugh places heavy emphasis on 'the local' level (i.e. 'local communities of formation and decision-making'), which he says is 'necessarily [and destructively] subsumed' under the universalizing tendencies of the state. Communion, Cavanaugh says, 'celebrates' the local while at the same time also 'effacing . . . the antithesis of local and universal'.[28]

While Cavanaugh's ideas may not be a perfect fit with Drop In, they nevertheless highlight important ways in which Drop In seeks to speak politically and theologically in and to the world.

Conclusion

In this chapter, we have explored the politics of mission in marginal places through a case study of a Christian outreach project known as Drop In, which seeks to connect with some of the most marginalized people in the community. Critiquing conventional interventions carried out in the name of 'development', we have been acutely conscious of the dangers of committing violence on people by imposing something generated from outside, by failing to listen, and failing to be open to difference and the multiplicity of ways in which any community might conceive of and realize public goods ('theirs not ours').

Drawing on Christian theology, we have argued there are ways that the church might guard against some of the worst pathologies of development. This includes reflecting on the cross as a means of subverting our natural will to power, on the importance of self-forgetfulness or self-emptying as a route to the full life that Jesus spoke of, and on ideas of human interdependence such that our own wholeness cannot be had while others suffer.

Drop In seeks to stand apart from state eligibility criteria such as those which govern the welfare state – or, worse, notions of 'deserving' and 'undeserving' poor – instead seeking to emphasize unconditional welcome for all in the manner of Christ. Drop In celebrates Holy Communion as a way of gently telling the Christian story, inviting people to let the story of their own lives and the Christian story intermingle with each other, in the hope that together we will catch a glimpse of a new heaven and a new earth wherein we all will be healed.

'Everyone must have the opportunity to come and see. All must have the chance to behold and test this new thing . . . What drives them to the new thing cannot be force, not even moral pressure, but only the fascination of a world that is changed.'[29]

Notes

[1] Gerhard Lohfink, cited in William Cavanaugh, 'Church', in *The Blackwell Companion to Political Theology* (ed. Peter Scott and William Cavanaugh; Malden, MA: Blackwell, 2004), p. 394.

[2] Harold Dwight Lasswell, *Who Gets What, When, How* (Whittlesey House: McGraw-Hill, 1936) http://www.policysciences.org/classics/politics.pdf (accessed 21 April 2015).

[3] Note that one of the principal foci of the Church of England's House of Bishop's pastoral letter 'Who is My Neighbour', released for the 2015 United Kingdom election campaign, was the arguably rather conservative and limited view of what it is to act politically, namely persuading Christians to vote. See Church of England, 'House of Bishop's Pastoral Letter on the 2015 General Election' (17 February 2015), press release https://www.churchofengland.org/media-centre/news/2015/02/house-of-bishops'-pastoral-letter-on-the-2015-general-election.aspx (accessed 21 April 2015).

[4] These insights are based on my own observations and reflections on inter-agency relationships both in the international aid community and in the parish. See also the OECD's aid effectiveness agenda for insights into the formal discourse about aid harmonization (OECD, Aid Effectiveness [n.d.] http://www.oecd.org/dac/effectiveness/ [accessed 21 April 2015]). It speaks to the point that there is a discourse about inter-agency co-ordination, which politically may not be all that it seems.

5 Indeed, there have been cases of consultants cutting and pasting large amounts of text from one country report to another, unfortunately forgetting to amend the name of the country!

6 Joe Hasler, 'Mind, Body and Estates: Outer Estate Ministry and Working Class Culture', pamphlet (n.d.) http://www.joehasler.co.uk/wp-content/uploads/2014/05/1.-Mind-body-estates-Booklet.pdf (accessed 21 April 2015).

7 With reference to the parish where I am vicar, the community was the recipient of £50 million under the Prime Minister Tony Blair-era New Deal for Communities. However, behind the façade of new buildings (houses, health centre, school), community life chances and health indicators remain as poor as they have ever done with the parish in the bottom 5–10 per cent nationally based on data on deprivation from Lower Super Output Areas. Moreover, a historical analysis shows that despite a succession of interventions to tackle poverty over the generations, the community has remained poor since its inception in the 1840s. See Martin Gainsborough, 'Liberal Interventionism and the Global North: The Case of Britain's Inner Cities', SPAIS Working Paper (2011) http://www.bristol.ac.uk/media-library/sites/spais/migrated/documents/gainsborough-11-11.pdf_(accessed 21 April 2015); and Martin Gainsborough, 'Scoping Document for a Joint Venture between Church Urban Fund and the Diocese of Bristol', draft report, 2013.

8 For writers who consider such issues in respect of international aid, see William Easterly, *The White Man's Burden: Why the West's Efforts to Aid the Rest Have Done So Much Ill and So Little Good* (Oxford: Oxford University Press, 2006); Paulette Goudge, *The Whiteness of Power: Racism in Third World Development and Aid* (London: Lawrence & Wishart, 2003); Linda Polman, *War Games: The Story of Aid and War in Modern Times* (London and New York: Viking/Penguin Books, 2010).

9 Julian Eckl and Ralph Weber, 'North South? Pitfalls of Dividing the World by Words', *Third World Quarterly* 28 (2007): pp. 3–23; Gainsborough, 'Liberal Interventionism'.

10 Angus Cameron and Ronen Palan, *The Imagined Economies of Globalization* (London: Thousand Oaks, CA: Sage, 2004); Owen Jones, *Chavs: The Demonization of the Working Class* (London; and New York: Verso, 2011); Ruth Levitas, *The Inclusive Society? Social Exclusion and New Labour* (Basingstoke and New York: Palgrave Macmillan, 1998); Nikolas Rose, *Powers of Freedom: Reframing Political Thought* (Cambridge, New York: Cambridge University Press, 1999).

[11] On the dangers of violence, including in areas we would tend to see as benign, see Martin Gainsborough, 'The Church as Emancipatory Political Project: Some Pointers from Political Theology for the Social Sciences', SPAIS Working Paper (2013) http://www.bristol.ac.uk/media-library/sites/spais/migrated/documents/gainsborough-01-13.pdf (accessed 28 April 2015). The paper explores diverse ways violence can occur beyond physical violence drawing on theologians such as Daniel Bell, William Cavanaugh and John Milbank. See also Stanley Hauerwas and Jean Vanier, *Living Gently in a Violent World: The Prophetic Witness of Weakness* (Downers Grove, IL: InterVarsity Press, 2008).

[12] Benedict Anderson, 'Old State, New Society: Indonesia's New Order in Comparative Historical Perspective', *Journal of Asian Studies* 42 (1983): pp. 477–96.

[13] Rowan Williams, 'The Christian Priest Today', lecture on the occasion of the 150th anniversary of Ripon College, Cuddesdon (28 May 2004) http://rowanwilliams.archbishopofcanterbury.org/articles.php/2097/ (accessed 28 April 2015).

[14] John Milbank, *Theology and Social Theory: Beyond Secular Reason* (Malden, MA: Blackwell, 1990), p. xxxi.

[15] Note, I do not have a problem with Alpha and Messy Church per se. It is just that these things often do not translate well into distinctive local contexts not least because they contain assumptions about such contexts which do not apply.

[16] Joel B. Green and Mark D. Baker, *Recovering the Scandal of the Cross: Atonement in New Testament and Contemporary Contexts* (Milton Keynes: Paternoster, 2000).

[17] For example, I was invited to a confidential police/city council briefing in November 2014 in relation to a child sexual exploitation case to be briefed alongside other 'community leaders'.

[18] Note how these labels do an injustice to the people concerned. Though they are inadequate, I am using them to set the scene as best I can. The point is that the people who we have got to know through the project can never be defined by such labels, which tend to limit and belittle them. Instead, we know people by name and they are simply the people they are.

[19] Of course, we often experience 'communion' over the sit-down lunch as much as we do during the formal Communion liturgy.

[20] We can count on the fingers of one hand the times we have had trouble in Drop In in terms of fights, people storming out, or throwing stuff around. This is over a four-year period.

[21] Daniel Bell, 'Only Jesus Saves: Towards a Theopolitical Ontology of Judgement', in *Theology and the Political: The New Debate* (ed. Creston Davis, John Milbank and Slavoj Zizek; Durham and London: Duke University Press, 2005), pp. 200–30.

[22] Bell, 'Only Jesus', p. 202.

[23] Bell, 'Only Jesus', p. 205.

[24] William Cavanaugh, 'The City: Beyond Secular Parodies', in *Radical Orthodoxy* (ed. John Milbank, Catherine Pickstock and Graham Ward; London and New York: Routledge, 1999), pp. 182–200.

[25] The point here is the constant promises of 'new deals', 'the end of child poverty', or any of the other promises that politicians frequently make, come and go with every successive administration but rarely result in much fundamental change (i.e. the poorer areas of Bristol remain poor). Thus, the promised or looked-for salvation never comes.

[26] Cavanaugh, 'The City', p. 184.

[27] Cavanaugh, 'The City', pp. 193, 196.

[28] Cavanaugh, 'The City', p.196.

[29] Lohfink, see note 1.

6

Case Study: Being Left with Some Difficult Questions

Martin Gainsborough

I don't remember exactly when I met Dan but he started coming to our Sunday Drop In – a kind of late breakfast club with prayers for people who were unlikely to come to our main church service. Dan had grown up in children's homes. He took medication for schizophrenia. He once told me how he had killed a man but had got off 'on a technicality'. He was an ex- or more likely a current heroin addict, and he looked like a man who had taken a lot of drugs.

Dan lived with Lily in one of the high-rise flats. Lily was in a wheelchair, having had one of her legs amputated. Though in her thirties, she had serious health problems. They were both on methadone. Their relationship was volatile but they stayed together. Lily clearly meant the world to Dan.

Dan in particular found Drop In a support. Often, he would come without Lily, tucking into the bacon sandwiches, playing pool and unburdening himself about what was getting him down, his worries about Lily's health, and the stress of being her main carer. Dan always asked us to pray for Lily.

One day, the church office and the primary school across the road were broken into. Not much was stolen but there was quite a lot of damage. CCTV evidence identified Dan as the culprit. Dan said he could remember nothing about it. It appeared he hadn't been taking his medication and was looking for money for drugs. The police were keen to prosecute, with the beat officer saying he wanted to get Dan off his patch. We spoke to Dan about the upset that the break-in had caused but decided not to press charges. However, the school took him to court.

On the day of the hearing, I accompanied Dan to the local magistrate's court. The barrister defending Dan did a good job. My presence in court – as Dan's vicar – was acknowledged as was my offer to remind Dan to take his medication. Dan avoided a custodial sentence, receiving instead a fine which would be taken out of his benefits. As we left court, Dan and I joked at how lucky he'd been. I could scarcely conceal my delight with the outcome.

Some months later, Dan announced that he and Lily were moving to a new place a few miles away, a bungalow which would be easier for Lily with her disability. I was sad to hear they were leaving but offered to help with their move, picking up a hire van on the day. Apart from their bed and a TV, their possessions fitted into a few carrier bags.

After they moved, I phoned Dan a few times but we fell out of touch. Then came news that Lily had died. I tried to call but the number no longer worked so I went round to see if I could find him. Dan answered the door, gave me a hug and told me what had happened. It sounded terrible. Dan kept bursting into tears. He told me Lily had been buried under an apple tree in Gloucestershire where her family had come from. Before I left, I prayed with Dan. I felt very inadequate.

The other day, I bumped into Dan as I was passing near his house. Life sounded as rubbish as ever. I encouraged him to come along to Drop In but I haven't seen him.

While there are times of laughter, happiness and meaning when the harshness of life fades into the background, it seems wrong to end on such a note – an overly rosy Christian optimism that is not born out by the facts. The reality is that for many people the suffering and the hardship never stop. There are no obvious signs of healing, the lifting of burdens, or the onset of 'full life'. Death, perversely, offers a kind of release. However, it leaves us with huge questions. What is the meaning of Dan's life or Lily's in the face of so much hardship, and how do we speak of the love of God in relation to them? *Kyrie eleison*, I cry for healing.

7

Case Study: Welcoming the Stranger

Martin Gainsborough

I meet up with Amir from the mosque, which is in a converted ware-house a stone's throw from the church. It doesn't look like a mosque. It looks like a warehouse. Amir shows me round. He shows me the classrooms where they bring the children for lessons after school. He shows me the facilities for washing before prayers. He tells me about the difficulties they are having with contractors working on convert-ing the warehouse. It sounds like they had had a dispute. Amir says they need more computers for the children. I say I would look into whether we have any going spare at the church.

The mosque is right next door to the George pub. Some would say this is unfortunate. I enter the George on a Thursday night wearing my collar. The air is thick with smoke as the pub ignores the smoking ban. People, nearly always men, are sitting round small tables in various states of inebriation. It's a dive if ever there was one. Locals joke that you have to wipe your feet when you leave. The carpet is threadbare. There is a large TV and a juke-box. The beer on tap tastes foul. You are best ad-vised to buy a bottle or can. Someone shouts across to me, 'You couldn't get rid of Mike for us – send him over to the Muslims or something.'

Mike is usually stoned on something as he scarcely copes with life. The pub has kind of taken him under its wing but he's the butt of many jokes. Someone swears and utters a kind of 'Ola, ola, ola' sound in a mock imitation of the Somalis.

Another night in another pub – this time the Three Nuns, another white working-class pub. The conversation once again comes back to the Somalis. 'The fucking council has abandoned us,' someone says, 'The Somalis get all the housing.'

'What about the rights of the original people?' someone else asks.

Usually I just soak it up, trying not to agree, trying not to disagree, trying not to laugh too much when the jokes are genuinely funny if un-PC. I worry that I lack moral courage in not speaking out but I am still quite new here. I need to get to know the people. Win their trust. Without their trust I can do nothing. On one occasion, I mutter something weakly about the 'need for us all to get on'.

'You may need to get on. We fucking don't', a bloke says to me.

Wednesday morning. I speed down the hill on my bicycle to the church. The area is alive with traffic and people dropping their children off at school. The sun is out. It's a sea of colour. The women look so attractive in their headscarfs and associated dress. I feel inspired by the diversity.

After morning prayers, I wander over to a Barton Hill leaders' meeting. It includes the head of the primary school, a local community organization called the Settlement, the head of the GP practice, and Amir and Khaalid from the Somali community. We get together monthly to compare notes, to update each other on things we are doing, and explore ways we can work together. It's been a great way to get to know Amir and Khaalid. I don't know them well but I think they trust us. A few years ago before the mosque project was born my predecessor had explored whether the church might do a joint project with the mosque so that they could worship in our buildings. It did not work out in the end but it laid the foundations for good relations.

Amir tells me he is going on a fund-raising trip for the mosque to the Middle East and South Africa. Could I write a letter of support from the church? 'Of course I could,' I say. 'I would be delighted.'

Amir comes round to pick up the letter a few days later. I print it out on headed notepaper and he asks me to sign multiple copies. I am sure it is the right thing to do but I wonder what people in the white British community would think if they knew.

One weekend I go with my family to a play put on by Somali woman. The play explores some of the challenges and tensions across the generations between parents who came to Britain as adults and children who have grown up here. It is in Somali and English. It is very funny and moving. I reflect that the concerns and worries of the Somali community are not that different from those of the white community, especially around our young people growing up. If only they knew! The play strengthens a resolve in me to get to know the Somali community better.

I talk to the church council about what they've done in the past with the Somali community, exploring ways we might get to know each other better. They tell me they once shared a meal or tea together. 'It was very awkward', someone says, and I can tell they are not keen to do more. I do sympathize with them. I have travelled a lot, spent long periods in other cultures. They haven't.

The mosque invites the church to join them for a planting day. They have cleared rubble from a series of flower-beds they are going to plant up with herbs and plants. I advertise it on Sunday. I tell people it's good for us to get to know the Somali community and do things with the mosque. I encourage people to come. On the day, just Sarah and I turn up. It's disappointing that not more people from the church come but we are warmly welcomed. We do some planting together until the rain comes down heavily. We shelter in the mosque. They give us tea and biscuits before we decide to call it a day.

We have set up a new venture at St Luke's. It's called Kids Kafe. It's a parent-and-toddler group and it meets on Friday morning, aiming to pick up parents dropping off their older children at school. The two women who run it have been out in the urban park, chatting to mums, many of whom are Somali. We are so pleased when the Somali mums start to come to Kids Kafe. It's still rare that we have events that bridge the Somali–white divide but it shows what is possible.

8

The Political Realm: Editorial Comment

Mike Pears and Paul Cloke

Those who live or work in, or are in some way involved in marginal communities will at once recognize the poignancy of Martin Gainsborough's analysis about the 'pathologies of development'. They describe a situation that for a small Christian community, a church or small voluntary sector organization can seem almost overwhelming in scale and complexity. Such groups are faced with difficult decisions about whether to 'join in' with the mainstream developmental structures or in some way 'opt out'. The challenges of joining in are manyfold. Not only do the 'pathologies of development' present groups with a range of difficult ethical dilemmas but the short-termism and complexity and constantly changing regulatory nature of the systems are daunting for those who are not well-trained and well-resourced professionals. Opting-out presents other challenges. The industrial scale of the development infrastructure tends to overwhelm the imagination and intimidate vulnerable creative expressions that seek to stand outside of the official mainstream; it is difficult to conceive of alternative approaches and figure out how they might work in practice.

The broad approach to political engagement taken in Chapter 5 helps us to understand that whether we join in or opt out we are nonetheless somehow involved in the political realm. Thus to opt out of direct involvement in organized development – which in some cases tends to happen on an industrial scale – is not to opt out of the political realm itself, but to be involved with it on different terms – as exemplified by recognizing the practice of Communion in the Drop In as a political act. In short, to be involved as a Christian community in marginal places is inescapably also to be involved in the political realm. The question is not about whether to engage with the political, but how well we engage.

The practical theological approach taken in Chapter 5 opens up some compelling resonances between the political landscapes as described by Martin and those presented in the gospel narratives. Eric Stewart, for example, investigates the ways in which political, economic, and by implication ideological discourses function in the first-century world and how those are presented in Mark's Gospel. He argues that in first-century geography the physical environment 'determines the character of the people' and 'furthermore, it places the centre of the world within Greek and then Roman territory'.[1] This creates a situation where 'all other cultures are measured by their adherence to Greek or Roman cultural tradition'; to be 'remote' from Rome is to be less civilized.[2] Roman territory was defined as civilized and its inhabitants were the beneficiaries of its security and prosperity; to be outside of this territory (that is in the wilderness) was to be uncivilized, dangerous, and foreign – the wilderness was indeed deemed the territory of demons.

In his gospel, Mark (like other first-century writers) draws on these geographical representations, but in his narrative he also inverts them to make a point.[3] Controversially he presents Jesus' first action in Roman Gentile territory as casting out the demon 'Legion'. Jesus contests the dominant imperial narratives of civilization and purity by exposing 'disorder and death (hence the location of the "legion" among the tombs)'.[4] By cleansing the demoniac Jesus shows that it is he, not Rome, that is the source of true civilization and thus calls into question the whole legitimacy of the Roman project. However else one reads this passage, it is difficult to escape the view that Jesus was engaging in a political activity – both in his actions and his teaching – and that, whatever else this entailed, it involved challenging and exposing the claim that political and economic structures and institutions were equally serving the interests of all (thus sustaining a 'civilized' system) while at the same time ruthlessly and violently assimilating the poor or the foreigner as slaves or expelling them into the outer regions or the wilderness.

Mark's narratives are characteristically dramatic, but this should not tempt us to dismiss them as politically naive. Drawing on the culture and language of the day, they vividly express the ubiquitous and ruthless nature of self-interested expressions of power and the manner in which those powers are embedded in everyday patterns of life such that they are deemed to be keepers of the peace and maintainers of the proper order of things. While most of the contemporary stories related in this book series are not as dramatic as the narrative of Jesus and the Legion, they nonetheless find resonance with Mark's portrayal of power and in particular the manner in which social constructions of power, including political and economic, are encountered by ordinary people in their everyday routines. Along with other authors, Martin has very ably and helpfully shown that you do not have to look far in marginalized urban areas to witness the inhumanity of 'the system' that orders daily life; indeed even its outwardly benevolent expression (for example in 'raising standards' and 'tackling poverty') is experienced by so many it claims to serve as humiliating, coercive and forceful.

Furthermore, these accounts appear to invite us to focus differently. They discourage a narrow consideration about whether or not we opt in or out of the organizational structures of aid and development. They point out to us that the political, social and spiritual arrangements of power do not confine themselves to these institutions, but they are the very waters in which we all swim. Indeed, as the case studies suggest, whatever our social, political or religious standing, we all in some way have to deal with the everyday political reality. Rather what we are encouraged to do concerns 'telling a different story' to that of the state or 'opening up a different space' (or a 'differently storied space'), not on the basis of social or religious position or particular need but to really get to know each other as people, to understand each other's humanity.

Being involved in this kind of 'differently storied space' entails a particular kind of presence or involvement which, in the introduction to this book, we have described in terms of ethnographic attentiveness. Such an approach seeks to get under the surface of normal life to make space for another way of 'seeing' the world; the sense of which comes across in Martin's reflexive writing style and the way in which he has made space for his own experiences to give new shape to his appreciation of 'the way the world works'. In relation to the political realm it gives rise to insights that strongly contest the generally accepted discourses about 'the poor' and how government services and voluntary organizations (including the church) might best address 'their needs'. It brings to light the reality that for many the 'suffering and hardship never stop' and begs troubling questions about the real 'meaning of life in the face of such hardship'. What is also clear is that the daily lives of those facing hardship is formed by a rich and complex tapestry of relationship and experience; it is certainly not possible to reduce such experiences to a series of 'problems' or 'needs' that can be 'solved' or 'provided for' through the institutional provision of various agencies. And furthermore, that the 'happy ending' stories and 'positive outcomes' that such agencies depend upon for their own survival look much less convincing in real life than they do on pieces of shiny publicity and annual reports.

Equally significantly, Martin's auto-ethnographic approach draws attention to the personal and inner aspect of the political realm as well as to wider social and structural aspects. To be involved in the political realm is to acknowledge that the powers we see at work elsewhere are also prevalent in our own lives. This resonates with a number of familiar biblical texts which have themselves been interpreted in political terms: that in the exodus, Israel might have been taken out of Egypt, but despite forty years in the wilderness, Egypt was not taken out of Israel; and drawing on those stories of exodus the narrative of Jesus' temptation in the wilderness also emphasizes the critical importance of the inner life – the life lived before God – in relation to issues of power and status.

As we write these chapters there is no sign of an easing-up in the relentless development of austerity politics and the prevailing rhetoric which denigrates and ostracizes those who do not fit in with mainstream political thinking about how society should work. It is clear that to be involved in mission in marginal places is not just a theological act; it is also a political act. The questions that arise are not about whether to be involved, but how to be involved – where the 'how' invites us to focus on the telling of different stories and on participating in the creation of new spaces.

Notes

[1] Eric C. Stewart, *Gathered around Jesus: An Alternative Spatial Practice in the Gospel of Mark* (Cambridge: Clark, 2009), p. 92.
[2] Stewart, *Gathered*, p. 92.
[3] Stewart, *Gathered*, pp. 179–80.
[4] Stewart, *Gathered*, p. 184.

Part III

9

Understanding the Social Realm

Gordon Cotterill

*Love consists in sharing what one has and what one is
with those one loves. Love ought to show itself in deeds
more than in words.*

St Ignatius of Loyola

Introduction

To understand mission in the social realm is to understand that the world
is different; it's not only that things have changed, but consistent social
transition has made areas once easy to define too fluid and variegated to
label. Within this complex context the church is required to persist with
its calling to be love to others and to find increasingly appropriate ways
of engagement through its presence in the ever-shifting sands of community. How God is made known through the church in these days and
in these places should be the focus of ongoing reflection with particular
consideration given to the sense in which the indwelling of the logos or
essence of God is embodied in and through us.[1] The spiritual exercises
of Ignatius, culminating in a contemplation on the love of God, still
speak powerfully to the contemporary social context as they draw attention to the way in which the social and benevolent love that is *agape* can
help bring stability to the friability that defines the social dimension.
'Love ought to show itself in deeds more than in words.'[2]

The purpose of this chapter is to explore how this incarnational love of God is embodied by the local church and expressed within a rapidly changing social realm. Two particular case studies are found at the end, but the chapter is written with them in mind as conversation partners throughout. These case studies represent the ministry of the Salvation Army in two distinct areas. Naomi Clifton, together with her husband John, has explored the experience of being the Salvation Army in Ilford, east London, with its characteristic inner-city melting-pot of variety and difference. The second conversation is with Adam Bonner who, as part of the leadership team of Sutton Salvation Army Church in south-west London, found the narrative of hospitality a driving force of transition as the church realigned itself to its immediate community and surroundings. Both situations show a commitment to hospitality and embrace in understanding mission in fluid and changing communities. It is to a consideration of the nature of this changing scene that we turn first.

The Social Realm in Flux

The cosy inner-city images of a *Call the Midwife* community, where doors are left open and children have a myriad of 'aunties', no longer exist. Communities are now characterized by transience, fragmentation and social variegation, so that needs and issues once obvious now create an abstract mosaic for the church in mission to encounter. In other words, where the role of the church once seemed clear, things have changed to such an extent that it now urgently needs to rethink and re-imagine ways of serving and engaging.

Involvement over the years with emergency food provision provides an anecdotal insight to this shifting social scene. While today food banks are an unfortunate fixture, in my early ministry within the Salvation Army providing emergency support was a more common part of our experience. The vast majority of clients supported were those fighting addiction with the result that alcohol- and drug-related causes for the need of a food parcel were the most common cases that we dealt with, followed by persistent budgeting problems and homelessness.

Today the picture is changing. While addiction incidents are still apparent, the shrinking of the social sector along with the rise of austerity politics mean that others are now emerging who need support. These include an increasing number of those with mental health issues who slip through a welfare system that sanctions individuals for missing appointments; or those unable to meet the demands of providing evidence for their job-seeking; and an increasing number from households that financially struggle to keep up with mortgage repayments following changing employment circumstances, or those whose benefits have been changed or are being reassessed. The increased use of casual-based contracts, such as 'zero hours contracts', is showing its impact on those for whom it provides a wholly inadequate economic household framework. We seem to see more and more folk who have no recourse to public funds and while some of those are not unexpected – not least migrants unable to claim most benefits or forms of assistance – the picture of those squeezed into the margins contains surprises. Stagnant incomes, alongside increasing prices for such things as food, fuel and energy, are forcing many more to become dependent on food-bank support as they fail to keep up with the demands for living. Indeed, a recent report states that 'today people across the UK will struggle to feed themselves and their families. Redundancy, illness, benefit delay, domestic violence, debt, family breakdown and paying for the additional costs of heating during winter are just some of the reasons why people go hungry.'[3]

Coupled to this, the landscapes of our cities are changing rapidly. Craig Taylor, quoted in *London: The Information Capital*, points out that 'most a-z's are half dead, because documenting a city as alive as London will always be an impossible task'.[4] Areas known in 1889 in the work of philanthropist and social researcher Charles Booth for being middle- and upper-middle-class have journeyed into deprivation and overcrowding and out again as they are re-gentrified. Areas once known as 'inner city' are being transformed as what was once viewed as 'low-grade' housing stock is being upgraded, and refashioned areas of urban living become highly sought after. The continual cultural shift of areas shaped by new waves of immigration brings further layers of distinctiveness to the ever-changing social landscape.

The once easily identifiable attributes of inner-city living are no longer constrained geographically and there is a distinct shift of poverty towards the suburbs and outer regions of the city to areas whose interwar housing stock is now in turn increasingly tired. The fragmentation to which the church is called to bring cohesion is no longer as hidden in the so-called leafy suburbs of our cities as perhaps it once seemed to be.

One implication of this is the need for an increasingly fluid understanding of what constitutes marginality. Once-accepted criteria, whether political or economic, now seem inadequate as they provide too narrow and limited definitions which fail to describe the increasing variation and complexity of marginal places. What terms might we use, for example, when we see a community that appears to be socially flourishing despite its economic challenges? Living in 'contented poverty' may seem totally incongruous but in some instances can be a reality. Alternatively, although perhaps economically secure, the experience for some of living within gated communities or in luxury riverside wharf accommodation can be of a deep social poverty, with distant or faceless neighbours and a diminished sense of shared life and neighbourhood.

In their book, *Beyond Homelessness: Christian Faith in a Culture of Displacement*, Steven Bouma-Prediger and Brain J. Walsh make some helpful contributions in thinking about the way we might broaden our understanding of what constitutes marginal living. They look beyond the normal conventional definitions of homelessness to consider the juxtaposition of the under-housed and over-housed, exposing the irony that an impressive property portfolio is as 'homeless' as the stereotypical images of homelessness. The defining issue here, they argue, is the lack of connection with place: 'To be home is to experience some places primal, as first, as a place to which one has a profound sense of connection, identity, and even love. To be emplaced is to have a point orientation. Homelessness, is then, a matter of profound and all-pervasive displacement. Homelessness is a matter of placelessness.'[5]

They go on to suggest that the street homeless, while vulnerable, often have a stronger sense of place and connectedness. Our experience of dealing with homeless people in Sutton would suggest that, in fact, there is little of the primal connection or identity that Bouma-Prediger and Walsh observe in their case studies. However, despite the measure of romanticism their premise may contain, the concept of what constitutes homelessness is well made. In Sutton, our engagement is indeed with those who are highly disconnected and displaced, exacerbated by a local provision of services that effectively constricts any real chance of immediate help. Firm policies mean that to be homeless in Sutton is a tough option, and the majority of cases quickly move on.

Bouma-Prediger and Walsh helpfully explore the theme of 'displacement' and move ideas of homelessness beyond the usual stereotypical definition. Likewise, if we are to move conversation regarding marginality beyond merely economic and fixed spatial constructs, it may be useful to think of it more in terms of 'fragmentation' and employ what might be termed as social and emotional criteria to begin to examine it through the lens of isolation, hopelessness and fear.

Marginality and the 'Corrosion' of the Social Realm

No one had noticed how bad Rose had got, largely because Rose lived by herself in an isolation broken sporadically by the visit of a neighbour with groceries. Rose was ninety-four and was dying when her neighbour came to us for help, 'I only get her groceries but thought you ought to know!' The smell hit the back of my throat as I walked into the dark flat. I spoke gently with Rose, she was hardly coherent but through faltering breaths was adamant that she was not going to hospital. I looked closer. I noticed her feet were wrapped in plastic bags. Intrigued, I got on my knees to see why. Her legs were a heaving mass of gangrene, the bags an attempt to stop the infection oozing onto her settee. I rang for the ambulance wishing I had seen beyond the door long before. Rose's story, like many others in the inner city, is one of loneliness, isolation and rejection.

Rupert lives within close proximity of the Salvation Army in Sutton, south-west London. Once high-flying in finance with an attractive property portfolio, Rupert found his dream of a long and well-funded retirement with his wife of sixty-two years shattered when she died, leaving him alone. Rupert's story, like many others in the suburbs is story of loneliness, isolation and rejection.

So what constitutes marginality? Rose and Rupert present an interesting juxtaposition, in many ways diametrically opposed, yet in others completely overlapped. The stories of these two very different people in very different places point towards the kind of multifaceted poverty identified by Henri Nouwen that encompasses the economic, physical, emotional, mental and spiritual.[6] What joins these stories is the common thread of rejection, isolation and loneliness and it is these experiences which are so deeply destructive, even corrosive, of the social realm.

George Monbiot, questioning the very existence of society, argues that we are currently living in the 'age of loneliness', hallmarked by 'heroic individualism'. Studies reveal that loneliness – which Monbiot describes as a 'life denying ideology which enforces and celebrates our social isolation' – is achieving epidemic proportions in both the young and old with an impact that is quantifiable: 'Ebola is unlikely ever to kill as many people as this disease strikes down. Social isolation is as potent a cause of early death as smoking 15 cigarettes a day; loneliness, research suggests, is twice as deadly as obesity. Dementia, high blood pressure, alcoholism and accidents – all these, like depression, paranoia, anxiety and suicide, become more prevalent when connections are cut. We cannot cope alone.'[7]

The factors that contribute to fragmentation and marginal living are complex. The following snapshots of four individuals who frequent the Coffee House at Sutton Salvation Army may serve to illustrate how a particular aspect of current social policy is also playing its significant part. On 1 April 2013 a new era for the state benefits system was ushered in as part of government policy; and these are examples of its impact on real lives.

Barry the sanctioned

Barry, who is a recent but frequent visitor to the Salvation Army either through need of a food bank, our computers or simply a chat, was completing his application for a loan. Barry, who needs help to get through his chaotic life, misses his benefits appointment and is sanctioned. No money for two weeks. His first solution? A bit of 'reduced' label-swapping in ASDA failed so a loan with an eye-watering 4,124 per cent APR it is.

Susie the displaced

Everyone seemed to know Susie. Her energy drive for building community would put most churches to shame; the vanguard of community transformation in so many ways, the bastion of local justice, standing up and against all things unfair in this part of Sutton. In the few months I knew her, I saw nothing but investment into others around her, no doubt about it – a pillar of this community beyond its cliché.

Well Susie is no longer here. She went very quickly. She has moved on, taking her young family away from the support structures and friends they knew. Now she's in a different but unfamiliar part of south-west London, all thanks to her misfortune to have, in old money, a boxroom, deemed now a bedroom. So, unable to withstand the 14 per cent cut to her housing benefit, Susie has gone, shoehorning her family into new communities and schools.

Janice the reassessed

It takes one look at Janice's make-up, perhaps ten seconds of conversation, maybe five minutes to detect her fear of any male, maybe several years to understand the life of brokenness that has shaped Janice's experience of life and realize why she receives the benefits she does.

Here is why the benefit changes of 1 April were no joke. Janice was required to undertake reassessment and is now deemed fit for work. Why? Because in one interview with a stranger she happened to mention that she looked after her mother. I'm no doctor, but that does not make Janice a carer nor signal new opportunities for employment.

Sally the reassessed

Sally is a victim of having brilliant parents who brought her up to be fiercely independent. Suffering cerebral palsy would be an inaccurate description, as there is nothing to suggest that Sally is suffering anything, for her attitude to life is a gift to anyone who spends time with her. But the reality is that, without complaint, Sally gets on with life hampered bodily through infirmity to both her arms and legs as well as living with learning difficulties. I can't blame the assessor for not seeing past her 'go get life' demeanour, but Sally will struggle to find full-time employment where she is under pressure to keep up and perform. We know that because she volunteers for us under close and supportive supervision.

Because she does so well in spite of her daunting challenges, her benefits have been slashed because she is now deemed available for work. She's no longer on Employment Support Allowance, but now under the additional pressure of Job Seeker's Allowance. She and her parents are very worried.

These stories highlight how the complexity of marginalization requires careful understanding, creativity and authenticity in shaping a response. The changing and indeed increasing pressures within the social realm demand more of churches to create alternative flourishing environments of hope. They also call for a clearly articulated prophetic voice which addresses the deepening polarization in society, a voice that needs to be heard in the minutiae of everyday local involvement as well as on the national stage.

The Church's Response to Changing Patterns of Social Marginalization

This chapter argues that the mission of the church must adapt in the light of the ever-changing patterns of social marginalization which have been described. However, the mission of the church is also predicated on the constancy of the attributes of God and his ever-faithful presence and compassionate activity in our world. Thus, as we pray 'your kingdom come, your will be done, on earth as in heaven' our eyes are opened once again to the remarkable characteristics of a heavenly father who opens his arms wide in generous hospitality and compassionate embrace. As we seek to participate in what God is doing by embodying these characteristics through our own practices we are discovering that the biblical mandate to welcome the stranger and embrace the enemy has potency even in the changing landscapes which are dominated by individualism and loneliness.

Engagement at the margins of the social realm demands an investigation of radical hospitality existing beyond merely meeting particular social needs: as suggested already throughout this series, encountering marginality, building social capital and community involves embodying shalom, through embrace and hospitality. My purpose here is to emphasize how crucially important it is for our praxis within the social realm to happen within a framework of hospitality and in the understanding of what constitutes shalom and radical embrace. Again the latter has been well explored in Book 1 of this series,[8] but it is worth being reminded that in a culture dominated by consumerism and self, the embrace of others through hospitality takes any abstraction of love and makes it concrete.

The embrace and inclusion of others through hospitality develops openness and safe places that bridge the divide where individualism fragments society. This kind of embrace demands more than a social-capital view of reciprocal relationships which says, 'I do it for you if you do it for me', and also more than those that even might say, 'I'll do it for you without expecting anything in return', but it recognizes a two-way flow of vulnerability, allowing ministry by the most unlikely.[9]

In order to help us imagine the particular shape that our participation in this way might take, and to help us understand theologically the ways that such engagement might bring about practical transformation within society, we will look at Luke Bretherton's discussion of the parable of the Great Banquet.[10]

The Great Banquet: Radical Hospitality, Embrace and Shalom in Practice

In his painting *The Potato Eaters* (1885), Van Gogh captures not only what he thought of society, but also the mystery of otherness-in-togetherness which is the essence of hospitality. Five impoverished, hard and ordinary lives come together in sacramental beauty; the 'togetherness' reflects the sense of divine hospitality which we as a church aspire to embody. Christine Pohl points to this intrigue as a means of sensing God's presence: 'A mystery of hospitality is how often one senses God's presence in the midst of very ordinary activities . . . as we make room for hospitality, more room becomes available to us for life, hope, and grace.'[11]

The parable of the Great Banquet represents a context lesson in what Anne Morisy defines as a generalized reciprocal relationship[12] where one moves beyond 'I'll scratch your back if you'll scratch mine'. Jesus himself sets the scene by insisting that it is too easy to be hospitable to friends and family who will be obliged to return your kindness. Giving insight to generously making room for life, hope and grace for those on the margins, Jesus exhorts his listeners to instead invite those with nothing to return. There is an urge to discover commensality, in other words a seeking to occupy without competition the same space with others, irrespective of independent values and customs, and to be with and contribute to others different to you; there you are likely to find a dignity in living, completeness in life.

Within the home of a prominent Pharisee, Jesus exposes hypocrisy as he deals with their objections, pointing out their prestige and selfishness while also illustrating the failure in attending to and caring for the poor. The parable is an exercise in missing the point made to a presumptuous nation feeling the smugness of their invite. Jesus makes sure that the danger of missing the banquet as a result of self-obsession is seen as a reality and unpacks the obligation of the Abrahamic promise[13] to be a blessing to all nations. The banquet has been prepared and the invites sent far and wide, but the excuses begin to come in. The response of the host? Go and bring in the poor, the crippled, the blind and the lame. Whether the narrative of kingdom realignment was lost on Jesus' audience we do not know, but the established Judaic boundaries of inclusion and exclusion had certainly been challenged.

Bretherton uses this biblical narrative to consider how the church, in its own practices, might act as a conduit of God's blessing and purpose into our own contemporary society. He finds four countercultural moves within Luke 14:15–24 that provide helpful context for our social praxis and which merit further exploration.

Dramatic asymmetry

The first move comes as an unexpected response to rejection. In the face of invitations turned down, we do not see revenge but an open invitation to all outcasts. This, Bretherton argues, subverts the culture: to identify with the poor and the outcasts and not resort to violence in the maintenance of power through hospitality 'steps outside the accepted patterns of competitive social relations that preserve honour and prestige among the elite'.[14] Bretherton identifies this as 'dramatic asymmetry'. Where the usual guests proved unworthy of the invitation, we now see the outcast honoured. Hospitality is reconfigured, with relating to each other at its heart rather than the preservation of affiliations of power, prestige and reputation.

In the parable the strong identification with the margins not only challenges conditions for inclusion but also creates a critical mass to counter the fragmentation produced through power, prestige and patronage; the antithesis of shalom. The symmetry of rich and poor, powerful and weak becomes dramatically asymmetrical with the excluded now included.

In our experience, community organizing undertaken by schools, churches, mosques, synagogues, unions, youth groups and universities committed to social justice and the common good represents an example of radical hospitality and embrace, where normal patterns of social relations and power brokering become asymmetrical. My first involvement with London Citizens (now called Citizens UK) was with the Strangers into Citizens campaign, where momentum grew initially from churches concerned at the welfare of some of their congregants who faced destitution. The impetus for giving status to those who had been living and working in the UK for many years culminated in a rally in Trafalgar Square calling for an irregular and extraordinary (one-off and one-time-only) general amnesty, regularization, naturalization and British citizenship for illegal immigrants in the United Kingdom.

Although this is now a defunct campaign, the asymmetric impact is worth noting. Despite the rejection of the proposal, the theory and practice of community organization was impactful. Endorsements from the Liberal Democrats, councils, churches and even Mayor Boris Johnson, who wanted to lead the debate for an amnesty for long-term illegal immigrants, showed something of the asymmetry of power. If the parable of the Great Banquet were overlaid with contemporary issues, perhaps the invite would have gone out to the illegal immigrants and the central theme of the banquet would have been amnesty and regularization.

The beginnings of such community organization are to be found in Chicago in the 1930s particularly focused around the work of Saul Alinsky within the poorest areas of that city. Now an international movement, the essence of all its expressions is the intentional building of relationships through listening campaigns and consultative exercises that are owned not by the listeners, but by those who need to be listened to. Together there is a strength that builds the capacity of local communities through a solidarity and common purpose. The Living Wage campaign is a current example of a stated aim of Citizens

UK to 'reweave the fabric of civil society' as it tackles family fragmentation exacerbated by low wages with parents choosing between time with family or earning enough to survive. Other examples of community action include the development of community land trusts and affordable housing, safer streets through CitySafe, and movements like Just Money among others. Angus Ritchie describes this as 'rethinking sovereignty' as citizens engage in reflection, negotiation and action to reshape their common life. 'Community organizing challenges some common assumptions about sovereignty. In political theory, discussions tend to focus on the legitimacy and limits of state power. By contrast, community organizing sees the state as one among a range of actors – businesses, journalists, and above all active associations of citizens. The movement recognizes that sovereignty is, and should be, diffuse.'[15]

Nick and Kerry Coke of the Salvation Army, together with John and Naomi Clifton, add a compelling argument for community organizing within the local church. Their conclusions offer insight to rethought sovereignty. They argue that this kind of asymmetric approach demands more than speaking up for the voiceless, more than doing things for others: there is a need 'to abandon the notion of being a voice for the voiceless by committing to help the voiceless find their voice. To pledge not to do for others what they can do for themselves.'[16]

Naomi Clifton, working out of Ilford Salvation Army, speaks of meeting the temporal needs of homeless people through their night shelter and associated ministries as not being enough. Addressing human suffering needs to be persistent and an integral and intentional part of our strategy of engagement in the social dimension: what is needed is a long-term commitment to work towards changing the actual housing situation. It has been through putting community organizing into practice that this has been expressed, with the voices not usually heard brought to prominence – demonstrating something of the dramatic asymmetry that Bretherton refers to. Naomi's account of this forms the basis of the case study in Chapter 10.

Economy of blessing

Second in Bretherton's exegesis of Luke 14:15–24 is what Brethertonton calls a conversion of the 'gift of heart' to the 'alternative economy of gift' or, as he describes it, to 'an economy of blessing'. The guests are undeserving, there is nothing that they had that the host wants and the host has no real reason for his generosity. This is more than just doing good, and in a culture where to be magnanimous would be to reinforce the self-sufficient status of the giver, Bretherton points out that the host within this parable does not remain self-sufficient; his vulnerability is exposed as he pursues the recipients of his invitation. This is hospitality of receiving and not just giving.

What is certain is that to bless should never be an exercise of power. However, being the source of blessing can easily slip into magnanimity, and churches need to be aware of this as they offer what they have to those who they perceive have not. The alternative economy of gift that Bretherton suggests allows for the dignity of reciprocity: the Great Banquet only happened because people turned up, people gave of themselves and made possible what the host had envisaged and hoped for. The host in return was blessed.

Sitting in a circle of street homeless men was a blessing when Brian pointed to each person in turn saying, 'You're my friend . . . you're my friend; in here I feel safe and wanted, in here I am with you, out there I am with them.' This is an alternative economy of gift. Learning that you receive so much more than you give identifies with the host in Jesus' parable. Hearing that Simon, who had slept on the streets for several years, was worried about me the night he sheltered from a heavy night of snow under a golf umbrella was an alternative economy of blessing.

Being vulnerable enough as a church to be blessed from the margins takes humility; to be open to receive from the unlikely undermines any magnanimity and subverts the often unintentional power that comes from being in the privileged position to bless. Naomi Clifton identifies the impact of the conversion of the 'gift of heart' to an 'alternative economy of gift' at Ilford Salvation Army's night shelter as she describes the impact of the economy of blessing that Bretherton identifies in the parable of the Great Banquet.

The night shelter commits to be 'a place of transformation', Naomi explains. We have come to learn that an ethos of hospitality creates an environment where transformation takes place on multiple levels within the same sphere. At the most basic level, the night shelter changes the situation of people sleeping rough on the streets, but it's not just the lives of those sleeping at the shelter that are transformed. Volunteers have discovered skills they didn't know they had, found a place to belong and a purpose to share in. For some, like Hannah, this has led to changes in career as they discover a vocation that captivates them. For many volunteers, the night shelter is a forum for discipleship as the team shares a reflection from the Bible and prays together before each shift. It's a setting that generates difficult questions of faith as we grapple with unanswered prayer and why bad things happen to good people. The shelter provides opportunity for the fruit of the Spirit to grow in our life and forces us to examine our attitudes and assumptions about others.

Naomi reflects that hosting the night shelter has been transformative for Ilford Salvation Army. She notes how it has fixed the focus of their mission firmly in serving Christ as they encounter him in the hungry, the homeless, the captive and the stranger (Matt. 25:40).

The double flow of blessing in Naomi's reflection captures a counter-cultural *kairos* moment. Rather than mission being something we do for others it becomes something we are together, a transformational relationship for all caught up in its sending movement. Mission is not what we magnanimously do for others but is about what we become together, bringing the kingdom into being. This is the reality of 'heaven on earth'. Richard Rohr identifies with this economy of blessing, which he describes as a surrendering of superiority. 'Such surrendering of superiority, or even a need for such superiority, is central to any authentic enlightenment. Without it, we are blind ourselves (John 9:39–41) and blind guides for others.'[17]

Sacramental embrace

Bretherton recognizes within this parable a counter-cultural sacramental embrace of others through hospitality as he captures the 'who, how and why' of mission in the social dimension:

> The parable of the Great Banquet articulates the nature and the proper form of the church's relations with its neighbours. The church is to participate actively in the life of the world as slaves and envoys of the true king, in a manner akin to Jesus, extending an invitation to those, like they were previously, who are not worthy guests, who are marginalized in the wider society, who do not consider themselves invited, and who have not even heard there is such a banquet available.[18]

The church represents the envoys sent to invite those that are considered unwanted, those unaware that they too have the right to be included. The host of the banquet puts out the call to those isolated by society: the poor, crippled, blind, and the lame; today we share the same responsibility to seek out and invite. In the UK as the state continues to shrink, the impact of austerity on the vulnerable brings impetus to the church to 'go out and seek' often the vilified and rejected, those whose currency in hope and choice is fast becoming bankrupt. Today, the host of the Great Banquet might encourage his envoys to go out into the streets and invite the benefit dependants, those scratching to get by on allowances for living with disability, the sanctioned and those forced out of their homes because of the 'bedroom tax'. Some areas of media would seem to scapegoat real people and the lives of those deemed to be work-shy scroungers. Television programmes and newspaper columns dedicate themselves to promoting the caricature of benefit Britain and to legitimize government policy. There seem to be votes to be gained by promising to crack down.

As we saw earlier in the chapter with the snapshots of four lives profoundly affected by new government policies, these are not statistics but real people that an upwardly mobile society does not want; and there are many such others every week who access community through the Coffee House as we offer an embrace and an invite to those coming under increasing pressure to survive. The benefit cuts, bedroom tax, cuts to legal aid, increased community charge, universal payment, on-line applications when those who need to fill them in are often computer-illiterate or do not have enough income to run a computer, benefit sanctions, reassessment of employment and support allowances, increased demand at food banks, increased hidden homelessness, increased displaced families – all this is a perfect storm of poverty that we will need to be prepared for. There are individuals who need a counter-cultural sacramental embrace.

Richard Horsley and Neil Siberman[19] point out that within Jesus' life he suggested that God was establishing his kingdom by creating an alternative society. The actual society Jesus inhabited was under the pressure of debt and taxation, where close-knit villages were being transformed into badly fragmented communities of alienation, where neighbourly responsibility in times of shortage meant that neighbours were now themselves debtors. The problem Horsley and Siberman identify is that Roman legal standards had begun to take precedence over the values espoused by the Torah[20] so that the political and legal processes of the day were usurping the divine dream of kindness, justice and righteousness, as articulated for example in Jeremiah 9:24.

Where such dissonance has taken place along with the associated experiences of exclusion and indifference, transformation begins to take place through the practices of sacramental embrace. Miroslav Volf makes some key observations about the theology and practices of embrace. In exploring open relationships towards the other he points out the unacceptable destructiveness of exclusion, seeing any form of exclusion as an exclusion of God. The parable of the Great Banquet gives insight into the beauty of the new community in which exclusion is supplanted by embrace. 'The spirit of embrace creates communities of embrace – places where the power of the exclusion system has been broken and from where divine energies of embrace can flow, forging rich identities that include the other.'[21] There is a responsibility for the church to take up the posture of embrace in troubling social contexts so that it gets caught up in God's movement of love towards people and in doing so participates in and makes known the unrelenting love of God.[22]

Taking this responsibility seriously also means that the church in mission needs to be aware of and pay attention to the possibilities for what could be called 'compromised embrace and hospitality'. While working with homeless men within the ministry of the Salvation Army's Faith House, I discovered the ease with which the street homeless saw inauthentic or compromised hospitality. I heard of feeding programmes dependent on attending evangelistic meetings, food served after worship to ensure attendance, a loss of interest and relationships dropped when 'decisions' were not forthcoming, even the suspicion of being treated like numbers to meet funding targets and criteria, when all that was needed was the authenticity of embrace. It seems while 'the mystery worshipper'[23] assesses how songs are sung and sermons are preached on a Sunday, what the homeless people of London are continually assessing is hospitality. In my time with Faith House I discovered that a street code exists to guide homeless people as to what kind of place is safe or not; what kind of place serves food or not; what kind of place is friendly or not; where is good to sleep or not. A simple chalk mark is left on a building to indicate the level of welcome and embrace; it is a fascinating code called the 'Homeless City Guide'.[24]

While the idea of manifesting the unrelenting love of God would seem axiomatic, the danger of distraction and disconnect for the church is real when there is a focus on the church rather than God's kingdom. Elsewhere I have identified the problem in the following terms:

> [A] theology that does not allow for mission in its fullest sense is not a theology, and a church that has no theology has an identity crisis . . . Even in an era when mission is high on the agenda, there is always the risk of an identity issue or some other disconnect if our theology of mission is not secure.

> A church that is unaware of its essence, that is disconnected by a delusion that mission is something it *does* rather than something it *is*, is a church

in peril. This disconnect can flourish wherever mission is reduced to conceptual or theoretical discussions or wherever it is seen as the key performance indicator, an output to measure to determine successful church life. We have to recognize that an identity crisis is lurking around the corner if 'mission' ever becomes a simple, fashionable buzzword, thrown into any discussion to gain kudos, or if it becomes a euphemism for something else, something which dilutes its very nature as an attribute of God.[25]

In his 1988 book, *Mission in Christ's Way*, Lesslie Newbigin warned about the separation of the message of the kingdom from the name of Jesus, a warning we might well still heed today:

> When the message of the kingdom of God is separated from the name of Jesus two distortions follow, and these are in fact the source of deep divisions in the life of the church today.
>
> On one hand, there is the preaching of the name of Jesus simply as the one who brings a religious experience of personal salvation without involving one in costly actions at the points in public life where the power of Satan is contracting the rule of God and bringing men and women under the power of evil. Such preaching of cheap grace, of a supposed personal salvation that does not go the way of the cross, of an inward comfort without commitment to costly action for the doing of God's will in the world – this kind of evangelistic preaching is a distortion of the gospel. A preaching of personal salvation that does not lead the hearers to challenge the monstrous injustices of our society is not mission in Christ's way. It is peddling cheap grace.
>
> On the other hand, when the message of the kingdom is separated from the name of Jesus, the action of the church in respect of the evils in society becomes a mere ideological crusade.[26]

Mission in the social dimension – if it is to be authentic, if it is to attract the right 'chalk mark' on our buildings – needs to be integrated. Anything less cheapens the grace that should be central to our embrace of others. It is important that the church is watchful of mission becoming dualistic and undermining of authentic community engagement and that it can identify its symptoms quickly. The reality in practice is that sometimes it is too easy to sleepwalk into a situation whereby initial desires and intentions, while noble, are corrupted and at odds with authentic grace-centred mission.

Seeking Authentic Engagement with the Social Realm

Practical theology

To avoid any such compromise, a church engaging in mission needs to be intentional in its evaluation of its life in community. Reflection on the kingdom implications of community engagement need to be proactively woven into the planning and evaluation of the church's activity. The key here is a practical theology rooted in sustained theological reflection. Judith Thompson, Stephen Pattinson and Ross Thompson talk about the concept of 'negative capability' as a means of bringing subjectivity and maturity to a church's self-evaluation, where negative capability is: 'a readiness to let go of the security based on long-held opinions and assumptions, and accept for as long is needful, a state of doubt, uncertainty and mystery; and a willing suspension of disbelief when the next step is taken, to look anew at what can be learned from the exploration of text and tradition that has been undertaken'.[27]

Helen Cameron recognizes a new energy for mission in the local church and offers insight to how missiological and practical theological thinking can helpfully inform one another, sustaining authenticity as local churches are mobilized.[28] Cameron offers the Pastoral Cycle[29] as a tool for the kind of theological reflection which is essential for any church that is seeking a more authentic and practical expression of its core values in its own locality while at the same time being realistic about how it is also inextricably linked to and shaped by the surrounding culture. The church needs to reflect, know itself and acknowledge what it presents as cultural signs. In this way the church may become more aware of how its own values are perceived by the community and how they can be better expressed through the planning and development of projects in the future.

Priorities of Christ in mission

Keeping within the priorities of Christ in mission is another means of authentic engagement. At the heart of the Cape Town Commitment[30] is a call that we should not lose the authenticity of the kingdom message. With my colleague Andrew Grinnell, I argued in a 2013 publication that Christ's distinctiveness calls the church to be shaped by humility, integrity and simplicity as an alternative to the prevailing culture that champions greed, power and the lust for reputation. 'It is to Christ, his humility, integrity and simplicity to which we need to continually turn if we as a church are to position ourselves against "all that exploits, squanders, and disfigures the world for selfishness, greed, and self-centred power" as a living demonstration of wholeness, healing and salvation.'[31]

If, as a core aspect of its mission, the church is to imagine, hope for, and indeed embody 'embrace of the other' as an alternative social arrangement, then it can start nowhere else than with the person and priorities of Christ, where radical embrace and hospitality reside. Likewise, if we are to see the embodying of God's passion for the world in the life, death and resurrection of the person of Jesus himself as the driving force behind our sent acts of love into our communities, there has to be an alignment with the life of Christ that centres on the announcement that the reign of God is at hand. The central teaching of Jesus concerned the kingdom of God; Jesus proclaimed the kingdom in his ministry, his actions pointed to the kingdom and its values. This theme not only shaped Jesus' sense of mission but represents the essence of mission passed on to his followers. Our challenge is to ensure that the outworking of our calling to mission reflects this message.

Therefore, mission in the social realm, if it is to avoid a woefully impoverished identity, needs to be shaped by the message of the kingdom, continually working to discover and understand more deeply the reign of God that Jesus announced and orientate to it. A church seeking its definition within the fundamentals of kingdom living will find the separation of 'my personal salvation' from 'God's healing reign' nonsensical.[32]

Conclusion

In this chapter I have considered the challenges to mission posed by the rapidly changing patterns and arrangements of the social realm. I have attempted to look beyond some of the more familiar constructs of economy and geography to think about the ways in which social factors such as isolation and loneliness have powerful marginalizing effects on people from all kinds of backgrounds. In the darkness of loneliness, rejection and isolation, the church will be a light if its actions in society are shaped by faith, hope and love: 'faith toward God and his action in Jesus Christ; hope toward God's future; love, toward both God and our neighbour.'[33]

To engage with this in our communities is to participate with God's kingdom purposes, namely radical and sacramental hospitality and generous, open-hearted embrace that is seen in the life and message of Jesus. Anything less is to toy with a theology of mission absent of authenticity and lacking prophetic connection to the contemporary social realm. Our communities need to be loved and, as churches, a vulnerable sharing of ourselves, our time and our resources is a practical way of expressing love into the burgeoning chaos of society. As Stanley Hauerwas has put it, our call as church is to be a people 'capable of maintaining the life of charity, hospitality, and justice'.[34]

Notes

[1] Col. 3:16.
[2] St Ignatius of Loyola, *Spiritual Exercises* 231–7.
[3] 'UK Foodbanks' (n.d.) http://www.trusselltrust.org/foodbank-projects (accessed 2 July 2015).

[4]   J. Cheshire and O. Uberti, *London: The Information Capital: 100 Maps and Graphics that Will Change How You View the City* (London: Penguin, 2014), p. 32.

[5]   S. Bouma-Prediger and B.J. Walsh, *Beyond Homelessness: Christian Faith in a Culture of Displacement* (Grand Rapids, MI: Eerdmans, 2008), p. 4.

[6]   H. Nouwen, *Bread for the Journey: A Daybook of Wisdom and Faith* (San Francisco: Harper, 2006), reading for March 18.

[7]   G. Monbiot, 'The Age of Loneliness Is Killing Us', *The Guardian*, 14 October 2014.

[8]   Paul Cloke and Mike Pears, eds, *Mission in Marginal Places: The Theory* (Milton Keynes: Paternoster, 2016).

[9]   This develops Ann Morisy's discussion on social capital in her book, *Journeying Out: A New Approach to Christian Mission* (London: Continuum. 2006), pp. 45–54.

[10] L. Bretherton, *Hospitality as Holiness: Christian Witness amid Moral Diversity* (Aldershot, England: Ashgate, 2006), p. 128.

[11] C.D. Pohl, *Making Room: Recovering Hospitality as a Christian Tradition* (Grand Rapids, MI: Eerdmans, 1999), p. xiii.

[12] Morisy, *Journeying Out*, pp. 45–54.

[13] Gen. 12:1–3.

[14] Bretherton, *Hospitality*, p. 132.

[15] http://www.theology-centre.org.uk/wp-content/uploads/2013/04/BiT Winter 2010 Ritchie.pdf.

[16] J. Clifton, N. Coke and K. Coke, *Marching towards Justice: Community Organising and the Salvation Army* (London: Centre for Theology and Community, 2015), pp. 48–9.

[17] R. Rohr, *Eager to Love: The Alternative Way of Francis of Assisi* (Cincinnati, OH: Franciscan Media, 2015), pp. 101–3.

[18] Rohr, *Eager to Love*, p. 135.

[19] R.A. Horsley and N.A. Siberman, *The Message and the Kingdom: How Jesus and Paul Ignited a Revolution and Transformation* (New York: Penguin Putnam Group, 1997), p. 54.

[20] Horsley and Siberman, *Message*, p. 54.

[21] J. Volf and M. Volf, 'A Spacious Heart: Essays on Identity and Belonging', in *Christian Mission and Modern Culture* (Valley Forge, PA: Trinity Press, 1997), p. 60.

[22] D. Bosch, *Transforming Mission: Paradigm Shifts in Theology of Mission* (Maryknoll, NY: Orbis, 1991), pp. 389–90. See also, S. Hauerwas, *The Peaceable Kingdom: A Primer in Christian Ethics* (Notre Dame, IN: University of Notre Dame Press, 1983), p. 67.

23 http://shipoffools.com/mystery/

24 'Homeless Code in the City', *The Pavement* (19 May 2009) http://www.thepavement.org.uk/stories.php?story=130 (accessed 10 November 2014).

25 G. Cotterill, 'Introduction', in *Call to Mission: Your Will Be Done* (ed. G. Cotterill, D. Taylor, D. McCombe and J. Mitchinson; n.p.: Shield Books, 2013), p. 6.

26 L. Newbigin, *Mission in Christ's Way: A Gift, a Command, an Assurance* (New York: Friendship Press, 1988).

27 J. Thompson, S. Pattison and R. Thompson, *Study Guide to Theological Reflection* (London: SCM Press, 2008), p. 104.

28 H. Cameron, *Resourcing Mission: Practical Theology for Changing Churches* (London: SCM Press, 2009).

29 Cameron states that 'the pastoral cycle is a process for thinking theologically about a particular situation with the aim of finding new and more faithful ways of acting in the future . . . It consists of four stages . . . Experience – what is happening?; Exploration – why is it happening?; Reflection – how do we evaluate our experience in dialogue with the Bible and Christian Tradition?; Planning – how will we respond?' (Cameron, *Resourcing Mission*, pp. 8–9).

30 Lausanne Movement, *The Cape Town Commitment: A Confession of Faith and a Call to Action* (Peabody, MA: Hendrickson, 2012).

31 G. Cotterill and A. Grinnell, 'Calling the Church back to Humility Integrity and Simplicity' in *Call to Mission: Your Will Be Done* (ed. G. Cotterill, D. Taylor, D. McCombe and J. Mitchinson; n.p. Shield Books, 2013).

32 Cotterill and Grinnell, 'Calling', p. 92.

33 N.T. Wright, *Virtue Reborn* (London: SPCK, 2010), p. 177.

34 Hauerwas, *Peaceable Kingdom*, p. 109.

10

Case Study: Ilford, London

Naomi Clifton

During four winters, over three hundred people have experienced hospitality at the night shelter in Ilford. Frank is a born-and-bred East-Ender. A die-hard West Ham supporter, he has been an alcoholic for over thirty years and on the streets for seven years. Cezar is a Romanian national with no record of exercising his treaty rights and now finds himself destitute on the streets of London. Rahul has a Master's degree in public administration, overstayed his visa and no longer has documents to demonstrate his country of origin as being India. Jim left school with no qualifications, can barely read and write, and worked in manual labour all his life. Arrested after an incident in a pub, his relationship with his girlfriend broke down and he found himself homeless on release from prison. Each guest can tell their own story of the chain of events that led them to sleeping rough on the streets. But there are common themes: relationship breakdown; financial difficulties; mental health issues; drugs and alcohol; migration.

The shelter is only possible because of the commitment of over one hundred and fifty volunteers from a wide range of backgrounds. Salvationists are joined by members of other churches: Catholics, Baptists, Pentecostals, Methodists and non-denominational. I've experienced a more meaningful unity of the body of Christ at the night shelter than I have in any other ecumenical setting. We are also joined by people of other faiths and none. The current volunteer team includes Muslims, Sikhs, Jews, atheists and agnostics. We are a diverse community brought together to meet a common need.

At the night shelter we are intentional about building relationships with our guests. We learn people's names and celebrate their birthdays. We encourage volunteers to sit down and eat a meal with our guests, knowing that Jesus is at work when we share meals together just as in the meals we read about in the gospels. It's when we spend time with our guests that we discover that one is a wonderful artist while another is a gifted musician; one was once the lead singer for a popular band in his home country and another can beat just about anyone he faces at checkers. It's in these encounters that we see past the stereotypes and see people created in God's image, members of our community with so much to give.

The night shelter commits to being 'a place of transformation'. We have come to learn that an ethos of hospitality creates an environment where transformation takes place on multiple levels within the same sphere. At the most basic level, the night shelter changes the situation of people sleeping rough on the streets. Our guests have somewhere safe to sleep and good food to eat. The shelter keeps people alive during the coldest months of the year and, for a proportion, a sustained period of good sleep and the support of the shelter community results in improved engagement with support workers and a longer-lasting solution to their homelessness.

All these individual journeys are important and significant, but if we are to look for more long-term processes of change we must also be committed to seeking ways of changing the housing situation of Redbridge. Part of the way we try to do this is through our active membership of Redbridge Citizens, the local alliance of Citizens UK. Citizens UK was founded in 1996 when thirty institutions, including one from Redbridge, formed the East London Communities Organization (TELCO). Self-identifying as a 'power organization', TELCO trained local institutions in the craft of community organizing, based on the theory and practice of Saul Alinsky, so that standing with their neighbours they have the power to challenge politicians, councils and businesses. It depends on the belief that when people work together they have the power to change their neighbourhoods, cities and ultimately the country for the better.

As the local elections came around in 2014, we as Redbridge Citizens had a decision to make about our involvement with this. Citizens UK have a strong tradition of organizing assemblies to hold power to account, using drama, laughter and serious business to challenge politicians to act on the priorities of our institutions, as identified by listening campaigns. In community organizing, power is defined as the capacity to act. We didn't know if we had that power. Could we fill a room? Could we get the politicians there? If we presented our 'asks', would they say yes or laugh us down? It was a risk but we decided to go for it.

On Tuesday 6 May 2014, ninety-three citizens gathered at Ilford Salvation Army hall to hear how the three electoral candidates for leader of Redbridge Council would respond as we asked them to work with us in tackling the priority issues that had been raised by listening campaigns in our six member institutions: housing, social care and the living wage. The diverse crowd, including members of the Christian, Muslim, Sikh and Jewish communities, listened as two mothers shared the challenges they and their families faced because of the borough's housing shortage and the impact of disrepair in council homes on their families' health. The three councillors were pressed to make commitments to pay a living wage to all care workers, create a register of private landlords, explore the possibility of a community land trust in the borough, and to meet regularly with Redbridge Citizens to work together in addressing the issues raised at our assemblies. At the end we joined together in singing the Redbridge Citizens' anthem: 'Fill your hearts with joy and gladness, working for the common good. We are citizens of Redbridge, helping in our neighbourhoods' – words hastily written the night before to the tune of 'Europe' but sung with gusto by a crowd enthused by the commitments of the councillors.

A lot of hard work had gone into the assembly: negotiations with politicians; a script carefully crafted; conversation convincing members to turn up. But this was just the beginning. Citizens UK doesn't ask politicians to do something *for* us, we ask them to do something *with* us. So in the months that followed, a small delegation met the newly elected leader and deputy leader of the council to follow up on their commitments.

One of these was to explore developing a community land trust (CLT). A CLT is a way to develop genuinely affordable housing by taking the land into shared ownership. This removes the inflationary considerations of the land value from the cost of rent or purchase, meaning they can instead be linked to the value of labour, i.e. the median income of a given area. Citizens UK have already pioneered the first urban CLT in the UK and we believe developing one within our borough will benefit local people struggling to find affordable places to live.

Seeking a public commitment from the council to explore possible sites for a CLT, one hundred members of Redbridge Citizens, including volunteers and guests from the night shelter, gathered on the steps of the town hall. One of the beds from the shelter was set up to symbolize all the local people who cannot afford to live in the area and are being moved out of the borough or simply don't have accommodation. A Muslim and a Christian volunteer from the night shelter placed a cardboard house over half the bed and then challenged Councillor Wes Streeting, Deputy Leader of Redbridge Council, to put in place a second house as a sign of the council's commitment to working with us to find innovative solutions to the borough's housing shortage. Days later, a small group attended the Neighbourhoods and Communities Service Committee meeting to press the Cabinet Member for Housing further on committing to identify possible sites for a CLT. One of the delegation, a night-shelter guest, said it had given him a boost to try to do something about the housing shortage rather than just complain about it.

11

Case Study: The Coffee House, Sutton

Gordon Cotterill and Adam Bonner

Sutton Salvation Army is located well. Not because of its centrality to Sutton, just off the high street, but because it is part of what was once the notorious Benhill estate. In recent times we have undergone a significant change in the nature of our engagement with our locality. The story of this transition, while painful for some, has facilitated an exciting encounter of re-imagination and opened up space for creative possibility as we have sought to move away from weekly 'evangelistic forays' into the heart of the estate based on an open-air meeting, to one based on authentic relationship and available 'presence'.

As a result of this journey, what is now at the centre of our missional expression as church is the Coffee House. And gradually, this professionally run coffee shop, priding itself upon the quality of service and coffee, has become the heart of community for many. Every week people encounter a kind of hospitality and sense of relationship that we pray will point beyond who we are, and through it we are discovering a form of evangelism that is not that hard to do!

The Coffee House represents the essence of Sutton Salvation Army in mission to its community; statistically it could be measured but it is its stories that need to be heard. It is where Rupert comes for community since his wife died. It is where Julie, despite her additional needs, comes to volunteer. It is where Christine can come and talk through her crumbling faith since her dad died. It is where Jimmy with cerebral palsy can come to help clean the tables and vacuum. It is where a support group for those with personality disorders finds a welcome, or where members of our local estate feel they can belong. It's where folks can find help in getting back into employment (in the Job Club), while at the same time being a hub for the church community and various family and friends who pop in when they can.

This isn't the latest in a line of social enterprises, or a clever innovative social outreach; it is more than a programme: it is simply a blurred encounter between what we represent as a church and the community to which we belong. And that blurring of who we are as community is growing. Sitting in the Coffee House, Hazel looked up from her latte and smiled, 'You need to know how important this place has become to us', and the group with her nodded in enthusiastic agreement. For Hazel, Thursday is community; it's the day of the community choir, something that came together at the Coffee House almost by accident but has since become a community of hope where not only is there singing, but the once-lonely now encounter others and share experiences with each other.

For us, as a new local narrative and understanding of what it is to be visible has emerged, a new trust has grown too; a new sense of life together has been established, no longer excluding those 'outside' of the church, but offering an inclusive welcome to all, expressed through our intentional availability. The doors are now open every day in hopeful anticipation of encounter.

More widely, as a mark of the relationship that has been created between the church and others within the Benhill estate, we are now invited onto the estate and seen as an active and welcomed neighbour, valued for our open-door presence. For example, we have been welcomed onto the Benhill Residents Association and have been party to something of a change of emphasis there. The 'not in my backyard' items are dropping down the agenda and concerns around how to build community are taking more prominence. The encounter with church is becoming so blurred that when a neighbourhood collaboration project was proposed to encourage the estate to be 'good neighbours', we just sat back, smiled and supported!

12

The Social Realm: Editorial Comment

Mike Pears and Paul Cloke

Gordon Cotterill's thoughtful and experience-laden chapter provides an excellent framework for considering how local mission in particular marginal places might be focused on the social realm. He alerts readers to two essential threads of appropriate mission. First, mission, at heart, requires an emphasis on *ways of being* rather than ways of doing. Doing-oriented mission can often involve strongly self-referential motives, such as a knowing achievement of performance indicators, or a desire to publicize the significance and achievement of Christian involvement in social good works. At worst, such desires find expression in 'badging' key projects in terms of who is *doing the doing*, rather than in terms of how social needs are *being* met; a sense of 'look what we bright shiny Christians are doing' rather than 'look at the social injustice and marginalization that afflicts individuals and families in contemporary society'. Ways of being involve an intentional positioning of mission in local community as a deliberate alignment of faith-action with the needs of the surrounding community (and not with the needs of the church). Ways of being need to be kingdom-shaped, eschewing the assumed middle-class birthrights of control, power and reputation for more cross-shaped attributes of humility, integrity and simplicity. Once that is achieved we can think about how being connects with doing.

Second, mission needs to be *an embodied reconfiguration of hospitality*; reconfigured in the sense that missional *giving* of hospitality needs to be constituted around the needs of those *receiving* hospitality. Rather than Christian mission aiming (somewhat paternalistically) to give care to the care-less, and voice to the voice-less, reconfigured hospitality involves engagement in a reshaping of common life in a community in such a way as to ensure that local people are able to find their own voice and shape their own care. An integral part of such embodiment is the development of a prayerful instinct to extend Christian embrace beyond people like us or people who like us (where embrace is often focused) to a deliberate seeking out of the vilified, rejected, hidden and vulnerable. As Gordon so clearly shows, the social geographies of marginalization are far more complex than is often imagined in the targeting of activity in terms of obvious social need. Embodying reconfigured hospitality, then, is likely to involve extending the social relations of who we share things in common with, and becoming more alert to the myriad ways in which people become disconnected from place and community.

Gordon's example of the Coffee House provides a fascinating picture of one kind of setting in which radical ways of being hospitable can be practised. As he indicates, however, there is no one-size-fits-all model, and intentional mission in the social realm needs to be tailored to local specificities and needs. As such, mission requires a longitudinal approach, taking time to understand and discern local material and spiritual conditions rather than jumping in with a preconceived strategy that supposedly guarantees an ability to hit the ground running. So much contemporary mission seems to depend on a capacity to narrate stories of 'success' in order to encourage participants and wider supporters and to demonstrate the utility of the work vis-à-vis external expectations of achievement. Miraculous conversion is usually thought to speak louder than developmental hospitality. However, being radically hospitable may require us to deflate the pressure of having to come up with 'success stories' so that mission that is more sensitive to context can emerge and flourish without the expectation of instant gratification. Longitudinal mission seems likely to develop over a number of stages, of which five are prompted by the account provided in Gordon's chapter.

1. Developing an Awareness of the Contemporary Shaping of Social Conditions

Social awareness and discernment are often hampered either by a reliance on outdated understandings of social change or by an (often unknowing) set of assumptions derived from personal social relations and experience. In fact, social change is happening very fast in the UK, and even seemingly stable communities are continually being challenged by changing times. Currently, social geographers are recognizing two particular sets of social issues that are destabilizing society and community in the European context. The first, and most evidently mediated, is *migration*. The flight of millions of refugees from war-torn, politically unstable and economically destitute parts of the world to countries in the Global North (and particularly Europe) has figured extensively both in the reporting of world affairs and in the political debates about asylum, integration and national identity in the UK. In fact the bulk of recent migrants have ended up in neighbouring states; a piece of evidence often hidden from the moral panic being expressed about 'our' borders, 'our' resources and 'our' identity. Nevertheless, both longer-term patterns of migration, and more recent in-movement of refugees and economic migrants has meant that many urban communities have faced complex issues relating to multiculturalism, multiple religious identities and the difficulties of achieving mutual hospitality across ethnic divides.

The second key social issue is increasing *inequality*. The gap between 'haves' and 'have-nots' is widening significantly, not least due to the impacts of austerity government on the financing of the welfare state. The welfare safety net has now been so strongly impacted by financial cuts that there are gaping holes through which different individuals and families fall – as evidenced by the seemingly now permanent landscape of food banks, hostels for homeless people and advice centres that punctuate the urban landscape. Poverty and social exclusion are now to be found in complex social layers, including among people in work as well as those receiving benefits. Wider problems of disconnection can occur throughout the socio-economic spectrum including many examples of those 'haves' who experience sudden powerlessness, for example through unemployment, stress and anxiety, and mental illness. Inequality is bound up in deep-seated power relations, whereby the powerful are increasingly likely to purify and gentrify previously common spaces by driving out and marginalizing the less powerful by economic and regulatory means. Mission needs to understand these wider conditions and relations before focusing on the local conditions of community.

2. Developing an Awareness of Localized Social Relations

Longitudinal mission will need to apply this broader appreciation of social change to its local territory, understanding the drivers of marginalization, displacement and disconnection, and gaining an awareness of how these drivers affect or bypass the local community. Essentially, as Gordon has emphasized, this task centres on developing relationship with and *listening* to local people. Places will usually have distinctive features, connected into the outside globalized world but formulating and developing local senses of culture and dwelling. Place-specificity may involve struggles to maintain traditional social and cultural forms that are embedded in a perceived sense of community. If so, such struggles will inevitably produce variegated identities of 'insider' and 'outsider' as well as more ambivalent social locations, and the idea of community will be reproduced in terms of these identity struggles. Elsewhere the pace of change may have overwhelmed any such sense of perceived cohesion. In-movement of gentrifiers, or of culturally 'different' groups may be impacting on a dwindling remnant of self-proclaimed 'authentic' residents. Listening to the voices of different local people – ensuring that our listening is not governed by our social stereotypes of need or by our natural inclinations about who is easier, or more difficult, to listen to – will gradually help develop a local social awareness. Walking the streets of the community, seeking discernment about the spiritual landscape of the community is a helpful aid to the prayerful understanding of local conditions.

This development of awareness is an essential part of a mission focus that empowers local people rather than assuming to speak on their behalf.

3. Practising Generosity and Reconfigured Hospitality

These initial periods of longitudinal mission – where the emphasis has to be on listening to and understanding local people, working out how power relations and social change are impacting local community, and discerning and joining in with the wind of God's Spirit in that place – will often require patience and deliberate inactivity in terms of 'bigger projects'. However, these periods of localized 'induction' and community-based 'training' represent ideal opportunities to practise simple ways of being generous and hospitable in mission. For example, mission needs to be soaked in reflexive self-examination about our openness to different types of people.

- To what degree is our potential for generosity governed by implicit prejudice or overly rigid ideas about who deserves what?
- To what extent are we ready to lay down the worldly norms of what Gordon terms 'competitive social relations' in order to act with humility, integrity and simplicity?
- Does our embrace and hospitality stretch to people who are not like us and who (at least on first impressions) don't like us?
- Are we willing to cross social and cultural divides in our listening, learning and sharing, even if in some places this involves developing integral relationships with people of other religions, ethnicities, social backgrounds and frameworks of morality, ethicality or politics?

One good way to be reflexive on these issues is to practise *random* acts of kindness and generosity. Such generosity can start as a training exercise in ensuring that our generosity is not conditioned by preconceptions about who *deserves* our missional attention, but will hopefully develop into a fully-fledged element of *being* missional. If small-scale acts of kindness (the unsolicited giving of gifts, buying coffee, paying for groceries, offering help, giving away garden produce, and myriad other ways) can be undertaken randomly, that is regardless of the character and nature of the recipient, then a posture of unconditionality can be developed that helps to establish a radical form of hospitality that goes beyond the idea of simply meeting particular social needs.

4. Serving Those in Need

In due course these stages of listening, awareness and practising unconditional generosity may lead to insights that point to intentional acts of community-building that respond to particular perceived needs. Some of these acts may well reflect wider models of response to specific social problems – as reflected, for example, in food banks, medical centres, advice centres, shelters for homeless people and so on.

However, the message of Gordon's chapter is that as well as being ready to respond to these often visible social needs we need to bring kingdom-based generosity and vulnerability to more hidden, less obvious needs. For example, schemes to introduce healthy food, bulk-buy fruit and vegetables, bake bread, produce inexpensive meals and so on may meet locally specific food needs, and may indeed change our own values and practices around food purchase and preparation. Invitations to share a meal can be extended to the kinds of local people whose experience is of being rejected, vilified, lonely, isolated, disconnected. Spare rooms can be opened up to welcome homeless people, refugees or others with less obvious needs for shelter and company. Friendship and support can be offered to those for whom a 'buddy' is an answer to loneliness or disconnection from bureaucratic requirements.

These examples are just examples. The key message here is that longitudinal mission develops an awareness of local social conditions and relations, a discernment about how God's Spirit is groaning and moving in that locality, and a vulnerable desire to join in with what God is doing. This process needs to be far more than the deployment of preconceived projects as some kind of local franchise of Christian response to social need. It needs to reflect the slow and reflexive building of a locally relevant community of unconditional embrace.

5. Wider Political and Ethical Engagement

Finally, it will be important to square the circle of social engagement by connecting localized missional awareness of and response to social needs with a wider commitment to solidarity with other people in other localities who are vulnerable to, and suffering from, the power relations that drive much of contemporary social change. Localized relations and responses are the predominant scale for mission. However, the very attributes discussed here about localized mission also apply to the task of speaking truth to powers at a larger scale. Rather than envisaging a series of self-sufficient and isolated pods of missional being in different locations, we need to explore ways in which these pods can also act communally to engage at national and international scales to use local awareness and local experience of hospitality and embrace to speak kingdom values into the politics and ethics of nations. Justice needs to follow love's embrace.

To reiterate, these elements of mission in the social sphere are certainly not intended as any kind of one-size-fits-all model. Rather they are suggested as *provocations* for localized awareness and discernment. Equally, it is clear that localized mission cannot and should not attempt to tick all of these potential boxes. That way leads to local insensitivity and burn-out. However, immersion in a longitudinal process of missional being that includes listening, awareness, radical hospitality and small elements of reshaped common life that are relevant to and owned by local people can provide a helpful starting point in aligning mission to the surrounding community in a way that is shaped by the message of the kingdom.

Part IV

13

Understanding the Environmental Realm

Paul Ede and Sam Ewell

Introduction

From favelas, barrios and slums in the majority world to postindustrial western cities, degraded industrial land, reduced access to sufficient quality food, proximity to toxic pollutants and disinvestment in environmental concerns by city authorities are all common signifiers of a marginal urban community. Noah Toly asserts that 'where creation care is concerned with the global environment, it must be concerned with the city . . . because both global sustainability and global environmental justice are at stake in our urban engagements'.[1] In the urban margins the damaging links between environmental, social and personal spheres are revealed so sharply that the need for integrated responses (integral mission) is undeniable.

Paradoxically, as environmental concerns have become mainstream, in post-Christendom[2] the western church has itself become marginal. In academic circles a re-evaluation of major biblical-doctrinal categories (e.g. the centrality of land, resource distribution, new creation) and the resultant implications for missiology and creation care is occurring across the ecumenical spectrum;[3] but at the local level, congregations remain alarmingly resistant to mobilization and response. This is especially true in communities distanced demographically from the bulk of the church. In the marginal places where it is most needed, the church has marginalized environmental mission.

Right at the heart of this situation is the colonization of our imaginations by the ideology that only industrial-scale solutions (corporatized, commercialized and therefore far removed from our responsibility) will make any headway. Our contention, however, is that aggregated local practical action – no matter how small – is a critical part of the response that is required[4] and that a vital linkage between mission and the environmental realm lies in cultivating community-based ecological care at the margins. For at the margins we can unfetter ourselves from obligation to existing power structures of thought and practice. At the margins precise responses to ecological challenges can find the space and freedom to flourish. At the margins lack of resources can engender surprising creativity.

Our framework is intentionally contextual, following an approach articulated, for example, by Michael Frost and Alan Hirsch in *The Shaping of Things to Come*.[5] Their contention is that to move in a new missional mode for a new missional context, the forms and practices of the church (ecclesiology) should emerge out of the practice of mission rooted in the local context (missiology). To generate fresh yet faithful forms of mission and subsequently church life, it is crucial to root such innovation and exploration in Christ-centred biblical theology (Christology). Recent application of the biblical theme of abundance to ecological and economic crises is but one vital insight that arises by beginning with Christ: the One who comes into the world to bring 'abundant life' (John 10:10).[6] Our vision for radical, counter-cultural ecological praxis at the margins combines the concept of abundance with the Christ–mission–church framework. For we believe that abundant community (church) emerges from the practice of entering the abundant kingdom (mission), which in turn emerges from a vision of abundant life (Christ himself).

In doing so, we explore two dimensions of environmental mission; namely, rehabilitating degraded urban land for community use, and urban gardening and food production. Then we offer two case studies from the margins: Clay Community Church in Glasgow, Scotland, and its work in restoring unproductive land; and the history and work of Casa da Videira, a communal food co-operative in Curitiba, Brazil.

Rehabilitating Unproductive and Degraded Urban Land for Community Use

Christology: Christ and urban land rehabilitation

The problem of unproductive, toxic or derelict urban land has been an issue for urban populations since ancient times, but today has reached an unprecedented scale. Now as then, those cast out of society are left to cope with the burden of life on the most damaged, unwanted land. In biblical imagination, degraded land is also tied up with the sins of the people and the oppressive urban systems that resulted.[7] Consequently, the response of the 'pure insider' was often to scapegoat the sinfulness of others in their degraded place, while the response of the 'impure outcast' was often to internalize the inevitability of their habitation of the places of degradation. Such arrangements seem to link degraded land associated with urban centres with social settlements that define sinfulness in society. These patterns are deeply embedded and resistant to biblical patterns of shalom. Counter to such social and ecological paralysis, however, the Bible offers a redemptive vision for a renewed people in relationship with land that is flourishing once more. At the heart of this vision stands the person of Christ portrayed in terms of three important images: the Tree of Life, the Destroyer of the Destroyers of the Earth, and the Healer of the Land. The source of abundant life is thus revealed in three different redemptive modes, each offering rich grounding for the practice of environmental mission at the margins.

Jesus Christ as the Tree of Life

The motif of the Tree of Life, which has been largely neglected in western thinking about Christ, vividly positions the Messiah as Creator and Redeemer of all of creation. For people daily confronted by wasted, unproductive land as they leave their homes, it is critical to offer a portrayal of Christ as Originator and Creator of their place, no matter how degraded it currently is. Without the awareness that

God through Christ (Col. 1:15–17) made creation 'very good' (Gen. 1:31), there can be no reason to think that the land is valued enough by God for him to redeem it. Being attentive to the symbolic language surrounding the image of the 'tree' as it unfolds in the biblical narrative and is drawn into the story of Jesus helps to illuminate and deepen our understanding of who Christ is, and his mission.

In the creation narrative of Genesis, the Tree of life, an integral part of sustaining life in Eden, was closed to humanity through the Fall; now Christ, who was himself crucified on a tree (1 Pet. 2:24; Acts 5:30), has become the Tree of Life to us, opening up and nourishing us in the life of the resurrection. In Revelation the image returns, book-ending the Bible with the same motif: in the new creation suffused with the presence of Christ, there will be a Tree whose leaves are for the healing of the nations (Rev. 22:2). To think of Christ in this way stresses God's inexorable goal of integrating and re-integrating all of creation; his reconciling purpose through Christ's shed blood is not limited to humankind, but rather envelops the whole of the created order in which humankind is also embedded, as Paul asserts in Colossians 1:19–20. To speak of Christ as the Tree of Life gives back to disempowered, dislocated and discouraged people a story of hope and a God who invites participation in his own abundant agency and power to transform their environment.

Jesus Christ as Destroyer of the Destroyers of the Earth

As Creator, Redeemer and Sustainer of creation, Christ must set himself to arrest 'anti-creational practices'[8] (sin) whenever they emerge. In biblical thought, just as Christ's redemption is conceived as embracing the whole created order, so 'sin' is presented as having a destructive effect on the entire created order. Sin is seen as a self-interested, self-serving complicity with the powers that be – whether social, political or spiritual – powers vividly portrayed in Revelation as 'those who destroy the earth' (Rev. 11:18). The consequences of 'anti-creational behaviour' are, however, always seen as boundaried by divine providence[9] and framed within the longer-term goal of redemption, as witnessed in the pattern of prophetic warning alongside the offer of mercy and covenantal renewal, in which 'the land' is an integral part. It is ultimately in Christ's death on the cross, outside the gates of the corrupt city-system of Jerusalem, that the destroyers of the earth are overcome. The principalities and powers are put under his feet and the ultimate sacrifice paid to ransom from their clutches both urban elites and urban poor, opening up space for reconciliation and collaboration towards the flourishing of both city land and city inhabitants.

The commitment of God to act in such ways in creation speaks profoundly to marginalized urban communities and the land degradation that they endure at the hands of corrupt city-systems. Urban land degradation at the hands of corporate greed and bureaucratic inefficiency is not an inevitable and unchanging phenomenon! In developing faithful missiological and ecclesiological responses to the effects of sinful exploitation of land and the created order, inhabitants of marginal communities can take heart in calling city authorities to account in light of both the judgement the cross makes on neglectful power and the hopeful imagination that resurrection opens up for a new redemptive way. Naming anti-creational powers, and working to establish social and ecological justice with the future in mind is the empowering result of poor communities released by the 'Destroyer of the Destroyers of the Earth' into the realm of prophetic and communal political action.

Jesus Christ as Healer of the Land

Even if the urban promise turns sour and the land is sullied by cities that spiral into an anti-creational pattern, biblically we see that God offers access to a counteracting grace-filled narrative of redemption: Christ as Healer of the Land. In the grand vision that ends the book of Ezekiel, the river of God – the Holy Spirit – flows from the temple where right worship has been restored, through the Arabah, down into the Jordan Valley and out into the Dead Sea. There the salt water is 'made fresh' and its surrounding geography is restored to bounteous life. The Hebrew word for 'made fresh' is *rapha*, meaning 'healed'; fruitful productivity is restored to defiled land.

The full import of this prophecy and depth of hope for land healing is revealed when we consider that the Dead Sea was understood to be the wasteland left after the destruction of Sodom.[10] By Jesus' day, the height of the Festival of Tabernacles had become an acted parable of the prophecy of Ezekiel: a water-libation ceremony saw water flow from the altar symbolically through the east gate of the temple (through which the Messiah was expected to be revealed). John records that it is at this precise moment in the festival that Jesus provocatively stands and announces, 'If anyone is thirsty, let him come to me and drink. Whoever believes in me, as the Scripture has said, streams of living water will flow from within him' (John 7:37–9), thus identifying himself as the One who would instigate the fulfilment of Ezekiel's prophecy. The living waters promised would bring resurrection life to individuals, but also point to Christ's future capacity to resurrect the land. John outworks the full implications of this in the text of Revelation when he reveals Christ as the instigator of the new creation, weaving his portrayal of land and city redemption in Revelation 21–22 in part out of the text of Ezekiel 47. Christ fulfils the hope of Ezekiel's prophecy for the whole of creation: he will eventually heal (*rapha*) all the earth.

That Christ identifies himself as the Healer of the Land is good news for marginal communities struggling with the effects of degraded land because it reveals that he has mandated the agency and energy of his Spirit to energize and equip his people for the work of seeing such places flourish with beauty and life once more.

These three titles and their underlying theologies reconnect thinking about Christ and the Spirit with creation theology, defining potential new ways for thinking about mission and creation care. They are particularly resonant for at-risk communities blighted by degraded land, because they establish Christ's rulership over and capacity to redeem creation, reveal his agency in resisting the powers that neglect blighted urban land, and show how Christ desires to resurrect, heal and lift the curse from these spaces. Working towards these

ends entails physical, political and spiritual struggle. Having one's imaginative, cognitive and emotional worlds shaped by such theology
helps to energize and nourish us spiritually and enables us to more
effectively intercede in prayer. It also supplies a coherent narrative to
help us explain in relevant ways to those we are working alongside the
reasons for the hope we have.

Missiology: establishing the abundant kingdom through healing of land enclosure, land covetousness and land defilement

As Christ the Healer of the Land establishes his abundant kingdom
in marginalized communities, what might the mission of his people
look like with regards to rehabilitating degraded urban land? Walter
Brueggemann has identified three key forces that destroy the land in
Scripture:

1. Enclosure (unjustly preventing the poor from owning land that is
   rightly theirs);
2. Covetousness (wilfully monopolizing land ownership out of greed
   and a desire for commercial gain); and
3. Defilement (polluting the land in moral or physical ways so that it
   becomes unproductive).[11]

To heal enclosure, Brueggemann outlines the biblical ideas of inal-
ienable patrimony, or the idea that heritable land rights remain in
place no matter what (unjust) legal provisions are later put in place
(Jer. 32:1–15). Healing land covetousness involves land redistribution, which relates to the practice of Jubilee, and can be seen in the
vision of Ezekiel 48 in which the land will be reapportioned fairly
after the return from exile. Lastly, healing defilement, we have the
idea of restored fertility (Hos. 2:21–3), in which land polluted by sin
or physical contamination is restored. In all these dimensions land
can be brought once more into a biblical vision of productivity. We
should be careful, however, not to overly narrow our definition of

'productivity' here to a purely instrumental understanding; instead we should acknowledge the relational, aesthetic and intrinsic value of the land. Embracing the Spirit of Christ we can challenge the idolatry of the market god with regards to the privatization, instrumentalization, consumption and ultimately selfish destruction of mere 'nature'. This opens up redemptive categories of thought and practice which can lead to (re)-creative and imaginative missiological engagements with urban land.

These strands provide a framework for a variety of practical missional responses towards healing derelict and vacant local land which are sensitive to the needs of the local context. A justice-oriented approach might challenge the powers, whether social, political or spiritual, that lie behind land enclosure. This type of mission would seek redress and land redistribution in favour of the poor or creation itself, calling anti-creational forces to account prophetically and politically. Challenging land covetousness can mean a congregation beginning to take responsibility for its own complicity in the industrial-scale exploitation of (urban) land for commercial gain at the expense of human wellbeing and the wellbeing of creation. The subjection of creation to Mammon causes innumerable problems, from seed patenting to destructive patterns of food production to the psychological pathologies engendered when people are alienated and dislocated from the land. Responses here might involve enabling local communities to take ownership of local land and develop projects focused on community-based, equitable and sustainable food production. It could also mean defending local land for its instrumental value to non-human creation – establishing a nature reserve for the benefit of migrating birds against an area's exploitation for human ends is one such example. Of course, such an approach doesn't need to be a zero-sum game: there are creative ways of making land productive for non-human and human alike. Conservation efforts seeking to maximize benefit to both is known as reconciliation ecology.[12]

Exploring the meaning of Sabbath and Jubilee for the land in this context might also lead to strategies that enable resistance to the way a culture of covetousness reifies people as mere consumers. Finally, missiological activities can seek to restore defiled land to fertility. This might require work to cleanse the land of invasive species or the soil from contamination alongside other strategies such as food production, the protection of existing biodiversity, and beautification of such spaces through guerrilla gardening or wildflower seeding.

Ecclesiology: The emergence of abundant community

We now seek to explore ways that abundant community might emerge through congregational work to rehabilitate degraded urban land. Similar to developing church in a café, community centre, local school or place of business, brownfield rehabilitation offers a locus for mission in terms of a 'third place'[13] with a different set of challenges and goals. Such presence and commitment in a third place can profoundly shape the contours of church identity, structure and activity. A porous, self-emptying, humble approach that learns to accept hospitability on other people's terms and to pursue a communal call to the local common good becomes possible and creates spaces in which all can participate. The work of brownfield rehabilitation also offers unique capacity as a space and set of potential relationships in which both the local community and the land itself can disciple and grow the church to maturity in character, gifting and connectivity.

For example, we can grow in gentleness of character as we act gently towards the land, and can foster the use of Spirit-given discernment in understanding how the powers may be at work in keeping local land out of local hands. In addition, connecting with creation opens the doors to a host of creative opportunities to contextualize sacraments and rhythms of the church in a new, outdoor context. My own church, Clay Community Church, has developed an Easter dawn service on a local plot of land that we and local residents are looking to be assigned Local Nature Reserve Status. This revolves around a tree-planting Eucharist and liturgy inspired by African Pentecostals.[14] The ceremony serves to place the importance of our work to heal the land at the very heart of our liturgical calendar, rooting us to the plot of earth God has given us, and dynamically shaping our life as a church in fresh and invigorating directions.

Urban Gardening and Food Production

A central claim that runs through this chapter is that ecological care can be an essential element of mission in marginalized places, where the increased pressure of environmental and sustainability issues impact disproportionately upon at-risk communities. We have also claimed that, in order to engage with environmental and place-based desolation, we must cultivate a range of responses that are rooted in practical local action, while not being circumscribed by an insular localism. This second part complements and deepens the work of the previous section by turning to the twin practices of gardening and food production as another such response. In doing so, we return to the Christ–mission–church template as a framework for situating how they can offer important gateways to participatory expression, and therefore, a relationally based response to the issue of food poverty in both the Global North as well as the South. We again take the idea of 'abundance' as our key theme, developing the idea of community-based urban agriculture as offering crucial 'demonstration plots of abundance' as counter-signs of the breaking-in of God's economy of abundance.

Christology: Jesus as the New Gardener and the cultivation of abundant life

In the prologue to the Gospel of John, the ministry of Jesus Christ is identified with bringing 'life' into the world (John 1:4; cf. 10:10); the very life of God, full of boundless energy, love and communion. That the incarnate Christ is the human bearer of this life means that the 'work of Christ . . . is not so much about the salvation of individual souls but about leading people into true, abundant, eternal, resurrection life'.[15] Thus, the Johannine Christ is not a gnostic bridge-figure to a divine realm of fullness that lies inaccessibly beyond material order of food, water, plants and bodies. Rather, as 'living water', 'bread of life' and the 'true vine' (John 4:14; 6:35; 15:1), the work of Christ manifests the divine life through the material order so that God's glory might be known on earth as it is in heaven.

As recent scholarship on the link between theology and food has emphasized, Jesus' ministry clearly shows us how central the sharing of food and table fellowship is to God's purposes to heal the world.[16] What is perhaps less obvious but no less vital is the connection between how we produce and access food as a means for receiving and sharing abundant life. In order to develop the linkage between the ministry of Christ and the work of food production, we want to develop the notion of Jesus Christ as the New Gardener – the one who 'came to cultivate the gardens of this earth and our lives'.[17]

Imagining Christ as the New Gardener brings together two complementary insights about gardening as an expression of mission. First, to speak of Jesus Christ as the New Gardener is to refer back to God as the first, or prototypical, gardener – 'the LORD God . . . planted a garden in . . . Eden' (Gen. 2:8–9) – and to remember God-as-Gardener places us as creatures who live in the hope that 'the wilderness [of our world] is made to be what it both should and will be: paradise, God's garden'.[18] Second, to imagine Christ as the New Gardener is to recall the basic human vocation to join with God's gardening in the world; the vocation to enact what Norman Wirzba calls 'Godly gardening'.[19] Gardening is more than the physical activities of weeding, watering, sowing, tending and harvest; it is a way of enacting our membership in creation and, as Wirzba contends, to do so in a distinct way: 'to develop into Godly gardeners . . . who work harmoniously among the processes of life and death, and in their work witness to the life-creating presence of God in the world.'[20] Put a bit differently, 'Godly gardening' always involves two cultivations, or two 'crops': what we grow from the soil, and how we grow from being with the soil; in other words, *what* we produce through gardening and *who* we become as we are 'gardened'.

It is no mere coincidence that upon Christ's resurrection in the garden of Gethsemane (a new Eden), John recounts that Mary mistakes him for a gardener (John 20:15).[21] Just as Adam's call was to steward creation in dependence on God, so we now see the New Adam, the One who has inaugurated the resurrection of humankind to fully respond to the call of God to steward creation in light of the coming resurrection of all creation. It is therefore appropriate to think of Christ as the New Gardener and see creation care as a vital aspect of discipleship as we follow him.

Missiology: food poverty and seeking the abundant kingdom

In the light of such a 'high' view of gardening, how might we cultivate 'Godly gardening' without losing touch with our emphasis upon sustainability issues and the conditions of urban deprivation? As a response to this question, let us explore how the practices of gardening and local food production offer a way of encountering food poverty as a missiological issue from the perspective of God's 'abundant kingdom'.

In a recent reassessment of food poverty and Christianity in Britain, Christopher Allen observes how two approaches to food poverty tend to dominate the theological landscape: a food-bank theology of charitable giving (on the right), and a 'social justice' theology that advocates higher minimum income and greater consumer access to food (on the left). While food charity and food capitalism (as Allen refers to them) clearly offer different approaches to food poverty, they also share a common premise; namely, that the issue of food poverty is fundamentally a matter of access to food. Allen argues however that these approaches are inadequate because neither addresses the issue of food production and, therefore, the sources of food inequalities. In other words, these approaches are inadequate because each position 'renders the exploitation of the earth and its inhabitants in food producing countries analytically invisible'.[22] What is needed, Allen argues, is a more radical Christian theology of food poverty, one which unmasks the injustices and false promises of capitalist food systems, while also casting an alternative theological vision centred around the twin principles of 'membership (digging, planting, growing, nurturing, respecting) and fellowship (hospitality, neighbourliness, communism, being with)'.[23]

As a complement to Allen's call for an alternative theology of food poverty, Fred Bahnson, a permaculture gardener and food activist from the USA, makes a vital distinction between the 'abundant mirage' and God's 'abundant kingdom'.[24] The dominance of the market-based food system and the global economy, he argues, projects an 'abundant mirage', inside of which we are conditioned to see a bountiful supply of cheap, convenient food. To call it a mirage is to highlight the falsity of this perception, not seeing for example: how the heavily mechanized and oil-based forms of modern agriculture depend upon unsustainable levels of energy consumption; how centralized production and distribution escalate dependence upon a food system in which greater numbers are left either 'stuffed or starved';[25] how the simultaneous rise in obesity and world hunger are two sides of the same coin. The task, then, is to engage broken food systems as well as food poverty from a missiological standpoint. The task is to see this as a mirage and not a God-given reality which we are called to embrace.

As Bahnson makes clear, what we are called to embrace is precisely that alternative reality of the 'abundant kingdom'. To seek and enter that alternative is to take seriously Jesus' claim to be the source of 'life abundant' as well as the inaugurator of an 'abundant kingdom'. The question remains: 'What kind of agriculture would make space for the abundant kingdom of God to take root and flourish among us?'[26] At a practical level, Bahnson clarifies how taking seriously our allegiance to Jesus and seeking the kingdom (Matt. 6:33) means recognizing that agricultural and eating practices are part of that kingdom. It means repenting of the illusion that we can and should exercise absolute control over the cosmos, much less absolute control over our food. More specifically, this sense of trust beckons us to recover and reincorporate agricultural practices that align with and serve the reality of the 'abundant kingdom'; namely those of regenerative agriculture. For whereas modern agriculture depends heavily on fossil fuels and capital-intensive machinery, regenerative agriculture depends on sunlight and labour-intensive care that enhance the quality of the soil base instead of depleting it. By respecting the natural patterns and cycles of the earth, as well as trusting in the abundance of creation, regenerative agriculture can serve as 'a means by which we can seek first the kingdom of God'.[27]

As a missiological expression of regenerative agriculture, gardens offer strategic sites of formation that enable us to discern the difference between illusion and reality; between the 'abundant mirage' and the 'abundant kingdom'. Indeed, gardens can become 'infrastructures of holiness' that make possible a renewed 'coming and seeing'.[28] Through gardening, we come to deepen our relationship with the soil, with neighbours and fellow gardeners, and cultivate an abiding relationship with the Creator as the source of every good gift (Jas 1:17). Through gardening, we see food poverty as a symptom of brokenness and dis-ease that spreads inside the distorted contours of 'abundant mirage' and, therefore, we see the issue of food production as a site of missional engagement. What's more, we see the 'abundant kingdom' in which our 'approach to eating [and food production] begins with the radical trust that God's abundance is enough'.[29]

Ecclesiology: becoming an abundant community

A final question remains: In what ways might our ecclesiology be shaped by engagement in gardening and local food production and attention to the abundant kingdom? Fundamentally, by refashioning our ecclesial imagination by offering us a way to navigate between the perceptions of scarcity linked to the hubristic sense of control over the environmental realm (on the one hand) and a disengaged sense of despair (on the other). Indeed, a 'third way' of enacting ecological care – and engaging with the issue of food poverty – is available within the logic of God's abundance. This way is nothing less than an invitation for the church to become an abundant community – a community that dispels the perception of scarcity by creating abundance with its gifts, associational life and practice of hospitality.[30]

Paradoxically, the perception of scarcity has become dominant inside the 'abundant mirage' discussed earlier. As the shadow cast within the myth of industrial progress and the rise of development, this perception of scarcity seems to have replaced, eclipsed or obscured the perception of an ordered creation that is 'good' and abundant, an order to which we relate in care and with limits (Gen. 2:15). According to the perception of scarcity, creation itself is not only limited and finite, but also defective. If scarcity is a basic condition of creation, then God cannot say 'good' over it. Indeed it would call into question the goodness of the Creator. Living with the perception of scarcity tempts us also to imagine ourselves as either 'like God' (Gen. 3:5) or 'less than human' – that is nothing except what we manage to consume. In other words, it turns us away from the humility and dignity of being creatures that bear God's image in a cosmos which God created out of love and deemed good.

Thus, we find ourselves in a vicious cycle in 'the world where the good life is measured and defined by the sum of goods and services'.[31] Modern industrial progress makes possible more efficient production of goods and services, and therefore, a greater capacity for consumption. On the one hand, we perceive this apparent abundance of commodities and imagine that the good life consists in having them. Yet, the threat of scarcity grows ever more menacing, precisely because the social space of consumer society conditions us to expect that our flourishing depends upon those institutions, systems, operators and experts who alone can provide what we need.

The paradox is that by assuming that we can overcome scarcity by consuming our way out of it, we end up escalating the conditions that give rise to the problem, a social imbalance between means and ends and, therefore, an environmental crisis linked directly to a widening gap between our needs and desires and our capacity to satisfy them.[32] Thus, within the social space of consumer society, we no longer inhabit a world that is created good and with abundance. We no longer inhabit a world of proportions, of action that is determined by what is good, fitting, and enough. We find ourselves in a world in which the means for enjoying what we need to flourish are not just limited, but scarce.

What an 'agronomic church' might learn in the garden, however, is that the means for creating a shared sense of abundance are limited, but never scarce. From inside the social space of the garden, we began to imagine anew how communities might dispel the false perception of scarcity as a basic condition by creating a shared sense of abundance through 'the invisible structures of an abundant community'.[33] As a way of illuminating some of what is meant by this term, John McKnight and Peter Block use the analogy of playing jazz as an apt description of the kind of social fabric that is woven around the activity of gardening. They note that in creating a jazz piece:

> What is operating is a clear structure, but if you are not part of the jazz culture, the rules and customs that make the music possible are invisible. Similarly, the properties of gifts, associations, and hospitality are the hidden structures of [abundant] community life . . . The jazz way is the community way of playing. The invisible structure of gifts, associations, and hospitality creates the possibility and are the rules of a competent community. They are always available and essential.[34]

Like jazz, gardening is a community way of playing that creates a social space in which people share their gifts, associate for a common purpose, and extend hospitality. Through gardening and food production, we imagine how the means for creating and sharing abundance are always available, and therefore, never scarce. This leads us to imagine that the same could be true inside the body of Christ (1 Cor. 12).

Conclusion

One of the distinct advantages of following a theological logic that moves from Christology to missiology to ecclesiology is the heightened awareness that ecological care is a pursuit that does not begin with the church as church, but with God. By beginning with Christ, we may sense the energy that comes with invitation to respond in faith, hope and love, doing so as an antidote to the anxiety that comes with the presumption that we must control environmental outcomes. Missiologically, the fundamental issue is not between action and passivity, but rather discerning which human action fits with our place within creation as bearers of the Spirit playing their part in the community of life. True, the environmental crisis is very much the work of our human hands. Yet, the way forward in understanding our place in the environmental realm does not lie in 'powering up' and escalating our impact on the world but rather in recalibrating it. It depends upon emptying ourselves (Phil. 2:5) and wagering upon the availability of a different kind of power (Rom. 1:16) and a different way of life (Eph. 2:10).

Ecclesiologically, the ability to do so has to do with the recovery of response-ability, or being able to respond to the call of Another. The good news is that in recovering this fundamental sense of response-ability, the church might also rediscover what it means to live as an abundant community. By getting its hands into both the garden and the wasteland, the church is not proposing a one-off solution to environmental issues, but is amplifying the range of responses. Through the direct actions of rehabilitating degraded urban land for community use, gardening and food production, the church is offering (or being offered) demonstration plots of abundant life: sites where even in the margins, we – and our non-Christian neighbours – might meet one another, tend the earth, and 'taste and see that the Lord is good' (Ps. 34:8).

It is worth reiterating that we are not peddling these particular areas of engagement as a panacea for all social ills in marginalized urban communities. In fact, we are suggesting that the search for panaceas is itself part of the problem. What is at stake is the cultivation of community-based places where an alternative imagination awakens; places where neighbours can stand, care and work together to offer counter-signs of shalom. Our experiences suggest that these counter-signs should be neither romanticized nor underestimated. Rather, we should receive them as tokens of God's in-breaking economy of abundance. At the level of imagination, these tokens offer holy interruptions that disrupt our 'default settings' regarding what is possible and desirable. At a very practical level, such tokens can make the difference between a family or even a community slipping into the indignity and misery of modernized poverty and the possibility of recovering the communal means to satisfy authentic human needs with dignity and joy.

Notes

[1] N.J. Toly and D.I. Block, eds, *Keeping God's Earth: The Global Environment in Biblical Perspective* (Downers Grove, IL: InterVarsity Press, 2010), p. 67.

[2] 'Post-Christendom' refers to the loss of centrality and influence within society of the narrative of the Christian faith and of the institutions of the church. For an excellent and helpful overview of this see, Stuart Murray, *Post-Christendom* (Milton Keynes: Paternoster, 2004).

[3] A (very) select overview of important and recent literature foundational for the study of the doctrine of creation is Jürgen Moltmann, *God in Creation* (London: SCM Press, 1985). Also the classic by Walter Brueggemann, *The Land: Place as Gift, Promise and Challenge in Biblical Faith* (Minneapolis: Augsburg Fortress, 2002). An excellent recent biblical theology of the environment can be found in Richard Bauckham, *Bible and Ecology* (London: Darton, Longman & Todd, 2010). For an engagement with eschatology and creation care, see Douglas Moo, 'Eschatology and Environmental Ethics' in *Keeping God's Earth: The Global Environment in Biblical Perspective* (ed. N.J. Toly and D.I. Block; Downers Grove, IL: InterVarsity Press, 2010), pp. 23–46. For overviews of the missiological debate, see Ernst Conradie, 'Missiology and Ecology: An Assessment of the Current State of the Debate', *Australian Association for Mission Studies* (2011) http://www.missionstudies.org.au/files/aams/ConradieKeynote2Ecology.pdf. (accessed 13 May 2015); also Willis Jenkins, 'Missiology in Environmental Context: Tasks for an Ecology of Mission', *International Bulletin of Missionary Research* 32(4) (2008): pp. 176–82. For recent work from a Pentecostal angle see A.J. Swoboda, *Of*

Tongues and Trees: Toward a Pentecostal Ecological Theology (Dorset: Deo Publishing, 2013). A helpful study of theology of the environment in the context of the city is Seppo Kjellberg, *Urban Ecotheology* (Utrecht: International Books, 2000).

4   We stress that to emphasize local responses is not to champion *localism*. What is needed is traction towards hands-on participation that acts first locally before moving towards wider influence, not least by creating pathways for these local responses to *aggregate* their impact into translocal networks. For an insightful account of why forging translocal initiative remains a foundational challenge for the urban food movement, see Kevin Morgan, 'Nourishing the City: The Rise of the Urban Food Question in the Global North', http://orca.cf.ac.uk/63716/ (accessed 17 May 2015).

5   Michael Frost and A. Hirsch, *The Shaping of Things to Come: Innovation and Mission for the 21st Century Church* (Peabody, MA: Hendrickson, 2003), p. 209.

6   As primary conversation partners here, we have turned to Norman Wirzba, *Food and Faith: A Theology of Eating* (New York: Cambridge University Press, 2011); Fred Bahnson and Norman Wirzba, *Making Peace with the Land: God's Call to Reconcile with Creation* (Downers Grove, IL: InterVarsity Press, 2012); John McKnight and Peter Block, *The Abundant Community: Awakening the Power of Families and Neighborhoods* (San Francisco, CA: Berrett-Koehler, rev. edn, 2012); as well as Eleazar S. Fernandez' essay entitled 'The Church as a Household of Life Abundant: Reimagining the Church in the Context of Global Economics', in *Theology that Matters: Ecology, Economy, and God* (ed. Darby Kathleen Ray; Minneapolis: Fortress Press, 2006), pp. 172–88. For a more general biblical primer on the theme of abundance in God's economy, see Daniel Erlander, *Manna and Mercy: A Brief History of God's Unfolding Promise to Mend the Entire Universe* (Mercer Island, WA: Order of Saints Martin and Teresa, 1992).

7   Walter Brueggemann, *Using God's Resources Wisely* (Lousiville, KY: Westminster/John Knox Press, 1993).

8   Terrence E. Fretheim, 'The Plagues as Ecological Signs of Historical Disaster', *Journal of Biblical Literature* 110(3) (1991): p. 386.

9   Gen. 9:11, 'I establish my covenant with you: Never again will all life be cut off by the waters of a flood; never again will there be a flood to destroy the earth.'

10 See Gen. 13:10–12 and Gen. 19, but also John Goldingay, *Genesis for Everyone, Parts 1&2* (London: SPCK, 2010).

[11] Brueggemann, *Land*, p. 195.

[12] Michael Rosenzweig, *Win-Win Ecology* (New York: Oxford University Press, 2003).

[13] 'Our first place is the home, our second place is work/school, and our third place is where we spend our time when we have time off. Anywhere people gather for social reasons could be a good place for missional engagement. Third places are pubs, cafés, hobby clubs, sports centres, etc.' (Michael Frost and Alan Hirsch, *The Forgotten Ways* [Grand Rapids, MI: Brazos, 2006], p. 145.)

[14] Paul Ede, 'Tree Planting Eucharist' (2011) https://www.scribd.com/doc/132831213/Tree-Planting-Eucharist-Booklet (accessed 13 May 2015); Inus Daneel, 'Earthkeeping in Missiological Perspective: An African Challenge', *Mission Studies* 13(1–2) (1996): p. 132.

[15] Wirzba, *Food and Faith*, p. xviii.

[16] In addition to the sources already referenced, recent contributions to the 'food and faith' conversation include Jennifer R. Ayres, *Good Food: Grounded Practical Theology* (Waco: Baylor University Press, 2013); Fred Bahnson, *Soil and Sacrament: A Spiritual Memoir of Food and Faith* (New York: Simon & Schuster, 2013); A. Francis, *What in God's Name Are You Eating?: How Can Christians Live and Eat Responsibly in Today's Global Village?* (Eugene, OR: Cascade Books, 2014); A.F. Méndez-Montoya, *The Theology of Food: Eating and the Eucharist* (Oxford: Wiley-Blackwell, 2012).

[17] Wirzba, *Food and Faith*, p. 62.

[18] N. Lash, *Believing Three Ways in One God: A Reading of the Apostles' Creed* (Notre Dame, IN: University of Notre Dame Press, 1993), pp. 121–2.

[19] Wirzba, *Food and Faith*, pp. 61–70.

[20] Wirzba, *Food and Faith*, p. 61.

[21] Tom Wright, *John for Everyone, Part 2, Chapters 11-12* (London: SPCK, 2nd edn, 2004), p. 146.

[22] Christopher Allen, 'Food Poverty and Christianity in Britain: A Re-Assessment', *Political Theology* (2015): p. 2.

[23] Allen, 'Food Poverty', p. 20.

[24] Bahnson and Wirzba, *Making Peace*, pp. 86–95.

[25] A turn of phrase taken from R. Patel, *Stuffed and Starved: From Farm to Fork, the Hidden Battle for the World Food System* (London: Portobello Books, rev. edn, 2013).

[26] Bahnson and Wirzba, *Making Peace*, p. 92.

[27] Bahnson and Wirzba, *Making Peace*, p. 101.

[28] See John 1:46.

29 Bahnson and Wirzba, *Making Peace*, p. 94.

30 For a more detailed account of this triad of gift-mindedness, associational life, and hospitality as properties of an abundant community, see John McKnight and Peter Block, *The Abundant Community,* especially pp. 67–82.

31 McKnight and Block, *Abundant Community,* p. 16.

32 W. Leiss, *The Limits of Satisfaction: On Needs and Commodities* (London: Marion Boyars, 1978), pp. 38–42.

33 McKnight and Block, *Abundant Community*, p. 81.

34 McKnight and Block, *Abundant Community*, p. 82.

14

Case Study: Clay Community Church, Possilpark, Glasgow

Paul Ede

The most economically marginalized communities are also the most affected by the legacy of poor-quality brownfield land, often contaminated with pollutants from historic industries, left vacant through disinvestment in the hope of future commercial gain. While this is to be expected in a postindustrial city, it remains an environmental injustice at the margins that urges naming. Possilpark in Glasgow is at the bottom of the league with regards to the indices of multiple deprivation in Scotland. Within its boundaries there is, ironically, no dedicated parkland for the community to enjoy. Large swathes of vacant and derelict land instead compound the deprivation, scarring our community geographically and psychologically. The land in Possilpark has paid witness to a long history of oppressive practices being greatly affected by all three of Brueggemann's anti-creational sins against the land. The estate where Walter MacFarlane built Saracen Iron Foundry was constructed through a system of enclosure during the agricultural revolution. The land was polluted not just physically by industrial practices but morally by the social pathologies that have resulted from the economic collapse of these industries. And the remaining land has more recently been subject to structural covetousness with the transfer of public land assets to City Property, an arm's-length enterprise organization which exists to resell this land to private interests for development.

Getting Started

Best practice in community development involves listening and seeing attentively with 'kingdom eyes' so as to understand from the inside out the rhythms, meanings and locations of the 'plot of God's earth given to us'.[1] There is a spatial as well as a relational component to developing such an awareness – and it takes time. In Clay Church we have all committed to 'living lives rooted in Possilpark';[2] some of us are relocators, some have come to faith here and remained. Practising faithful presence in a defined local space and becoming a known character by local residents develops trust and paves the way to receiving their insights.[3] Both outsider and insider perspectives are generative, particularly when a dialogue emerges attentive to the Spirit and with local people who aren't part of the church.

When my wife and I first moved to Possilpark, I spent many days wandering around the turf we had been invited into. I imagined myself as a child growing up there and explored the land from that perspective, squeezing through every nook and cranny I could find. In doing so I discovered an area of neglected greenspace called the Clay Pit, a stark contrast to the dumped-on brownfield land common here. In the midst of this shabby natural grandeur I heard the groaning of creation (Rom. 8) and Christ speaking about his desire to the heal the land of Possilpark and its people. Here, surely, was a local gem – an asset that had abundant potential.[4] Here began my journey into discovering new creation-rooted christologies (as outlined above) and, following Graham Cray's missiology where he assumes that the Spirit is already at work in every place,[5] to understanding that in our listening to God, the church and the local community we also need to allow the context itself – the land, nature and the environment – to have its own voice in this process.[6]

Accepting invitations from sympathizers with our kingdom vision already working in the area is a must: within a month of moving in we had the opportunity to join in with a seed-sowing project run by a local branch of Barnardo's on a site right in front of our new home (which now hosts a community garden). Here we first learned about an initiative spearheaded by local mums to see the land their children crossed to get to school rehabilitated into playable space, free of needles, weapons and discarded credit cards. There is no substitute for getting our hands in the soil alongside our neighbours – relationships, trust and vision germinate even as toiling in the soil bonds our souls to the land beneath our feet.

Pathways to Participation

There comes a point where listening must naturally give way to agency. The Spirit-filled agency of God's people, born of a hopeful conviction that the kingdom can and is breaking in to the present to bring change and transformation, is a key component in catalysing action for change. It should be affirmed and encouraged. But for it to be truly generative such agency needs to be submissive to the Spirit at work through others, hospitable to participation by the community and attentive to the small ways that the Lord is prompting the marginalized to have their own role. The way we use prepositions is important: doing things 'with' and not 'to' or 'for' is key. One value of Clay Church states, 'We aim to reflect Jesus by doing things with and not just for our neighbours; sharing our lives and working alongside them as catalysts towards the transformation of our community.'

In Possilpark there are many examples of how imposed, industrial-scale transformative interventions in the built environment have quickly been rejected and vandalized after the hype of the opening ceremony.[7] In Clay Church we have taken the approach of starting small, an approach which introduces change gradually, facilitates accessibility and flexibility and fosters the growth of confidence. With this in mind we have practised a variety of communal, fun, quick-win actions, such as investing in our backcourts and local nursery at the instigation of local mums. With our neighbour's encouragement and help we painted colourful murals on walls and pavement games on concrete slabs and tarmac, taking ownership of neglected public space on behalf of our children. Assuming responsibility for local planters and terrain features neglected by the council, we have also practised guerrilla gardening with simple tools and experienced the joy of seeing people taking delight in colourful flowers appearing unexpectedly overnight.

N.T. Wright has written that the creation of beauty is a key element of the meaning of the gospel.[8] Beyond the aesthetic, there is a political dimension to this kind of activity: a direct challenge to principalities of neglect, a statement that this space, our space, is worthy of beauty and investment. One member of Clay Church put it like this, 'I was thinking again about Jesus being a radical . . . There is something about putting a seed down on a piece of land – fighting power and money and individualism – counteracted just by putting down some seeds.'[9] We have also built simple wooden planters as memorials to commemorate our neighbours' lost loved-ones, enabling people to create something with soil and imagination to work through their grief and loss. In the process we made connections to the encouragement of Jeremiah to 'plant gardens' in Babylon (Jer. 29:5). Perhaps this was very practical advice from God who knew that re-rooting ourselves into the soil can help us process the deeply held grief that exile, loss and dislocation generates. Communities may find release and healing for themselves in cultivating new life as an expression of healing the land.

In addition, we have held our Sunday afternoon gatherings in the local public square of Possilpark (Saracen Cross), starting with a picnic and sharing our food with passers-by, and going on to spend a sunny summer afternoon digging and planting, chatting with local people, being available in as accessible a 'third space' as it is possible to be. These communal activity days not only blur the boundaries between church and community,[10] but also create opportunities for both practical service and sharing the gospel in creative and relevant ways. In them we also seek to physically express virtues (fruit of the Spirit) towards both creation and the community. Gentleness towards neglected earth combines with the expression of love for our neighbours. Learning patience in waiting for our activity to flower chimes even with the somewhat discordant necessity of developing forbearance when our work is trampled on by someone unaware of our efforts. We grow in our character through expressing both our relationship with the earth and our relationships with fellow human beings in such communal earth-keeping activities.[11]

Expanding the Work

Our confidence has grown in tandem with being interwoven in the relational network of our community, and we have become involved in the much larger work of having the Clay Pits site recognized as a local nature reserve. Taking ownership of a site that has been neglected by the local community has involved developing ways to be intentionally present there: a missiology of presence. We individually go to the site for our own personal devotional and contemplative time, especially those of us who strongly meet God in creation. But our mission is also proactive. We have held 'Forest Church'[12] picnics on summer Sunday afternoons instead of our normal gatherings, with nature-based games and contemplative exercises designed to connect us with Christ outdoors. We have seen success as we have engaged in prayer-walking, asking the Lord to fight on our behalf and open up the possibility that the current landowners of the site (Scottish Canals) would be generous with allowing their land to become a nature reserve. We have helped found a local group called Friends of Possilpark Greenspace out of the work of consulting the local community and lobbying the council for structural recognition of the site, a process of political engagement to secure the land for access by the marginalized over and against the land covetousness of commercial developers. Drawing together aesthetic, educational and recreational dimensions of mission we have been at the heart of volunteer staff for an annual event called Bats, Beasties and Buried Treasure. This draws families from across our community to spend the day connecting with nature through canoeing, mountain-biking, den-building, environmental art, storytelling and conservation walks (the latter run by A Rocha). Finally, we have developed a series of annual church events on the site, including an outdoor Easter tree-planting Eucharist and an annual celebration of the Feast of Tabernacles, rooted in the narratives of Ezekiel 47 and John 7. These are our tentative attempts to design an abundant community out of missional practices inspired by the Christ who is a Tree of Life and Healer of the Land to our community.

Notes

1   The 10th Mark of New Monasticism.
2   Clay Church Values, http://www.claychurch.org.uk/values/ (accessed 13 May 2015).
3   Paul Sparks, T. Soerens, and D.J. Friesen, *The New Parish* (Downers Grove, IL: InterVarsity Press, 2014), p. 59.
4   The Clay Pit was later declared an ecological gold mine by the A Rocha conservation advisor we invited to come and give an initial impression from the perspective of a professional ecologist. A Rocha can provide an excellent consultation to start up congregational earth-keeping initiatives.
5   Graham Cray, *Discerning Leadership* (Grove Books, 2010), p. 24.
6   P. Ede, 'How Do Spirit-Led Missional Connections Begin to Form?' in *Urban to the Core* (ed. Juliet Kilpin; Leicestershire: Matador, 2013), pp. 44–8.
7   See Jessica Lack, ed., *Five Spaces: New Urban Landscapes for Glasgow* (London: August Media, 1999).
8   Tom Wright, *Surprised by Hope* (London: SPCK, 2007), pp. 233–6.
9   Personal interview, conducted by Paul Ede, Sept. 2011.
10 Michael Frost and Alan Hirsch, *The Forgotten Ways* (Grand Rapids, MI: Brazos, 2009), p. 217ff.
11 For more on earth-keeping as a means of sanctification/discipleship see Paul Ede, *Urban Eco-Mission: Healing the Land in the Post-Industrial City - E169* (Cambridge: Grove Books, 2013).
12 Bruce Stanley, *Forest Church* (Llangurig: Mystic Christ Press, 2013).

15

Case Study: Casa da Videira, Curitiba, Brazil

Sam Ewell

From 2007 to 2010, I (Sam) had the privilege of becoming friends and working with the core members of Casa da Videira (hereafter, CdV). In 2010 when our family moved to the UK, I was sent as their 'reverse missionary'. We found inspiration in the idea of 'reverse mission(ary)' from Henri Nouwen, which he describes in his Latin American journal *¡Gracias!*: 'If I have any vocation in Latin America, it is the vocation to receive from the people the gifts they have to offer us and to bring these gifts back up north for our own conversion and healing.'[1] Ever since leaving Brazil, I have remained one of CdV's 'co-inspirators' (*co-inspiradores*) on 'reverse mission'; someone who has returned from the so-called mission field of the Global South in order to share stories and signs of good news with those in the north. What follows here is a glimpse of some of those of stories and signs.

In 2003, inspired by the horticultural metaphor of Jesus as the Vine,[2] Igreja do Caminho (Church of the Way) began a Christian charity called Casa da Videira (House of the Vine). Originally, Claudio Oliver, the founding pastor, envisioned CdV as both a Christian charity and a missional incubator that facilitated the outreach initiatives of the local church (such as urban agriculture, street ministry with homeless people, neighbourhood-based community-organizing, carpentry, as well as cultural and film productions). While CdV has always focused on relationally based alternatives to programme-based forms of mission, over the last ten years it has evolved from hosting a range of missional initiatives to operating as a 'grassroots ecclesial community'.[3] A community member describes the ethos that has permeated CdV as follows: 'Casa da Videira is a collective of friends and families who have decided to turn their lives, skills and homes into flourishing spaces for balanced, relational and abundant life. It is an expression of a way of life where community, simplicity, tradition, discipline and limits guide its members' lives in consonance with their faith and loyalty in following the steps of Jesus.'[4]

Getting Started

In 2008, the members of CdV became increasingly concerned about the widening gap between Curitiba's alleged reputation as one of the 'greenest' or ecologically minded cities in Latin America and the twin issues of urban waste management and food security. Based on the reflections around the triad of 'scripture, culture, and agriculture',[5] CdV launched Quinta da Videira (Homestead of the Vine) as their collective response. In this new configuration, three families relocated within walking distance of each other right to the 'edge' between sprawling gentrification and the last remnants of 'grassroots' residents, residents marginalized and threatened by municipal re-urbanization.

Through its urban homestead, the members of CdV began to experiment with the obstacles and possibilities of engaging the problems of urban waste and food security. They soon made a discovery: the recovery of a sustainable mode of food production in urban spaces lies precisely in the recovery of the biological nutrient cycle – what they call the 'cycle of life' (*ciclo da vida*). As a way of subverting the dominant 'waste management' mindset of diverting nutrients into landfills, CdV began to treat their own food discards and other peoples' 'waste' not as a problem 'to get rid of', but as a primary asset. In fact, the basic activity of their homestead was, in effect, organized as urban waste rescue mission in which:

- Vegetable and fruit discards from local farmers' markets and shops become the primary food source for livestock (e.g. chickens, goats and rabbits);
- Wood shavings from the local carpentry shop become a ready supply of carbon-rich bedding to animal excreta;
- Bedding mixed with used coffee grounds from McDonald's locks up ammonia to cut the pungent smell of animal urine, while also adding a vital source of nitrogen;
- Cultivating an army of earthworms generates rich compost from the animal manure that becomes the basis for year-round rotation scheme of raised no-till vegetables beds; and
- The worms, in turn, are fed to the chickens as a primary protein source and an alternative to dependence upon monoculture-based animal feeds (e.g. soy and corn).

In a real sense, the vision began on the fifth floor of an apartment building, by making a 'preferential option for the possible'.[6] In this case, 'possible' meant a worm bin and a vertical garden of lettuce and root crops growing inside recycled bottles. There Claudio started to experiment in finding responses for treating creation as creation and not 'rubbish', remaking soil and growing food not as someone who was looking for a solution to the issues of waste management and food security, but rather as someone who was inspired to sow seeds of possibility and co-inspiration. Looking back, Claudio would be the first to acknowledge his surprise at how those seeds would grow and the impact they would have. Following these steps, CdV's urban homestead produced enough food for three families, as well as providing for neighbours and a network of volunteers. In November 2011, again much to their surprise, they caught country-wide attention as the feature article in a national Brazilian newspaper; Oliver noted that they were ordinary people and the truly odd thing was how three families growing food together had apparently become exceptional and newsworthy![7]

Pathways to Participation: Subversive Cohabitation

As the members of CdV also discovered, sustainable urban agriculture is not just about planting and harvesting according to biologically sound principles. It is also about what happens around the planting and harvesting: reclaiming human contact with the earth, the delight of children playing with and caring for animals, the joy of collective work for the sake of the common good – all right in the middle of a fragmented, dehumanizing urban landscape. In other words, a basic insight of this community is that the way back to recovering the nutrient cycle is also the way towards recovering the humanizing social bond and participatory interdependence which sustainable food production both requires and makes possible.

When members speak of having their 'humanity' restored, they are not referring to a vague sense of fulfilment or an ideal of achievement but to the restoration of a fundamental relationship to the soil and to one another, and a deep connection to God by inhabiting a place together. As such, CdV represents a way of life that subverts the dominant modes of urban 'habitation' in which the home is no longer a centre of production, but has atrophied into a centre of consumption. Its search towards understanding what it might mean to inhabit a place began with a series of questions articulated by Oliver in 2002, beginning with, 'Is it possible to live out an experience that is authentically communitarian, biblically faithful, and genuinely spiritual and that can be established at a human scale? . . . What and whose interests are engaged when that path is chosen? . . . What "good news" can be given to those around us?'[8]

In grappling with these questions, Cdv are not looking for an 'ideal' church, but a possible way of being church that dwells with the tension of being a counter-cultural community without becoming a disengaged ecclesial ghetto in retreat from the world. Through dialogue with both tradition (the particularities of Christian wisdom) and with innovation (such as the insights of other grass-roots social movements like Transition Towns, Slow Food or Buen Viver) CdV offers an experiment in 'subversive cohabitation',[9] which is to say, a way of dwelling together for the sake of seeking the kingdom (Matt. 6:33). As Oliver makes clear, the fundamental motivation energizing what CdV does together is to receive and to share the abundant life that comes to us through the person of Jesus Christ (John 10:10).

> [W]e understand that what Jesus offers for us is this sensation of being alive, enjoying life, living abundantly. All this starts when we look to those pieces of life, sent to die as garbage, and reintroduce them into the cycle of life, respecting them as part of creation. It's a process that begins in the soil and ends at our tables. We harvest our veggies from this cycle, we breed our animals inside of it . . . Where the world sees garbage, we see nourishment; where the world sees death, we see life; in a world of loneliness, we discover community.[10]

In a space of about three hundred square metres, this community has shown that it is possible to untie the knots of unsustainable consumption and reweave the bonds of interdependence by cultivating not just a simpler lifestyle, but a 'demonstration plot for abundant life'.

Journeying and Expanding the Work

CdV's journey has been a consequence of a permanent cycle of questioning, observing and responding to each moment or context, or as they like to say, 'the embrace and celebration of contingencies'. This sensibility arises out of their understanding of the Christian life as a journey where the most important thing is not knowing where we are going, but with Whom, trusting in God's promise to be with us and recognizing that very often, 'The sign of God is that we will be led where we did not plan to go'. So when the city council repeatedly admonished CdV over legal restrictions against 'farming' in urban areas the members of CdV made a decision to respond to the invitation of their Mennonite friends to relocate and expand their operation, moving to twenty-nine acres surrounding an abandoned orphanage in a rural context, just outside Curitiba, in the neighbouring town of Palmeira, Paraná.

Here in the rural context, CdV finds itself responding to a different kind of marginality than it encountered inside the metropolis, a marginality generated by monocultures of soy and tobacco plantations, fracking, and the intense economic pressures that the global economy places on farmers whose livelihood depends on food production. Here, CdV partners with small-scale farmers to explore how an agro-ecological reading of the Bible can lead to an abundance of life as an alternative paradigm. Five years of experience with urban agriculture and nearly a year in the rural context has confirmed their intuition: food security is an issue that affects not only the urban population, but also the rural. In their partnership with the Mennonites in the region, CdV has launched an 'experimental station', to promote what they call *agricultura domiciliar* (home-based agriculture) as a way of amplifying responses to food security by bringing food production 'close to home' – whether that place be urban or rural.

Of course, this community's way is not the only way to respond to the economic and ecological crises generated by the predatory nature of global capitalism. Indeed, the collective witness of this community does not offer an 'ideal' way or blueprint model to be reproduced. Rather, by its demonstration plot it offers possibility and a sign of hope to say that another way is available, necessary and is happening. CdV takes seriously the ecclesial vocation to enact its faithfulness through 'subversive cohabitation', yet it does so without the ecclesial hubris of expecting that the church should exercise control over social issues in order to be effective. CdV also takes seriously the importance of 'creating infrastructures of holiness',[11] which enable us to see and seek the abundant kingdom as an available alternative. Such structures that do not circumscribe our action or range of influence, but rather offer a place to dwell, a place to take a stand. As an alternative to the Promethean endeavour that expects a 'better life' through the escalation of technical, institutional, and professional control over the environment (in general) and food production (in particular), CdV offers a witness that wagers its hope on a promise, upon the conviction that 'Jesus is the incarnation of the most frequent promise in the Bible: God with us.'[12] CdV is one community's attempt to follow the New Gardener and to receive, cultivate and share his peace.

Notes

1 Henri Nouwen, *¡Gracias!: A Latin American Journal* (Maryknoll, NY: Orbis, 2005), p. 188.

2 See John 15.

3 I borrow this phrase from Guillhermo Cooki's treatment of Latin American base communities from a Protestant perspective. See especially ch. 8, in G. Cook, *The Expectation of the Poor: Latin American Base Ecclesial Communities in Protestant Perspective* (Maryknoll, NY: Orbis, 1985).

4 R. Seifert, email correspondence, 1 July 2014.

5 This triad comes from Ellen Davis, *Scripture, Culture, and Agriculture: An Agrarian Reading of the Bible* (New York: Cambridge University Press, 2009).

6 By referring to Claudio's stance as a 'preferential option for the possible', I mean the way his activism operates through a commitment to doing what is 'possible' instead of clinging to a vision of an 'ideal' scenario.

7 See F. Sciarra, 'Agricultores, pecuaristas – e pós-graduados', in *O Estado de S. Paulo* 17 (23 November 2011): p. 5.

8 C. Oliver, 'Será Possível a Igreja?' (unpublished document, 2009).

9 I borrow this term from the essay by Eleazar S. Fernandez, 'The Church as a Household of Life Abundant: Reimagining the Church in the Context of Global Economics', in *Theology that Matters: Ecology, Economy, and God* (ed. Darby Kathleen Ray; Minneapolis: Fortress Press, 2006), pp. 172–88.

10 Bahnson and Wirzba, *Making Peace*, p. 107.

11 Bahnson and Wirzba, *Making Peace*, p. 107.

12 C. Oliver, *Relationality* (Philadelphia: Relational Tithe, 2010), p. 20.

16

The Environmental Realm: Editorial Comment

Mike Pears and Paul Cloke

The excellent chapter by Paul Ede and Sam Ewell provokes a number of crucial questions about the form and function of mission in marginal places. In particular it prompts urgent consideration of the basic question of why it is that, taken as a whole, mission has been far more likely to focus on social and economic issues than on the environmental realm. External commentators might be forgiven for summarizing Christian responses to the environment as 'they just don't care'. To do so would of course ignore several important initiatives occurring at different scales – from the international work of A Rocha to the kinds of local schemes illustrated in the case studies above. However, it is hard not to conclude that there remain significant barriers to everyday Christian involvement in missional environmentalism, and it is worth taking a moment to reflect why that might be. Two obvious problems spring to mind.

The first is theological. Popular theological understanding predominantly points to an emphasis on people rather than environment. For example, evangelical traditions have typically provided basic biblical inspiration for mission through key instructional verses that are easy to remember, grasp and build vision around. Consider for instance the motivational force for social justice in Matthew 25 to feed the hungry, give hospitality to the stranger, heal the sick and visit the prisoner, which has elicited very significant practical responses from faith communities wishing to enact these biblical practices of care and love. The result can be seen in the ways in which faith-based organizations play a seminal contemporary role in wider social movements ranging from providing accommodation for homeless people and feeding the poor and disenfranchised to establishing medical and on-street prayer-healing services and caring for offenders and asylum seekers. In these kinds of examples, Christians are literally practising the word, and for some the added bonus is that such practices provide ample opportunity for their propensity to want to see people 'saved'. It has been far more difficult to energize a 'saving' of the environment. Although there are a series of references in the Bible that call for attention to the earth, the lack of equivalent key instructional verses to those such as Matthew 25 may have contributed to a much more flaky missional response to ecological justice involving a sustaining, beautifying and transforming of the environment.

The second, related, problem is conceptual. Jane Bennett[1] has demonstrated how for most people there is an everyday conceptual distinction between the dull matter of things ('it') and the vibrant life of beings ('us'). Assuming human life to be the sole source of thoughtful subjectivity, we can tend to live by quarantining life from matter, and thereby ignore the vitality of matter and the lively powers of material formations. This tendency is especially resisted by people with a key passion for the non-human – notably in our experience people such as keen gardeners, or hill-walkers, who have found ways of living enthusiastically among the vibrancy of nature. Many others, however, have no innate grasp of the liveliness of matter, and require considerable encouragement to envisage more intelligent and sustainable engagements with the vital materialities that flow through and around us.

One way to go beyond the quarantining of life from matter is to acknowledge that human agency is itself intimately bound up with non-human materiality. The keyboard that we type on, the air we breathe, the food we eat, the reliance on electricity or petrol to make things work, the increasing role of technology in communication, our relationship with wildlife and pets, the ideas that shape the way we understand the world and so on, *all* point to the fact that human agency is what Sarah Whatmore[2] has termed 'a relational achievement' in which the very fabric of peoples' lives relies on the creative presence of organic beings, material things and discursive codes. We are so reliant on these 'non-human' elements that everything we do involves a relationship with them. In that sense we need to acknowledge that we are co-dependent on that constellation of things that we loosely call 'the environment', and we need to bear witness to the non-human beings, things and codes that form the vibrant materials that flow alongside and within us. As people, then, we need to understand that organic and inorganic bodies and natural and cultural objects will all affect us. And as Christians believing in a Creator and creative God, how much more should we be alert to the creativity that comes from our relational achievements with both human and non-human surroundings.

These theological and conceptual problems are simply but profoundly addressed by Jesus when he provides us with metaphorical pictures of who he is. The idea of a 'good shepherd' inherently emphasizes the care relationship between humans and animals. By saying, 'I am the bread of life', Jesus specifically reflects on that organic material which sustains life, nourishes the body and enables the fellowship of eating together. The metaphor of a door portrays a wooden entrance way that marks a material threshold between the inside and the outside. The description of vine and branches uses the qualities of plant material to emphasize the crucial significance of relational agency formed by being grafted into Jesus himself. In each case Jesus describes himself in terms of relationships and settings that transcend the human and embrace the non-human. These are not simply inert references to the everyday life of the times – they are distinct and meaningful references to the importance of life and matter together, bearing witness to the vital materialities that flow around and through us, and confirming that the spiritual landscapes in which we dwell are more-than-human, consisting of affective relations with organic and inorganic bodies, objects and technologies. That is why the environmental realm is an inherent part of the landscape of mission.

It reflects the mutually affective togetherness of life and matter, and helps us to get beyond human-centric postures that are too often controlling and colonizing in (and of) nature.

Paul and Sam's chapter provides a three-step framework with which to awaken an alternative imagination about the role of the environmental realm in mission. First, they identify the need to make the cultivation of community-based ecological care a central plank in the platform of mission. That is, the alarming resistance of local congregations to embrace the vibrant matter of relations between humans and the non-human needs to be overcome. This is especially crucial in mission to marginalized people who often dwell in the most damaged and unwanted tracts of land in the city. It is at these margins where creative initiatives to address local ecological issues can be most productive in changing local spiritual landscapes as well as material landscapes. In places which are rarely understood by residents as flourishing, a redemptive vision can be developed through simple acts of environmental renewal that can purposefully begin to provoke a sense of wellbeing and flourishing. Although such places might seem to provide a blank canvas for ecological care, it is highly likely that residents will already have passions (gardening, pets, food, communal use of a piece of land, tidiness and so on) that will form the nascent and actual cores of potential activity. A listening to, and understanding of, these localized passions would be a fruitful starting place for incarnational engagement with community cultivation.

Second, Paul and Sam demonstrate the hope to be found in Jesus for a return to flourishing. The biblical vision of the Tree of Life articulates a narrative of hopefulness for those whose experience may be marked by feeling disempowered, dislocated and discouraged. To such people, an invitation to participate in God's abundance and power through the transformation of their environment represents a significant and optimistic opportunity to be affected by vibrant matter. Rather than being told that environmental wellbeing exists elsewhere – to be visited but not lived among – they can have the opportunity to share in the cultivation of such wellbeing in their own dwelling-place. Moreover, a modelling of how Jesus sets himself against anti-creational practices can provoke and empower local communities into political and prophetic acts aimed at the establishment of ecological justice, and the invocation of the energy of the Holy Spirit can empower people's work to see their dwelling-places flourish with vibrant life once more. All in all, attention to the environmental realm offers the opportunity to create abundance and flourishing as life and matter come together in the hopeful pursuit of ecological justice, revelling not only in what we can cultivate, but also in who we become as we are cultivated together.

Third, the chapter articulates gardening and food production as strategic examples of ways to develop abundant community and bring life into the local world. The case studies illustrate the formative power of these simple practices in purposeful community-building, associational life and mutual hospitality. Even in the case of these examples, there is much scope for fitting activity to local landscapes and conditions. For instance, it is clearly important to develop schemes that are inclusive and embracing; being open to postsecular ways of working will be of paramount significance. A 'church garden' tended by Christians will be far less powerful than cultivation schemes involving partnership with all kinds of neighbours, perhaps on sites that already have communal purpose and status. This could mean working with existing community groups – nurseries, schools, health centres and so on – or it might point to initial 'guerrilla gardening' activity that sparks off a wider appreciation of how communal sites can be made beautiful or more productive. Equally however, attention to the environmental sphere may involve other strategic practices or sites – say involving pet celebrations, nature conservation, pollution monitoring, site clear-up or local energy schemes – and may involve elements of creativity through which local ecological justice can be interspersed with art, video or music. In some circumstances it may be appropriate to join in with existing organizations who are already working in the area; examples here could be participation in A Rocha's local schemes, or with the local Transition group. Similarly, local concern and action need to be linked to larger-scale ethical and political action so that love's local embrace can be fortified with a concern for wider justice. As always, the key to effective and locally significant mission involvement is a reflexive, listening and discerning awareness of what seeds of need, enthusiasm, passion and vision are already taking root in the community and areas involved.

It would be foolhardy to suggest that environmental mission will be straightforward or problem-free. Many such experiments have experienced difficulties associated with apathy, destructive opposition and carelessness – from within Christian communities as well as from beyond. Nevertheless, such mission offers powerful opportunities in and beyond the practical qualities of repairing and beautifying the earth in local settings. By promoting a redemptive vision for a renewed people in co-constitutive relationship with land that can flourish once more, mission can re-establish vital understandings of how God works both in and through human beings, and in and through the non-human beings, objects and discourses that so often form the vibrant materials that affect what it is like to be human.

Notes

[1] J. Bennett, *Vibrant Matter* (Durham: Duke University Press, 2010).

[2] S. Whatmore, *Hybrid Geographies* (London: Sage, 2002).

Part V

17

Understanding the Creative Realm

John Hayes

Introduction

Back in the 1990s, an artist who had spent much of his life working to develop artistic skills with children began tracking child development and passion for the arts. Or rather, he began to mark the attrition in children's confidence and interest in the arts. Over the course of many years Gordon MacKenzie noted that when children in first grade were asked if they were artists, all would enthusiastically raise their hands. In second grade about half the class would raise their hands, with diminished exuberance. Each year the number willing to raise their hands declined by about half, such that by sixth grade the number of students declaring themselves artists had diminished to one or two. MacKenzie reports that those holdouts lifted hands 'ever-so-slightly – guardedly – their eyes glancing from side to side uneasily, betraying a fear of being identified as a "closet artist"'.[1]

Artists see capacity

I worry that as we 'grow up' we graduate too quickly out of our artistic eyesight and so miss out on the insight that comes with creative expression. I believe that cultivating creative eyes is not just important for quality in art, but quality in mission – life itself, in fact. In more than thirty years of mission in the margins, I have found that the more we are open to tap into the creative Spirit of the living God, the more we will see release for people trapped into destructive structures, systems or syndromes.

In my experience, it is helpful to have artists on mission teams living in communities struggling with poverty because artists more naturally see the kingdom peeking out of unlikely places. Equally important, artists see capacity in 'multiply-deprived' communities where others see problems to be fixed. This ability to see assets first and foremost is not only an issue of empowerment, but an issue of accuracy. As Christians, and especially as mission workers, we can enter new communities assuming we have God's eyes. But more often than not, workers enter poor communities with eyes shaped by our culture. When we come into a materially poor context as a 'relocator' with the eyes of the mainstream, we find it hard to resist trying to remake the community in our own cultural image. In so doing, we can deprive neighbourhoods of the jagged beauties that are their birthright.

With the benefit of hindsight, it is now generally acknowledged that western mission history, especially in the colonial era, is filled with instances in which evangelization and westernization were effectively intertwined. Sometimes this fusion was intentional, other times unwitting.[2] Either way, the result for local communities has been a mixed blessing.

Entering neighbourhoods of 'brokenness', if we can come with creative rather than cultural eyes, we might instinctively get in touch with broken areas within ourselves. This helps us approach communities wrestling with poverty more as partners than patrons, and encourages us to lay a relational base before we seek solutions. This is easier said than done. I find we often rush the early 'courtship' of a new community; we become 'solutional' before we become relational.

In addressing the need for creativity in mission, I have the rare privilege of coming first as a visual artist and second as a minister. In this chapter, I will emphasize the role of art, particularly visual art, rather than creativity, generally. Art, though a subcategory of creativity, is personal to me in my ministry experience in the margins. 'What's personal is universal', Henri Nouwen has incisively observed. I have found this to be true, and I expect that the deeper I am able to mine my experience and communicate it, the wider the application for others will be. In an age of franchise that suggests generic approaches will help your church grow irrespective of context, we need to be reminded that going deep will carry us far. Additionally, I believe that if I can make a specific case for art as essential in mission, I will make the point for creativity, generally.

But first, why creativity? Why make the case for imagination and originality in mission when here in the UK we face steady decline in numbers expressing the Christian faith? Shouldn't we just get on with the work of communicating good news? Isn't creativity generally, and art specifically, a luxury we cannot afford?

I wonder if the decline in numbers and influence is precisely why we should get so serious about creativity as the people of God in the UK. Creativity in mission draws people. Moreover, in my experience, when people get a taste of how creative our God is, it is harder for them to walk away. Creativity subverts cynicism. Christ knew this when he spoke innovatively in parables, for example. But beyond his teaching style, he ministered in a creative mix of word, deed and power, and he found ways to be where people gathered. He ministered in homes, synagogues and public spaces, on the lake, on the shore and on the road; leaving large amounts of time unscripted such that people could take the lead in conversation and invitation to welcome him into their own spaces, homes and places.

The exodus story is also an example of the people of God creatively at work. One could easily argue that if ever there was a time a people were entitled to put as much distance between themselves and their former masters, this was the time. But instead, God led them on a circuitous journey designed to deepen identity and flush out dysfunctional behaviours ingrained from bondage. Immediately after crossing the Red Sea, they were instructed to camp and write a song. This was the first of many art moments – building altars and monuments and giving creative place names to key geographies. And most notably, the Hebrews were instructed to stop for months for the biggest art project of all, building the tabernacle. In the twenty-first century, mission workers are admonished to make faith practical, and rightly so. But biblical experience shows us the faith experience is better sustained when it grips the imagination. For example, InnerCHANGE teams that work with people for whom identity is particularly fragile or for whom identity formation will be especially healing, often name their teams. The San Dimas team, set up to minister to gang members and ex-offenders, took the name of the thief who came to faith at Calvary because gang members identified so strongly with him.

EARS TO HEAR; eyes to see

In the twenty-first century we no longer ask visual art to serve as picture text for timeless spiritual truths so, for most of us, Christendom painting, sculpture and the architecture of centuries past looks remote and 'dated'. Yet it can be argued that *predicatio muta* (silent preaching) was the highest ambition of Christendom art for the majority of the centuries dating back to the conversion of Constantine. As early as the sixth century, Pope Gregory the Great affirmed sacred art as 'books of the illiterate'.[3] Cathedrals were intended as 'sermons in stone', designed to bring heaven to people and people to heaven.[4]

But that time has passed. We have lost an artistic spiritual fluency that thrived for centuries, not simply among the learned, but pervading all ranks of society. It doesn't help our comprehension of past sacred art that much of the best of it has been ripped out of context and clinically deposited in museums. But even 'framed' in iconic settings we struggle to read and appreciate what we see in centuries-old places of worship. We no longer understand why Mary is typically serenely robed in blue, for example, or Mary Magdalene in red with loose flowing hair, or Peter in gold, white-haired and bearded.[5] We sigh encountering yet another Madonna and child, not realizing that artists in that day were working diligently to present the miracle of the incarnation – that Christ came among us in defenceless flesh. John Drury, art historian and former priest, emphasizes that, in the presence of past Christian art, twenty-first-century viewers, whether Christian or not, are now 'visitors to a foreign country'.[6] Art that was meant to be pedagogical now looks pedantic and arbitrarily formal.

In the meantime, church art that once inclined to the pictorial and was designed to educate, edify and encourage has long since given way to worship arts centred instead in experience. It is as if we have only ears to hear – not eyes to see. This is especially so in Protestant churches. We have inherited a similar suspicion of visual art to that held by reformers. That distrust was justifiable in its day, given many church leaders' sumptuous lifestyles and lavish expenditures on art. But we would do well, in our day, to recover a healthy appreciation for sacred art. I wonder if our inability to value sacred visual art combined with our scepticism of beauty opens us today to pernicious forms of pleasure instead. Our culture becomes increasingly self-oriented, bent on amassing stuff, status, success and security.

I do not intend to pit worship arts against visual arts. Both add depth and richness to our faith experience and our ability to glorify God. But my lament that centuries of Christian visual art go largely neglected and that comparatively little is being produced today is not simply nostalgic. Instead, I believe that healthy faith communities should be able to appreciate and access multiple art forms for spiritual growth. Sacred art can help us regain the ability to be still, to be awestruck. And I wonder if it can help us regain our balance in an over-messaged world in which we drink shallowly from our culture's running tap of words.

So where might we begin our journey of considering engagement with the creative realm?

In the Beginning: Lessons from the First Artist

In the beginning, God created the heavens and the earth. The earth was without form and void, and darkness was over the face of the deep. And the Spirit of God was hovering over the face of the waters. And God said, 'Let there be light', and there was light. And God saw that the light was good. And God separated the light from the darkness. God called the light Day, and the darkness he called Night. And there was evening and there was morning, the first day . . . And God said, 'Let the waters under the heavens be gathered together into one place, and let the dry land appear.' And it was so. God called the dry land Earth, and the waters that were gathered together he called Seas. And God saw that it was good. (Gen. 1:1–5, 9–10, ESV)

This is an exceptionally visual passage, and I recommend for accuracy's sake that we listen to it with our imaginations as much as we grapple with it theologically and structurally. There is an economy of words in this passage that is artistic. Art is as much about decluttering as filling in.

I love this image of God in that first moment when everything is a chaos of raw materials around him; chaos with potential for creativity, but also for intimidation. In the presence of an empty canvas or blank sheet of paper artists know there is a precarious moment that hovers between confidence and uncertainty.

Consider the beautiful phrase: 'The Spirit of God was hovering over the face of the waters.' I love the artistic, imagistic way the English translates the Hebrew as 'face'. What does the face of your community look like? How is God hovering over it? Are there doors the Spirit passes through easily that we'd love to see open to us in ministry?

It is important to note an implication here of God's dynamic activity. One of the things we have to get used to as ministers in the margins is how often and quickly the canvas gets reworked. Many times in our journeys among the poor we have seen emerging transformation blunted when an inner city gentrifies or a slum is bulldozed.

Looking closely at verse 3 gives us important insight into the way God works as an artist. 'Let there be light', he says. God does not command or demand that there be light. He simply speaks invitingly, creatively. Cultivating a climate of creativity on mission teams, in churches and in community work means we will need to create an environment of permission. This does not mean an environment with no agenda. A climate of permission that allows for exploration and failure inspires people to attempt things beyond themselves in the face of the dark void. Notice that the first thing God does is something visual artists typically do as the first order of business: he stakes out his light source and separates his lights and darks.

God follows that first moment of creativity by stepping back and appraising his work. 'It is good', he says with satisfaction. In this instance, God shows us that if we want to see the creative, imaginative eyes of our team members and neighbours opened, such that they see possibilities not readily visible, we need to foster an environment of affirmation.

Let me also point out that when God steps back to survey his creation, and tells himself, 'It is good', this is a confirmation that our God is not simply an engineer, a master builder, but an artist. An engineer would step back in satisfaction and say, 'It works.' Certainly I am oversimplifying, but I think God's use of artist's language here shows he is interested in something more than technical mastery – he is after a prodigal beauty.

The vibrant colour of this newly forming world, the intricacy, the design, the arresting but unnecessary aesthetics have no other purpose but to be beautiful. Luther famously pronounced: 'The poor need beauty as much as bread.'

Art as Re-Legitimating Beauty

Early on in my thirty-year journey living and ministering among the poor, I was baffled by the occasional decision-making I saw around me concerning the use of limited resources. When I first moved into the huge inner-city area of South Central, Los Angeles, I would see, for example, a family with limited means go without basics in life and then suddenly splurge on a hired limousine for their son's graduation. Weeks later, sometimes this decision-making would mean the same family would appeal to me, or a neighbour, for help. Pastor E.V. Hill of Mt Zion Missionary Baptist Church summed up this perplexing process in a phrase: 'Beg what you need, buy what you want.'

Abhijit Banerjee and Esther Duflo discuss this phenomenon at length in their masterful book, *Poor Economics*. In analysing health care data, the authors found that some slum residents postponed free immunizations that would deliver long-term wellbeing for their children tomorrow but would involve the short-term cost today of travel and time queuing at a clinic. They found that people – all people, not simply those struggling with poverty – wrestle with decision-making that pits our 'today selves' against our 'tomorrow selves'. On occasion, people choose a costly self-gratification today over a long-term interest that yields its benefits tomorrow.[7]

There are likely many reasons people living in poverty often prioritize 'luxuries' over necessities at critical points in their lives but I would suggest that one motive is a craving for beauty. It seems to be human nature to struggle with 'manna' for long periods, no matter how freely given. I believe that being made in the image of God means that we long to see the creative impulse in us find expression. In the West, much of what makes up the lives of people of limited means is generic. This is especially true of public housing, most of which is numbingly bland. My East-Ender friend, Ronny, says that council housing architecture is fine, 'But it doesn't stir you' (Figure 17.1).

Figure 17.1   **Tower Hamlets by Peter Anderson**
(www.fiercelyalive.com)

Art as Prophetic Statement and Activity: Two Images

Safe mission

The first Christian art we have record of dates from first- or second-century Rome, from the catacombs.[8] To me, it is fitting that Christian art should begin, literally, as an 'underground' expression, because one of the critical roles of art in mission is expressing prophetic truth.

Safe Mission (Figure 17.2) has grown out of a deeply held grief that mission from the West into the developing world inclines increasingly toward short-term forays, sending inexperienced 'missionaries' with improbable expectations using inappropriate technology in ways incompatible with local culture. *Safe Mission* is one of the largest pieces I have ever done and it was used as a banner for the Poverty Track of the most recent Urbana missions conference. Despite the fact that more than one in six people round the world live in slums, barrios or inner cities, and this demographic constitutes the fastest growing in the world (100,000 a day move to slums),[9] western mission is moving away from careful, long-term efforts and opting instead for vehicles that are quick, safe, yet aspire to great impact (hence the helicopter dangling the statue of Jesus). These short-term mission efforts are often efficient, effective ways for young Christians from the West to get valuable exposure in the majority world but they are costly in terms of resources and often superficial in terms of bringing lasting change. More important, they can be experienced by host communities on the ground as a misfire conveying a message of a western-style, stone-dead and bound Jesus.

I address the impersonality of much short-term mission, as well as the expectation to 'save and be safe' at the same time, by drawing a quasi-military helicopter creating a glare that means we cannot see the people inside. On the far left, I have placed a girl facing away from the activity overhead. She looks away not because she is angry or anguished over the message but, simply, because it is not relevant to her.

Figure 17.2   *Safe Mission* by **John Hayes**

"SAFE MISSION"
InterCHANGE 2012

Safe Mission is not a blanket critique of all short-term missions – indeed the optimist in me insists that much of it is helpful. And I am glad people are *going* intentionally to right wrongs, not merely 'write wrongs' from the comfort and safety of blogs or other communication vehicles. But I have found it not helpful that short-term efforts increasingly become ends in themselves on our terms. *Safe Mission* is a prophetic piece asking that we self-examine with the same energy we direct toward missionaries of previous generations.

Every creative venture involves unexpected discoveries. Early on in this piece, as I was sketching the hanging clothes in the far left-hand corner, I found I had to put my pencil down, I was trembling so much. It took me some time to understand that I was especially moved because I was drawing the intimacy of another's life simply because they did not have the economic wherewithal to cover it. In that instant of realization, I sensed God sharing: 'You're feeling a bit of what it was like to hang on the cross and suffer the indignity of watching your clothing publicly displayed at the foot.' I determined then to depict the presence of Christ in the drawing, not in the statue hovering without landing, but nailed to the reality of the slum in the form of three crosses. On both sides of the drawing I clustered telephone poles and aerials to represent the three crosses.

This is a deeply personal piece, not because it depicts a slum or barrio in which we have members. We have members and kindred spirits living in slums resembling this but not in this particular community. It is personal because it offers a glimpse into a country I could have been drafted to fight in when I graduated high school in 1972 had the US Government not stepped up to end conscription. By 1972, the Vietnam War had sagged into its darkest and most unwinnable state and as a 17-year old it was daunting to consider.

Creating this drawing was prophetic in process as well as intent. As one who works in society's margins, simplicity is a high value. I am at heart a painter and love the motion and emotion of pigment spontaneously moving across a surface. But when I picked up my art again in 1994, after a gap of twelve years, I wanted to find a medium simple in resources as well as execution. So I asked myself what I could do with just pencil and paper. Art doesn't get much simpler than that.

Furthermore, there was an austere beauty in the Saigon River slum panorama the day I was there that I felt was best captured in black and white. This is a large piece – much larger than pencil drawings typically run. But I am a believer that pencil can hold space and convey emotional content effectively with understated fidelity.

As a pencil realist I often wonder if as a 'serious' artist I don't already have two strikes against me. Pencil can be dismissed as simply a preparatory medium, and realism as suggestive of low imagination. However, I find pencil can be used for more than sketching; it can indeed accomplish finished works. And realism can be more than descriptive. It can be charged with layers of meaning. In this I have been inspired by Michelangelo who, late in life, produced a number of large, highly worked, 'presentation drawings' with sacred themes. His friend and one-time mentor, Vittoria Colonna, found herself flagging in faith in her twilight years. Michelangelo's faith, in contrast, deepened and intensified with time, and he created a series of drawings for her meditative encouragement.[10]

Working in pencil is satisfyingly elemental but slow. This is especially so in the way I work. I can work three to six months on a single piece. I often say that the point of pencil is the point. And the point cannot cover a large area quickly. In my view, the central asset of pencil as a medium is the lyric of line and line's ability to create a tide pool of intricacy in what, in paint, would be rendered as a single, solid field. People respond to my art often exclaiming about the intensity of detail – especially as it contrasts with sweeping areas of paper left untouched. But the intricacy with which I often work a few square inches actually has less to do with realistic detail and more to do with revealing a dynamic activity: a wrestling intensity in dark spaces that in paint might appear static. Paul Klee maintained that art is less about reproducing the visible than making visible.[11] It is important to me that the process of my art is resonant with the dynamism of fragile, febrile places in our world's cities.

I have stated above that pencil is slow. In point of fact, in comparison to today's accelerated world of instant image it is ridiculously inefficient. I have come to see that working laboriously – tediously,

even – is one of the ways I stand against a culture permanently fixed
to fast-forward. Working at the pace of pencil means I cannot create
all the pieces I have vision for, or even many of them. Every choice
represents a non-choice elsewhere. But pencil's limits help me express
myself purposefully, resourcefully, and this, in turn, puts me in step
with people living within limits in the extremities of our cities.

Incarnational mission in margins is very like working a pencil point
on a vast page. There can be long, slow seasons in micro-communities
drilling down to great depth in evangelizing, raising leaders, organizing and developing. Impact can be long in coming and proceeds from
costly choices. But the discoveries made, the intimacy along the way
and the intensity of meaning experienced are incomparable.

Safe Mission grew out of an experience in Ho Chi Minh City when
I was walking a street bordering the Saigon River. To my right, the
cityscape suddenly opened up and revealed a slum panorama stretching limitlessly to right and left vanishing points. I was gripped by the
scale and stark beauty of the fragile buildings reflecting in the stagnant water. Reflections, to me, are a reminder that the wrong-side-up
way we live our lives is only truly complete when we intuit the presence of the upside-down kingdom of God.

For years I've maintained that there is an intrinsic beauty in the
margins; sometimes a desperate and fragile beauty. But I haven't always been articulate about it. And I've recoiled when people have
described marginal communities as 'war zones'. We have a worldly
wise saying in the West: 'I'll believe it when I see it.' But in nearly
thirty years of living in the margins I have come to realize that often
'I see it because I believe it'. Where else in the world, for example,
except in slums and barrios, are there houses built entirely by hand,
by the residents themselves – fingerprinted to their economic capacity
and ingenuity. In nearly every other community, we live in structures
mass-produced by someone else, for someone else, with investment
capital from yet someone else, all in a chain of impersonality resulting
in indifference. Moreover, where else do houses exist that interlock in
order to maximize space? There is a beauty in this resourceful inter-
connectedness we know little of in our hyper-individualistic lifestyles.

The power of a poster: speaking truth to power

On a spring day in 1787, twelve men met in the upper room of a Quaker print shop in central London to calculate how to bring down the slave trade. Nine were Quakers, including one American. Three were Anglicans. The triangular trade was the globalism of its day, taking guns and enticements to the west coast of Africa, transporting slaves westward across the Atlantic in the notorious 'middle passage', and finally bringing sugar, rum, hemp and other exports back to the British Isles. For nearly a hundred years, Quakers on both sides of the Atlantic had formally worked for abolition of the trade and of slavery itself. But despite raising levels of consciousness, their efforts had resulted in no legislative change. Partly this stemmed from the fact that Quakers were dismissed as the shrill voice of a 'nonconformist sect'. But more generally, it seemed that for every person willing to cry out that slavery was not just, there were many more to intone that it was just reality. In the late eighteenth century, historians estimate that more than three quarters of the world's population served in some form of bondage or another.[12] A world without slavery seemed inconceivable.

Even Christians were conflicted on the subject. It didn't help the cause of abolition that winds and currents seemed to favour the triangular trade and that this was often interpreted as God's blessing on the lucrative traffic. One of the ironies of the trade was that many ships transporting slaves were owned by people of faith. Ship names like the *Blessing*, the *Annunciation*, and the *Jesus of Lubeck* reflected this. Furthermore, there were top Christian leaders who were slave-owners. The Church of England's missionary arm, the Society for the Propagation of the Gospel to Foreign Lands, owned a productive Jamaica plantation called the Codrington Estate. The governing board included the Archbishop of Canterbury. One might assume that conditions at Codrington were gentler than on other plantations. But the copious records left are no less incriminating. One practice, not atypical in the business but particularly ironic at Codrington given the owner's missionary purpose, was that slaves were branded across the chest, 'Society'. Ostensibly, this was done to reduce the number of escapes.[13]

Today we tend to forget how formidable resistance was. Hindsight into history often suggests an inevitability that in the moment was simply not there. Anyone who has pioneered real change knows how much it feels like one is stepping out into the unmapped dark. Similarly, in 1787, there was nothing to suggest that the world's first modern advocacy movement would succeed twenty years later. The abolitionist vision was put further out of reach a few years later when Great Britain went to war with France, and calls for emancipation were tinged with the unfavourable light of the French Revolution.

Thomas Clarkson, a 27-year-old son of a vicar, came to abolitionist views researching a Latin essay at Cambridge. Clarkson believed that British people would rally to abolition if they could be apprised of the suffering commerce in human cargo caused. 'If they knew it, they'd feel a just indignation.'[14] Clarkson and his abolitionist friends knew they needed to awaken empathy through identification.

In the end, however, it wasn't words that did the heavy lifting to awaken the British public to the barbarity of the slave trade. It was an art image, produced in 1788 (Figure 17.3).

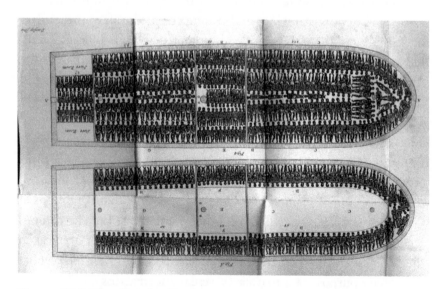

Figure 17.3 **The *Brookes* Diagram**

In late 1788, a member of the Plymouth chapter of the Society for Effecting Abolition fortuitously found a diagram instructing the crew of the slave ship, *Brookes*, in loading 'cargo' so as to maximize space and, consequently, profit. He sent the diagram to former slave-turned-abolitionist, Olaudah Equiano. In turn, Equiano sent it on to Thomas Clarkson who promptly printed seven thousand copies in James Philips's print shop. By the end of 1788, the *Brookes* diagram was hanging in sympathetic homes, pubs and commercial spaces and had been reproduced in newspapers all over Britain.[15]

The impact for the cause of abolition was incalculable. The *Brookes* poster remains one of the most widely reproduced graphics of all time, and it helped to revolutionize modern advocacy. In 2012, the *Brookes* diagram was listed in Scott Christianson's *100 Diagrams that Changed the World*. Even Clarkson was surprised at its effectiveness. He wrote: 'It made an instantaneous impression of horror on all who saw it.'[16]

I suspect that the Plymouth abolitionist who conceived the idea of presenting the public with a visceral image of the evils of the slave trade was, if not an artist, someone with a creative gift for the visual. The *Brookes* diagram helped move the British public from experiencing the savagery of the middle passage from third person to first person. In giving eyes to what had before been blind ignorance, it helped build the bridge from pity and paternalism to empathy and self-examination. People of conscience could not walk away from its visual power as they could an abolitionist speech, comforting themselves they were not directly involved. No one could look deeply into the poster's depiction of the packed slave trade and not contemplate what it might be like to lie naked on rough planks and feel flesh tearing away with the violent rocking of the craft.

The central image of the poster shows a cutaway of the decks from above, and taken in at a glance today, it appears to be a missile from hell. And yet, the poster was a mastery of understatement – it depicted the decks of the *Brookes* loaded with only 454 slaves, the maximum 'legal' limit. But the fact remained that the *Brookes* had carried upwards of seven hundred slaves in order to maximize profit. As on other slave vessels, African men and women had been laid on their sides or stacked like cordwood to pack in more than the permitted 454. So the full

extent of the horror of the middle passage was left to the viewer's imagination. The airless decks would have run with blood, pus and human
waste. In turn, this would have led to further infection and death.[17]

The *Brookes* diagram reminds us that speaking God's truth to power
need not always be verbal. In fact, the ongoing impact of the iconic poster
demonstrates the transcendent power of image, generally, when words
have long since passed on to become sound-bites or random clichés. The
Brookes image lives on as a symbol to animate current prophetic movements standing against modern-day slavery. Here in the UK, for example, it is often choreographed by students both to raise awareness and
galvanize public support against human trafficking and the commercial
sex trade. Symbols that are image-based inspire wordlessly and provoke
imaginative vision that holds a complexity beyond articulation.

Art as the Sign of the Cross

We were minutes away from doing a seminar in a room of people
overflowing into the hallway. It was the second day of the Urbana
mission convention. José, K.T. and I had agreed to meet ten minutes
before start time in order to pray in the hallway. K.T. looked ashen.
Fighting back tears, she showed us this message on her phone:

Dear InnerCHANGE family,

Just a few hours ago we got word that early this morning (2am), some
young men opened fire on a birthday party in the slum area called San
Pablito. Five were killed, including the 5 year old birthday girl. Please
remember us, as we will be engaging with the families in the next few
days and feeling the weight of the tragedy.

John in Venezuela

All three of us were staggered by the message from John Shorack, a
leader of our Caracas Team. Ironically, we had been asked to do a

seminar on violence in marginal neighbourhoods, a subject we typically shy away from because violence, especially for those who have never lived in an inner city, slum or barrio, can be naively sensationalized. We were shaken and sat quietly on the floor in the hall and prayed and listened. We sensed that we should proceed with the seminar as planned – but determined not to draw in this latest news. It was simply too fresh, too crushing, and we feared we could not do justice to the enormity of the loss in that moment.

The barrio of San Pablito overlooks the city of Caracas. In the decade and a half since John and Birgit Shorack pioneered an Inner-CHANGE team there, they have experienced a level of loss from violence that exceeds any of our fifteen teams around the world. Much of the bloodletting derives from a feud among three extended families that was sparked by coveted Air Jordan shoes making their debut on the hillside in the 1980s.[18]

We typically think of prophetic ministry as speaking truth to power. But there is a second dimension that is equally critical: speaking truth to the powerless and helping them find their voice. In Caracas, the tragedy of that birthday-party shooting gripped the San Pablito hillside as well as neighbouring barrios, driving people indoors and inward. The likelihood that the loss would spark a fresh wave of vengeful killing was almost certain and residents felt powerless to prevent it. Helplessness in the face of repeated acts of oppression or a legacy of tragedy is not an uncommon response. Moses, for example, found that when he returned to Egypt with the good news of God's intent to deliver the Hebrews, the people could not hear the message because of their 'broken spirit' (Exod. 6:9). Art can play a role in bridging despair and hope.

Together with a local leader, José Ramon, John organized neighbours to march for peace on four successive Sunday afternoons in January. Because the main thoroughfares of San Pablito form a T-intersection, John was acutely aware that, seen from above, the marchers were prayerfully tracing the lines of the cross. Arguably, the cross is the most powerful Christian image of all time, and certainly one of the most powerful in human history. More specifically for the purposes of San Pablito in that season of mourning, the cross has solidarity with people in suffering like no other symbol in human experience. John was conscious that the march was significantly more than a prayer walk. It was a moving art installation drawing on the power of the cross in its many dimensions of loss and grief, resurrection and renewal of hope.

The summer following the birthday massacre, the Caracas Team invited professional artist, Chris Abisuirez, to San Pablito for several weeks to help work with children still processing loss. Chris, a former graffiti 'tagger' who came to Christ in the ministry of our Los Angeles Team, is our most gifted visual artist in InnerCHANGE. He was also asked to help organize neighbours in a hillside mural project that would tangibly express peace. The mural drew in countless families and, when the project finished, neighbours realized they had never before been part of a creative project like it.

John and Birgit believe that the 'Paz' mural project was not simply a hopeful expression during the season it was created – it continues to act as a force for forging peace on the hillside.

Art as Lamentation

By the time the biblical story of Job gets to the nineteenth chapter, Job has lost his health, wealth, sense of purpose and, most devastatingly, his family. Likely he has even lost whatever perverse comfort he might have had sitting on the ash heap, an archetype of borderless pain. Now he is gripped in suffering's solitary confinement, the 'friends' no longer about. But suddenly he does something that perhaps only one who has endured much pain, or possibly an artist, would notice. He cries out with savage energy: 'Oh that my words were written . . . that they were inscribed in a book . . . that with an iron pen and lead they were engraved in the rock for ever!' (Job 19:23–4, ESV). It would be a stretch to say that Job is looking first and foremost to create a work of art. But certainly he wants to record a hyper-honest message, art's stripped-down raw material. He is not complaining. He is yearning for significance – not necessarily for himself, but simply that *there would be significance*. 'Art is a revolt, a protest against extinction', French novelist Andre Malraux has said.[19] Characteristically, Job is looking beyond himself to record something timeless.

Today, 'Amazing Grace' is likely the most widely sung hymn in the world,[20] and entire books have been written about it, so formidable is the cultural phenomenon the song drives. 'Amazing Grace' is pitch-perfect in expressing an unashamed purity of emotion. However, there are not very many markers along its journey from the pen of John Newton to its current status that we can chronicle with certainty. We know, for example, that Newton wrote the hymn in 1773, under the inspiration of 1 Chronicles 17, to accompany a New Year's Day sermon in which he took an annual personal inventory.[21] But we do not know the melody he chose, or if indeed he wrote one. Nor do we know how the now-famous tune was settled upon, nor who the author was of the famous 'fourth' verse that begins monumentally: 'When we've been there ten thousand years'. In fact, many of the people who shaped the song and gave it momentum are anonymous. Perhaps this is as it should be, enabling it to more easily become a song for everyone.

That 'Amazing Grace' was written by the captain of a slave ship (as Newton had been) who suddenly recognized his terrible guilt and consequently wrote a hymn that would be on the lips of every abolitionist would be the Hollywood version. But the evidence suggests that the hymn was not written with repentance for his role in the slave trade foremost in mind. And it was not widely sung during Newton's life by anyone, let alone the abolitionists. To me it is remarkably redemptive that 'Amazing Grace' came of age in the American South,[22] giving voice to slaves and that it should be they who championed the song as a message of prophetic hope.

'Amazing Grace' as a work of art is perhaps at its most poignant when it is sung as a cry of lament in the tradition of the biblical lamentations. In the early nineteenth century, 'Amazing Grace' also gave voice to the Cherokee as they forcibly made the devastating journey called the Trail of Tears; in the mid-twentieth century, during the

Civil Rights Movement in the USA, 'Amazing Grace' took on fresh meaning as a visionary protest song; and in June 2015, in a community in Charleston, South Carolina, ravaged by one of the most senseless, racially motivated mass murders in recent history, President Obama paid tribute to those who had died and broke into song. He needed a song big enough to express loss, but visionary enough to express hope. He chose 'Amazing Grace'. 'Amazing Grace' testifies to the power of art when it simultaneously rises to aesthetic, emotional and spiritual standards. Only the Spirit can do that.

Art as a Threshold to Eternity: The Disciple Who Journeyed Farthest Out

I cannot write about art and mission, particularly pictorial art and its aspirations, without discussing art as a vehicle for contemplation, instruction and faith-building. As members of a Christian order, InnerCHANGE people pursue a rhythm of life that includes regular spiritual retreats and days off. We have found spiritual rhythms essential for guarding sustainability in tough work in the margins, but also for nourishing powers of seeing with meaning. Some of us are revisiting the use of artistic image to stir contemplation and add richness and depth to our times of devotion. On days off, I often head to art galleries in London. I am particularly drawn to the National Gallery's collections of medieval and renaissance painting.

The Incredulity of Saint Thomas, painted by Guercino, is a favourite (Figure 17.4). I find it powerfully expressive on several levels. I find Thomas's rough humanity comforting and compelling at the same time. And I love the irony, if we rely on church tradition, that Thomas carried the gospel message all the way to India. It seems that the disciple with deepest doubt journeyed to minister farthest out. Most of all, though, I love Guercino's accessible Jesus. Stylistically, Guercino's fluid brushstrokes and dramatic lighting give movement and immediacy to the scene to remind us this event happened with real people in real time.

Figure 17.4 *The Incredulity of St Thomas* by **Guercino**
Photo © The National Gallery, London

Jesus is unquestionably the centre of the painting, flanked in almost antiphonal 'call and response' form by Thomas and Peter. On the right, Thomas responds incredulously to Christ's invitation to touch the wound. Peter, in turn, reacts to Thomas, amazed at the impropriety of the situation. It's a comforting commentary that 'the rock of faith' and 'the doubter' can co-exist in the same room. Guercino catches Thomas in the act of pressing his rough hand; his eyes focused on the wound miss the poignant expression in the eyes of Christ, brushed with tears. Despite abundant presence of visual rhetoric (the banner in Christ's hand, the royal blue of his robe, Peter depicted as aged and bearded), the intent of the painting is overwhelmingly human. Peter, ever protective of Christ but perhaps also filled with self-importance, is next to Jesus. He represents the church in necessary proximity to Christ. But Peter's fussiness also suggests the negative: the church can try to 'protect' Jesus from unpolished folk sincerely stretching for faith.

Jesus opens his robe – an astonishing moment of intimacy reinforced by delicate flesh tones. But he is not just opening it to Thomas – his open hand is extended as much to us as well. He is present, emotional, because he is with friends.

I like that one can appreciate the painting at face value but also dig for more. Guercino gives us a Jesus who is intensely physical, personal, vulnerable. His expression says he has gone to the cross, and now crossed over. He wears heavenly blue to remind us he is resurrected. The light source seems to meander, such that only Jesus is fully lit. Christ holds the flag of victory over death, the blood red cross on a pristine white field, but in this case, we can only see a fringe of white. It is more shroud than flag, blowing away, as doubt is intended to blow away. The colours are dark and brooding, but in the light of Christ's tender expression, they become dark and reflective.

Closing Thoughts: The Ragged Shoreline

To end, we come back again to take lessons from the original artist. After God separates light and dark he takes time in Genesis 1:5 to name them. It is not the names 'day' and 'night' in and of themselves I want to stress, but the process of naming. We name something usually when we are invested enough to care. Too often we ask the poor to settle for functional status and in the process sometimes eradicate community place names that had existed for generations.

As an artist, I find that verses 9 and 10 are some of the most beautiful in scripture. I hear them with my eyes. This is the day God calls out the dry land and orchestrates it to meet the seas. Imagine what it must have been like for God that first time, to hear water thundering against cliffs or rushing banks of sand dazzling like diamond dust.

Most experts in aesthetics maintain that asymmetry is essential to beauty and I am inclined to agree. I do not think a perfect world, before the Fall, meant that God created geometric pieces of land and uniform waves. I believe that on the third day of creation God de-signed ragged shorelines for land and sea to meet with artful beauty.

Most neighbourhoods in the margins have ragged shorelines, too. Some fall along immigrant or ethnic lines. Other shorelines are pat-terned along class or income lines. Shadwell, in London's East End, has ragged shorelines between Bengali immigrants and East-Enders, between a senior generation trying to hold onto history and a gener-ation of new arrivals trying to forge a new one. As always with ragged shorelines, there is potential for difference, for conflict. But there is also potential for interaction and reconciliation. Wherever there is a ragged shoreline there is vitality, potential for beauty, and possibility for the Word alive.

The urgency for creative initiatives in the margins is illustrated in an often-told story of the sixth-century Irish monk, St Aidan, and the gift horse. In order to facilitate the saint's considerable itinerant ministry, King Oswin presented Aidan with a prize mare from his stable. He very much admired Aidan and wanted to ease the burden of his exhausting journeys on foot. Aidan thanked the king but then promptly gave the horse away to the first beggar he met on the road. The king was deeply dismayed and asked the monk why he had given the valuable gift away when a horse of much lesser value would have suited the beggar.

When it comes to working with the poor, it is tempting to collapse into the notion that the cheapest and least creative responses are not only enough, but are most suitable. It is almost as if a remnant of the workhouse mentality continues to tether us to low imagination. As the people of God, I wonder if we have the opportunity to distinguish ourselves from generic and often disempowering mass approaches to people in poverty by means of life-giving creativity. Creativity springs from a deep personal place, and its unique quality to be both personal and universal helps counteract the impersonality of institutional so-cial service policies. This call for creativity does not begin with what we do – but how we see. Before we make visible, as Klee has sug-gested, we would do well to posture ourselves authentically with peo-ple in need so that we can glimpse the assets God is making visible.

In one of the most important advocacy movements of all time, the *Brookes* diagram shows us the compelling power of image to make visible realities hidden from view. But more than simply making visible, the abolition poster demonstrates art's ability, likewise, to make memorable.

Finally, 'Amazing Grace' shows us that art in particular, and creative work generally, has the ability to make meaningful. With laser precision, art can capture and focus expressions of truth that words can only grope toward. In awakening ourselves to hidden realities, we are reawakened to truth in its essence. In a world beset with issues of poverty and marginalization, in which the 'poor will always be among us', we must retain a transcendent awareness of meaning in which solutions will always fall short.

Notes

1   Gordon MacKenzie, *Orbiting the Giant Hairball* (NY: Viking/Penguin Group, 1996), pp. 19–20.
2   See David J. Bosch, *Transforming Mission* (Maryknoll, NY: Orbis Books, 1991), pp. 310–12 for comment on the history of the 'Western missionary enterprise' and colonialism.
3   Jennifer Trafton, 'Painting the Town Holy', *Christian History* 91 (Summer 2006): p. 14.
4   Henry Thorold, *Collins Guide to Cathedrals, Abbeys and Priories of England and Wales* (London: Collins, 1986), p. xv.
5   Beth Williamson, *Christian Art: A Very Short Introduction* (Oxford: Oxford University Press, 2004), pp. 55–6.
6   John Dury, *Painting the Word: Christian Pictures and Their Meanings* (London: National Gallery London Publications, 2002), p. ix.
7   Abhijit Banerjee and Esther Duflo, *Poor Economics* (London: Penguin, 2011), pp. 64–70.
8   Williamson, *Christian Art*, p. 4.
9   United Nations Human Settlements Programme, *The Challenge of Slums: Global Report on Human Settlements 2003* (London: Earthscan, 2003), p. 12.
10   Thomas Mayer, 'The Art of Grace', *Christian History* 91 (Summer 2006): p. 34.

11 Matthew Gale, ed., *The EY Exhibition: Paul Klee* (London: Tate Publishing, 2013), p. 8.
12 Adam Hochschild, *Bury the Chains* (Boston: Houghton Mifflin, 2005), p. 2.
13 Hochschild, *Bury the Chains*, pp. 61–8.
14 Thomas Clarkson, *The History of the Rise, Progress, and Accomplishment of the Abolition of the African Slave-Trade by the British Parliament, Volume I* (London: Longman, Hurst, Rees & Orme, 1808), p. 321.
15 Hochschild, *Bury the Chains*, p. 155.
16 Thomas Clarkson, *The History of the Rise, Progress, and Accomplishment of the Abolition of the African Slave-Trade by the British Parliament, Volume II* (London: Longman, Hurst, Rees & Orme, 1808), p. 111.
17 Hoschschild, *Bury the Chains*, pp. 155–68.
18 John Shorack, *Nail-Scarred Hands Made New* (Eugene, OR: Wipf & Stock, 2012), pp. 100–02.
19 Judith Herman, '27 Responses to the Question: "What Is Art?"' http://www._mentalfloss.com (accessed 27 June 2014).
20 One Newton biographer estimates it is performed ten million times annually (Jonathan Aitken, *John Newton: From Disgrace to Amazing Grace* [Wheaton, IL: Crossway Books, 2007], p. 224).
21 Marylynn Rouse, 'Amazing Grace: The Sermon Notes', the John Newton Project (www.johnnewton.org). In a telephone conversation with Marylynn (15 February 2012), she also made the point that hymns in the eighteenth century were frequently written without accompanying music, so there may not be an 'original' melody associated with Newton anyway.
22 The hymn passed into relative obscurity throughout the nineteenth century in its home country, but a geographic leap to the United States proved to act as fertile ground. It was introduced in the Second Great Awakening and continued on as a mainstay of camp revivals, accruing up to seventy verses. It seems that once in the powerful grip of the song, people struggled to let it end (See, Mark Noll, and Edith L. Blumhofer, eds, *Sing Them Over Again to Me* [Alabama: University of Alabama Press, 2006]).

18

Case Study: Called to Witness

John Hayes

15 July 2007, Addis Ababa, Ethiopia

My friend, Aila Tasse, and I sway in a crowded public van as it lurches through driving rain in downtown Addis Ababa. Passengers stare stoically ahead, culturally giving space to one another despite the fact they are smashed together in a mix of body heat and wet clothes. My face is pressed against the fogged window, and I use my sleeve to clear a circle. We stop momentarily in the flow of traffic and I glimpse two spectral men across the road, squatting under a scrap of plastic sheeting they hold aloft. Gusts of wind and rain seize the plastic and it gives off a sound like shuffling cards. A channel of muddy run-off water courses between them. They appear used up – too old to work, too indomitable to lie down and die. I have to glance away, emotionally drawing a shade. But my eyes are drawn back to the two men and for a flicker my vision is transformed. I sense this makeshift shelter pillared by human arms is none other than the house of God.

Aila and I are on our way to meet leaders in one of the city's poorest slums. He is the founder and director of Lifeway, a mission that develops leaders and plants churches among remote rural peoples and in very poor slums throughout East Africa and the northern areas of sub-Saharan Africa. The missionaries of Lifeway are all non-western. I am conscious that I am experiencing a rare opportunity to see hallowed ground that, but for Aila, would be closed to me.

The van lurches to a stop and Aila and I climb out of the van like we're unfolding from an airline luggage compartment. I follow my friend across a vacant lot of sucking mud and journey into one of the poorest sections of the city, nicknamed 'Beirut', because of its volatility. We thread our way down a passageway so narrow the iron sheeting grabs at my shirtsleeves.

We make a sharp turn in an alleyway slick with emerald sewage. Eventually we emerge into an open space inside the slum so packed with people, it feels like wading into a tide. We pass clusters of street kids, wide-eyed with curiosity and delight. Aila explains to me that several children inhaling deeply from ragged long sleeves are sniffing glue. I know we are already a bit late for a leadership class that Aila has asked me to help teach, but instinctively I hold out open hands to brush the small fingertips reaching out to me. One of the smallest boys stretches out a hand in slow motion and I pause. He appears shrunken in an oversize homemade smock. It takes a second for his smile to emerge and the light in his eyes seems to rise from the bottom of a pool. 'Chuck Norris', he calls out. I smile back and remember that I currently have a beard.

We come to a concrete block building that Aila has permission to use for training local leaders and pastors. I am warmly introduced to a gathering of men and women and then, spontaneously, heads bow and slowly the crowd begins to sing hymns in Amharic. The sound is ancient and seems to rise out of the ground. I am reminded that Ethiopia's church is one of the world's oldest, tracing its lineage directly to New Testament times. The sound washes over me and I experience a powerful sense of encounter with the Ancient of Days.

I have the privilege of introducing some practical training. For me this means interactively sharing insights choreographed to biblical story and drawing out best practices from local leaders who know their context. We focus on the Mark 2 story of four men carrying a paralysed man to Christ. In the passage, the four friends arrive at the room where Jesus is teaching and healing only to discover the door is too crowded to pass through. They go to the roof, innovatively tear an opening and lower their paralysed friend to Christ. I know that learning that sticks will come from sparking their imaginations, their 'eyes to see'. The gate to fresh vision is through the eyes more than the ears. This is one of the reasons, I believe, that the Bible is 80 per cent story. I hope they will see Mark 2 visually – not only in the text, but in their context around them. Who in the community is immobilized? Who possesses the intentional solidarity of the four men?

In the class, we begin to reflect together on what it is like to carry people in need to Christ in the slums of Addis. The leaders really warm to the subject as we collectively read this dynamic passage and let it speak to us in its multiple levels. They feel keenly the disappointment these men on mission must have experienced when they discovered that, despite their best efforts, they could not access Jesus because of the throng at the door. We update the passage to twenty-first-century Addis and talk about how it feels to carry communities immobilized by hardship to Christ only to encounter closed doors and the reality that churches have already spent most of the budget on their own plans and programmes. We move from that posture to share stories of creative, upside-down ways in the slums we can 'get to the roof' and take the 'lid off the system'. And we remember that this Jesus of Mark 2, who promptly served the paralysed man lowered to the floor, is the same Jesus of today who will immediately meet us in our actions on behalf of others and not send us to the back of the line.

One pastor blurts out that in his experience in the slums the numbers of Mark 2 feel reversed: 'I feel like I have four paralytics in my community trying to gain the help of a single healthy man.'

He speaks with such candour and warmth that I am deeply touched. He is not complaining, simply drawing attention to a compelling reality. Members of the class laugh sympathetically. 'Seriously, what do we do with such overwhelming need?' they ask.

The pastor confides that with so few who are able-bodied, it is often easier to insulate himself and his church from the unremitting agonies of the slum.

I want to tell them that they are right – they do lack resources; to tell them that we will help and that, over and above help, we will rather bring InnerCHANGE staff to come to live with them and share lives in ways we mutually discover the riches of God. But this is not a time for answers or promises that create expectations, no matter how well intentioned. This is my first trip to East Africa, and I am here primarily to learn from my friend Aila, and to assist him in any way I can. And I know that the numbers of missional Christians willing to live in such elemental conditions are few.

So instead, we talk about the assets every community possesses to spark transformation from within, even if those assets appear to be only the size of a mustard seed, or just a 'few loaves and fish'. We talk about passages in the Bible where God works with a remnant, how Jesus fed five thousand people from a child's lunchbox. As the leaders begin to share small-scale responses they are engaged in to reach the desperate around them, I quietly sit back and listen.

That night as I reflect on the day, I ask God to allow us in Inner-CHANGE to come to Addis one day to partner with the kind of leaders I met that evening. It is only my fourth day in the city and already my capacity to take in new images, my 'camera', is full.

My thoughts come like scribblings of graffiti. I close my eyes to see, and re-see, the two men resolutely holding the scrap of plastic in the driving rain.

Glancing at the clock I realize that in London with the time change, Deanna is tucking my youngest daughter, Alexandra, into bed. She will be secure, loved, wreathed with stuffed animals. I wonder where the boy I touched hands with will sleep tonight. Wherever it is, I expect he will count on glue to take the chill edge off the night air. As I turn off the light, I calculate that he is likely the age of my daughter. His frail stature makes him look at once, older and younger. I cannot get over the sense of finality I had in making contact with him, like touching the lid of a coffin.

I see the world in pictures. Surprisingly, perhaps, I have never used a camera in ministry to record anything. I am not sure I'd know how to take pictures without being invasive and, more important, I find I look deeper knowing there will be no record but memory. But either way, I wonder if there are moments so ineffable in poignancy they are not meant to be captured on film. Not meant to be framed, boxed, blogged, museum-ed or archived. They simply belong in the portfolio of the heart. Anything else would be a form of trespass.

There are times when God opens windows for us, and us alone, simply to witness. And in that witness to let God fill our eyes with a longing for beauty and the beauty of longing for a kingdom that is upside-down and not readily visible if we are looking with the world's eyes.

19

Case Study: Life in a Paper Cup

John Hayes

InnerCHANGE missionary Susan Smith is exceptional in the cross-cultural discipling of leaders and is one of our most creative teachers but, admittedly, she struggles with what we might term 'evangelism'. So when she was asked by prison authorities in Kampong Cham, Cambodia, to reach out to hundreds of inmates she paused.

Prison in Cambodia is exceptionally grim – not merely in terms of the barely survivable conditions, but because the prisons combine short-term inmates with others doing life. Factor in a deterministic Buddhist world-view suggesting current punishments stem from sins in a former life and the result becomes a fatalistic despair difficult to penetrate.

Furthermore, few inmates are literate. Susan felt moved to do an art exercise. As many inmates as possible filed into the courtyard, not because they were eager, Susan clarified, but because they were bored. Susan passed out hundreds of sheets of origami paper and instructed her listeners to crumple them. 'Even if your life is crumpled and ready to be thrown away, God can make something good from your life.'

Inmates were intrigued with this soft-spoken foreigner fluent in Khmer. Susan instructed the people to smooth the paper, fold it diagonally and tear off an edge to make a square. 'The extra – like your sin – Jesus wants that part – you don't need to keep it', she said.

By this time everyone was listening, and inmates who couldn't crowd into the courtyard were now peering through the windows surrounding it.

'Fold up the rest to make a cup. You may feel like you have no value, but God can make something useful from it. Now pour water into the cup. Your life can be a place God's Spirit can live, to refresh you and others.'

For many of the inmates, creating something useful and beautiful out of crumpled paper was the first art project they'd ever done.

'Now drink the water.'

Afterward, Susan shared: 'I cannot remember ever getting applause during a sermon in church but, by this time, people were clapping, laughing, almost cheering.'

20

The Creative Realm: Editorial Comment

Mike Pears and Paul Cloke

Chapter 17 is not about how art might be 'used' in the service of mission; such a view would be completely at odds with what John Hayes has described here. Indeed it would be no less than a corruption of the creativity that he talks about – a kind of domestication of art that would be the loss of its very essence. Neither is the chapter about how mission might 'reach' or be relevant to the creative community or the community of artists. While this would certainly be a valuable discussion, it would be still to miss the point that John has so ably conveyed.

This chapter is about the essential creativity of God and the manner in which that creativity is gifted to people and communities. The artist's perspective with which John approaches Genesis 1 brings to the fore the profound sense that 'being creative' is indispensable to 'being human' and that to be creative is at the heart of participation with God. The 'creative realm' therefore does not describe a distinct section of society nor does it apply only to those with a particular artistic inclination. Rather it identifies something that is fundamental to being made in the 'image of God' and is an indispensable characteristic enabling participation with God in his creation.

The crucial link which this chapter makes between creativity and participation raises a number of important questions for those involved in mission that we might think of in three particular ways. The first asks: Where do we see this kind of creativity occurring? John has argued that the mainstream or predominant culture tends to diminish creativity, indeed that there is evidence that the 'artist' gets trained out of us as we grow up. It is not of course that art – even 'good' art – is not to be found in the mainstream; but rather that creativity seems to contain within it a particular quality that tends to flourish in marginal places because these situations evoke a different 'seeing' of the world.

As we write this, news comes of the deaths of both David Bowie and Alan Rickman and, interestingly, part of the radio reviews that I (Mike) am hearing involves discussion on the particular link between Bowie and Rickman's working-class backgrounds and the creative impacts of their lives. Frank Cottrell Boyce, talking about Bowie's creativity, reflects that 'innovation can come from anywhere . . . [but] usually comes from the outsider and from the margin, and if we close the door to those margins then we really diminish our entire culture'.[1]

Australian writer Terry Veling argues that 'living in the margins' is the essential site from which insight and understanding are gained:

> I suggest that hermeneutics provides an alternate way of looking at marginality; the space of the margins is a site of vital creativity, a creativity that is generated in the ongoing interplay between belonging and non-belonging, attachment and alienation, tradition and innovation. Rather than seeing marginal space as a typically narrow, withdrawn, alienated space, we need to allow the margins to breathe, to be the very life and breath of the book – to make wide the margins.[2]

The concept of marginality is complex and is discussed elsewhere in this series. However the sense conveyed here is that creativity emerges from, or even erupts out of, places and encounters that are disturbing, dark and outside of the 'normal' or the mainstream. Thus the context of God's creative acts in Genesis 1 are the darkness and emptiness of the 'face of the deep'; likewise creative energy is released in the anti-slavery movement through a diagram that brought mainstream culture into a visual encounter with those who had been utterly marginalized as non-human. John has beautifully articulated the place of creative encounter as 'ragged shorelines [which] meet with artful beauty'. His testimony from many years of involvement with poor slum communities from around the world is that these 'ragged shorelines' are the creative sites which open one's eyes to see both beauty and darkness in new ways.

If places of 'inter-face' open up particular kinds of possibility for 'seeing' afresh, then the second question to raise is: How does the Christian community participate in these creative marginal spaces? One answer would be by an intentional inhabiting of marginal places by purposeful location, or relocation, of the Christian community. The sense of call to participate in marginal locations is motivating a small but significant movement of Christians in a number of countries, including the UK, and InnerCHANGE is an inspiring example of the kind of communities that are being formed as a consequence. These communities could be described by the term 'intentional' in that they intentionally embrace marginality in two specific ways: they seek to maintain critical distance from the norms of western lifestyle that exclude unwanted others and exploit the resources of the planet, which often results in such communities being embedded or incarnated in socially and economically disadvantaged places. They also maintain critical distance from the mainstream institutional church which is viewed by many in such communities as uncritically embodying the values of middle-class, affluent western society rather than the radical convictions portrayed through the gospels.[3]

In practice, identifying marginal spaces and establishing relational connections with the communities in them is extremely challenging. The significance of this chapter is that it helps to present this challenge in a new light by moving the focus on marginality away from a primarily negative concept of social and economic deprivation and towards a positive concept of zones of creativity as primary sites for 'participation' in the creativity of God. Sadly, experience would seem to show that viewing marginal living in this light is not usual. While a number of intentional Christian communities have demonstrated a remarkable capacity for creativity,[4] many struggle with unrealistic expectations and overwhelming pressures (both from within and without) and never find the creative space or inspiration that would give them life. John, I think, brings strong encouragement to us that a more intentional nurturing of creativity, or more specifically of co-creativity with those in marginal situations, is an indispensable part in shaping and establishing intentional Christian communities. If this is the case, then we need to enquire further as to what the Christian convictions and spiritual practices would be that might enable faith communities to more deeply inhabit the creative margins. If such communities are to engage with the 'whole social-symbolic order' as an effective voice from the margins questioning its 'rules, terms, procedures, and practices' and 'seeking alternate theologies, spiritualties, and practices',[5] what foundations are they to stand on and what grounds are they to be rooted in? These are difficult questions to wrestle with and, although there are some helpful traditions and movements to learn from, they can only be properly explored through hard experience and practical struggle.

Third, this chapter also raises a series of questions about the way that the creative realm is implicated in the social-spatial arrangements of power. How exactly does the creative process assist in challenging unjust and inequitable arrangements of power? How is the creative process related to transformation of individuals and places and indeed can any meaningful transformation take place apart from a creative process? Can creativity itself be subverted or co-opted and if so what expression might this take?

Perhaps what this chapter helpfully brings into focus is that an essential starting point in addressing this area has to be the confession that questions of power are not only about the world 'out there' but they are also about the self, the world 'in here'. It is an important issue, indeed one that is addressed at length elsewhere in the series, and John brings it into view as a central part of his discussion. John has argued that 'cultivating eyesight' is critical for mission, not only as a participation in the creativity of God himself, but also in mitigating our own tendency to participate in colonial patterns of mission that impose dominant cultural norms on host communities. The way that creative insight enables self-awareness in the individual and in the intentional Christian community, in particular an awareness about our own real vulnerability to misuse or abuse others for our own benefit, is sensitively exemplified in John's story of his visit to Addis Ababa.

Alongside this he has also shown how artistic intuition and creative practices can open up ways of engaging with and even dramatically challenging widely accepted cultural and social discourses which give support to profoundly unjust and unequal ways of living. His powerful example of the way in which Thomas Clarkson's use of the *Brookes* diagram dramatically affected public opinion demonstrates how well-placed public art can effect a shift in the balance of power. Intriguingly, between John's writing of the chapter and this editorial response, we have seen the way that a single photograph shared on social media dramatically changed the rhetoric on immigration in the course of a single day. The moving picture of 3-year-old Aylan Kurdi, who drowned while fleeing the war in Syria with his family, caused a substantial surge in offers of practical hospitality for asylum seekers and, at least for a while, caused a strong and emotional counter-narrative to the constant stream of anxiety and outright hostility which had previously dominated reporting on the subject. As John has argued, one image achieved in a moment what years of political lobbying had failed to change.

The role of the creative realm and the use of art in contesting unjust and inequitable arrangements of power is an important area that will be explored in more detail in Book 6 of this series, *Placing the Powers*. We want to briefly note here however the particular importance of the creative *location*; it is not the subject matter of an image alone, nor the temporal moment of its release that effects a catalytic engagement with social and economic arrangements of power – it is also the 'placed-ness' of the image.

Social geographer Tim Cresswell presents a detailed analysis of the effect of 'where' art is found in his study of the story of graffiti in New York. Well-structured graffiti communities began to appear in the city in the early 1970s during a period of severe austerity in which poorer communities, comprised largely of ethnic minorities, suffered

disproportionately. Graffiti represented a struggle between subordi-
nate and dominant cultural groups and in effect contested 'the system of dominant, "appropriate" meanings in the urban fabric' which
was presided over by the city authorities.[6] The 'city government were
fuming at the suggestion that graffiti should be considered art' and
their anti-graffiti campaign linked the 'out-of-placed-ness' of graffiti
with a breakdown of moral order in the city.[7] While the campaigns of
city authorities failed significantly to address the graffiti 'problem' the
gradual relocation of graffiti from everyday street space to 'art' space
began to empty it of its power to radically critique the ideological values that were being purveyed through city-spaces. The movement of
the counter-cultural to across-the-counter art represented a 'subver-
sion of the subversive' largely through a change of location: a movement from the illegitimate space of the street to the 'site of *legitimate*
creativity', namely the art gallery.[8]

Discussion about the creative location suggests that missional engagement in the creative realm might also involve the practice of curation. This act of curating, which is reflexive to local culture and
seeks to embody the Jesus-centred values discussed in Book 1 of this
series[9] – for example in terms of radical hospitality – could be seen as
a way of opening up and holding spaces that nurture new and exciting
creative expression. In John's terms such spaces could be understood
as embodying the ethos of the 'ragged shoreline' or in Veling's language they could be expressive of the 'wide margin'. There are perhaps
questions to explore here about the extent to which people who are
already involved in the creative industries are involved in the curation
of these kinds of spaces or indeed how those who convene Christian
worship might be willing to extend their involvement through co-
curating such spaces in the wider community.

In conclusion, creativity is profoundly missional. It can stir a deep
sense of hope that even in – or perhaps especially in – the darker
places moments of creativity and artistic insight can spark a sequence
of redemptive and transformative happenings. In particular it is an
indispensable quality of any movement of mission that seeks to be
involved with issues of physical deprivation and social exclusion. This

raises important questions for the wider Christian community. How do vulnerable and fragile intentional Christian communities make room for and nurture the God-given creative impulse in the challenging contexts in which they are embedded? Likewise, how does the institutional church recognize and learn from the creative challenge that comes from marginal communities, and how does it encourage and support such communities while resisting the temptation to co-opt them or dominate them for its own purposes? These are, we believe, critical questions if the church's mission in marginal places is to be shaped by the creative inspiration of the Spirit.

Notes

1   Frank Cottrell Boyce in conversation with Paddy O'Connell on BBC Radio 4, *Broadcasting House* (17 January 2016).
2   Terry Veling, *Living in the Margins: Intentional Communities and the Art of Interpretation* (Eugene, OR: Wipf & Stock, 2002), p. 2.
3   Veling, *Living in the Margins*, pp. 3–7.
4   See, for example, Mike Pears, 'Convictional Communities and Urban Social Justice' in *Working Faith* (ed. Paul Cloke, Justin Beaumont and Andrew Williams; Milton Keynes: Paternoster, 2013), pp. 85–110.
5   Veling, *Living in the Margins*.
6   Tim Cresswell, *In Place/Out of Place: Geography, Ideology and Transgression* (Minneapolis and London: University of Minnesota Press, 1996), p. 57.
7   Cresswell, *In Place*, pp. 33, 49.
8   Cresswell, *In Place*, p. 55.
9   Paul Cloke and Mike Pears, eds, *Mission in Marginal Places: The Theory* (Milton Keynes: Paternoster, 2016).

Author Biographies

Adam Bonner

Adam has a background in youth work and community development. He is the Executive Director of Public Engagement at Livability (previously the Shaftesbury Society).

Naomi Clifton

Naomi, with her husband John, has been an officer at Ilford Corps of the Salvation Army since 2011. She studied history at the University of Cambridge before working as a primary-school teacher for three years. Alongside her pastoral responsibilities, Naomi teaches church history at William Booth College.

Paul Cloke

Paul is Professor of Human Geography at the University of Exeter. His recent research has examined the role of faith in combatting social exclusion and marginalization, and is published in *Faith-based Organisations and Exclusion in European Cities* (Policy Press) and *Working Faith* (Paternoster Press). Paul has written widely on the intersection of faith and social science. He is Fellow of the British Academy and Academician of the Academy of Social Sciences, and is highly experienced in publishing having produced more than thirty books and more than 220 academic articles and chapters. Paul is part of Exeter Vineyard Church.

Gordon Cotterill

Gordon has been a Salvation Army officer for twenty years, beginning his ministry in Poplar in the East End of London. Following this, Gordon was appointed as the Spiritual Programme Director of William Booth College, London, where he taught mission studies, spirituality and spiritual formation, together with Old Testament studies. Drawing on his experiences of inner-city mission he contributed to the book *Call to Mission: Your Will Be Done* (Shield Books, 2013) and has written articles on theological education published within the Salvation Army. He and his wife Catherine are currently leading Sutton Salvation Army Church in south-west London.

Paul Ede

Paul is a church planter and practitioner of incarnational mission at the margins, based in Glasgow, Scotland. With his wife Esther he has planted Clay Community Church in the community of Possilpark, a community with a particular passion for environmental mission in a neighbourhood blighted by urban wasteland. He has a Master's degree in urban mission through Aberdeen University.

Sam Ewell

Sam is a US national and permanent resident of Brazil, where he served as a missionary from 2003 to 2010 with his wife and three children. Since 2010, the Ewells have resided in Birmingham, UK, where Sam has recently completed his PhD on Ivan Illich and Christian mission entitled 'Prolonging the Incarnation' (publication forthcoming with Wipf & Stock). As an ordained minister and member of Companions for Hope, a small missional community in Winson Green, Sam combines community organizing, prison chaplaincy and urban agriculture as a platform for cultivating abundant community from the margins of inner-city Birmingham.

Martin Gainsborough

Martin is Professor of Development Politics at the University of Bristol, minister of an inner-city parish, and a member of the General Synod of the Church of England. He has interests in the politics of development, theology and theopolitics, and is currently engaged in two research projects: one examining the power effects of the way in which development studies is traditionally taught and its implications for practice, and another looking at ways in which atonement theories may help us break free from some of the recurring pathologies of development. He is the author of *Vietnam: Rethinking the State* (Zed Books, 2010).

John Hayes

John lives on an inner-city housing estate in London's East End together with his wife Deanna and their two daughters. In 1985, John founded InnerCHANGE, a Christian mission order working for inside-out kingdom transformation in slums, barrios and inner cities on five continents. He is an artist and also the author of *Sub-Merge: Living Deep in a Shallow World* (Ventura, CA: Regal Books, 2006) as well as a contributing author to *Living Mission* (Downers Grove, IL: InterVarsity Press, 2010).

Mike Pears

Mike is the director of Urban Life, a learning and research network which develops innovative and pioneering approaches to ministry and mission in marginalized and deprived places. He has been involved in urban mission for over thirty years in a variety of contexts including Peckham (London), Vancouver (Canada) and Bristol and is currently a member of a small intentional community in a large urban estate. Mike completed his doctoral studies at the International Baptist Theological Seminary Centre (VU Amsterdam) in theological and ethnographic studies of place and is a tutor in missions studies at Bristol Baptist College.

Chris Sunderland

Chris was formerly a research biochemist, working in an Oxford laboratory at the cutting edge of biotechnology. He was ordained and became vicar of the tower block estate, Barton Hill in Bristol. He is now a social entrepreneur, one of the founding directors of the Bristol Pound, a local currency project that has attracted widespread attention and is developing a new food cooperative, called Real Economy, designed to get fresh food to people in the toughest circumstances. His latest book, is *Rise Up – With Wings like Eagles (Earth Books, 2016)*.

Samuel Thomas

Sam works for YMCA Exeter. He currently oversees the volunteer strategy for the organization and runs the Perspectives Project which exists to empower, coach and mentor men caught up in the criminal justice system. Sam has a PhD in human geography from the University of Exeter and is a contributory author to *Working Faith* (2013) and *Faith-based Organisations and Exclusion in European Cities* (2012). His PhD thesis is an ethnographic exploration of incarnational expressions of the Christian faith in socio-economically deprived neighbourhoods.

Andrew Williams

Dr Andrew Williams is a lecturer in the School of Geography and Planning, Cardiff University. His research focuses on the relationships between religion, welfare and neoliberalism, with particular regard to food banks, homelessness and faith-based drug services. His latest book is *Working Faith: Faith-based Organisations and Urban Social Justice* (co-edited with Paul Cloke and Justin Beaumont, Paternoster, 2013).